# 100 HIKES in

# CALIFORNIA'S
## CENTRAL SIERRA & COAST RANGE

**Second Edition**

THE MOUNTAINEERS BOOKS

# 100 HIKES in

# CALIFORNIA'S
## CENTRAL SIERRA & COAST RANGE
### Second Edition

## Vicky Spring
### Photos by Kirkendall/Spring

THE MOUNTAINEERS BOOKS

**The Mountaineers Books**
*is the nonprofit publishing arm of The Mountaineers Club,
an organization founded in 1906 and dedicated to the exploration,
preservation, and enjoyment of outdoor and wilderness areas.*

1001 SW Klickitat Way, Suite 201, Seattle, WA 98134

First edition, 1995

Published simultaneously in Great Britain by Cordee, 3a DeMontfort Street,
Leicester, England, LE1 7HD

Manufactured in the United States of America

Editor: Christine Clifton-Thornton
Cover and book design: The Mountaineers Books
Layout: Marge Mueller, Gray Mouse Graphics
Mapmaker: Tom Kirkendall
Photos: Kirkendall/Spring
Cover photograph: *Small creek below Hungry Packer Lake in Sabrina Basin area of John
Muir Wilderness (Hike 32)*
Frontispiece: *Banner Peak rises above Thousand Island Lake in Ansel Adams Wilderness
(Hikes 20 and 21)*

*Library of Congress Cataloging-in-Publication Data*
Spring, Vicky, 1953-
  100 hikes in California's Central Sierra and Coast Range / Vicky
Spring.— 2nd ed.
      p. cm.
  Includes index.
  ISBN 0-89886-896-3 (pbk.)
  1. Hiking—Sierra Nevada (Calif. and Nev.)—Guidebooks. 2.
Hiking—Coast Ranges—Guidebooks. 3. Sierra Nevada (Calif. and
Nev.)—Guidebooks. 4. Coast Ranges—Guidebooks. I. Title: One hundred
hikes in California's Central Sierra and Coast Range. II. Title.
  GV199.42.S55S67 2004
  917.94'4—dc22
                            2004004183

# CONTENTS

## HIGHWAY 198

## HIGHWAY 180

## HIGHWAY 168

## HIGHWAY 101

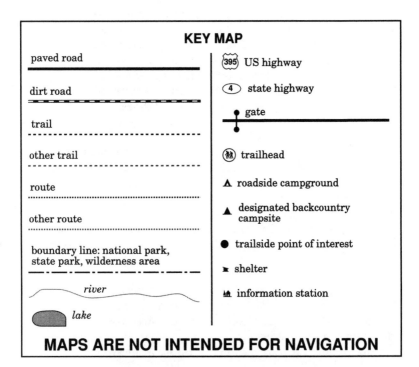

KEY MAP

paved road

dirt road

trail

other trail

route

other route

boundary line: national park,
state park, wilderness area

*river*

*lake*

(395) US highway

(4) state highway

gate

(⋀) trailhead

▲ roadside campground

▲ designated backcountry
campsite

● trailside point of interest

⚑ shelter

⛫ information station

## MAPS ARE NOT INTENDED FOR NAVIGATION

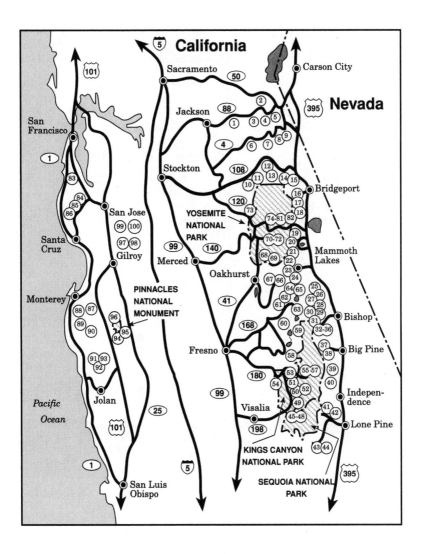

California

Nevada

Pacific
Ocean

PINNACLES
NATIONAL
MONUMENT

YOSEMITE
NATIONAL
PARK

KINGS CANYON
NATIONAL PARK

SEQUOIA NATIONAL
PARK

San
Francisco

Santa
Cruz

Monterey

Jolan

San Luis
Obispo

Sacramento

Jackson

Stockton

San Jose

Gilroy

Merced

Oakhurst

Fresno

Visalia

Carson City

Bridgeport

Mammoth
Lakes

Bishop

Big Pine

Independence

Lone Pine

# HIKE FINDER

**Mileage :** Round-trip or loop-trip distance, in miles
**Hiking time :** Time needed by average acclimated hiker under normal conditions
**Elevation :** Total elevation gain from start to destination and back to start
**Hike type :** DH = day hike (no camping); BP = backpack (camping permitted)
**Difficulty :** Potential difficulty rating: E = easy, M = moderate, D = difficult, D* = difficult under any circumstance
**Trail open :** Month trail is normally open
**Permits :** Wilderness permit information, by case number described in the appendix

For a complete discussion of categories, see the Introduction.

| | MILEAGE | HIKING TIME | ELEVATION (FEET) | HIKE TYPE | DIFFICULTY | TRAIL OPEN | PERMITS |
|---|---|---|---|---|---|---|---|
| 1. Cole Creek Lakes | 28 | 2–4 days | 3,400 in, 1,740 out | BP | D | mid-July | 1 |
| 2. Emigrant Lake | 8 | 4 hrs | 810 | DH/BP | E | mid-July | 1 |
| 3. Showers Lake | 9 | 5 hrs | 720 in, 400 out | DH/BP | M | late June | 1 |
| 4. Fourth of July Lake | 10 | 6 hrs | 787 in, 1,196 out | DH/BP | M | mid-July | 1 |
| 5. Granite and Grouse Lakes | 12 | 7 hrs | 1,324 in, 900 out | DH/BP | E | August | 1 |
| 6. Bull Run Lake | 7.4 | 4 hours | 860 in, 560 out | DH/BP | E | July | 1 |
| 7. Paradise Valley Loop | 15 | 2 days | 2,170 | DH/BP | M | mid-July | 1 |
| 8. Noble Lake | 9 | 5 hrs | 400 | DH/BP | E | mid-July | 1 |
| 8. Asa Lake | 14 | 8 hrs | 950 | DH/BP | E | mid-July | 1 |
| 9. Raymond Lake | 21.2 | 2–3 days | 1,200 | BP | M | August | 1 |
| 10. Crabtree Trail | 13 | 6 hrs | 1,030 | DH/BP | M | July | 1 |
| 11. Whitesides Meadow | 12 | 6 hrs | 1,280 in, 880 out | DH/BP | M | August | 1 |
| 12. Kennedy Lake | 15 | 8 hrs | 1,450 | DH/BP | M | July | 1 |
| 13. Emigrant Wilderness Loop | 39.5 | 4–6 days | 4,460 | BP | D* | mid-August | 1 |

| | MILEAGE | HIKING TIME | ELEVATION (FEET) | HIKE TYPE | DIFFICULTY | TRAIL OPEN | PERMITS |
|---|---|---|---|---|---|---|---|
| 14. Latopie Lake | 9 | 5 hrs | 1,576 | DH/BP | M | late July | 1 |
| 15. Cinko Lake | 30 | 2–4 days | 2,200 | BP | D | mid-July | 2 |
| 16. Tamarack Lake (Hoover Wilderness) | 9 | 5 hrs | 2,560 | DH/BP | M | mid-July | 2 |
| 17. Crown Point Loop | 22.5 | 2–3 days | 3,340 | BP | D | August | 2 |
| 18. Hoover Lakes | 13 | 7 hrs | 1,780 | DH/BP | M | mid-July | 2 |
| 19. Koip Peak Pass Traverse | 23.7 | 3–4 days | 3,743 | BP | D | August | 3 |
| 20. Island Pass Loop | 21 | 2–3 days | 3,477 | BP | D | mid-July | 3 |
| 21. Thousand Island Lake Loop | 18.9 | 2–4 days | 2,760 | BP | D | mid-July | 3 |
| 22. Ediza Lake | 20 | 2–4 days | 2,620 | BP | D* | mid-July | 3 |
| 22. Shadow of the Minarets Traverse | 16.2 | 2–4 days | 3,580 | BP | D | August | 3 |
| 23. Mammoth Crest Traverse | 12 | 7 hrs | 810 | DH/BP | D | July | 3 |
| 24. Valentine Lake | 10 | 5 hrs | 1,840 | DH/BP | M | July | 3 |
| 25. McGee Creek–Steelhead Lake | 11 | 6 hrs | 2,150 | DH/BP | D | mid-July | 3 |
| 25. McGee Creek–Big McGee Lake | 14 | 8 hrs | 2,280 | DH/BP | D | mid-July | 3 |
| 26. Tamarack Lakes (John Muir Wilderness) | 9.5 | 5 hrs | 1,900 | DH | M | mid-July | 3 |
| 27. Little Lakes Valley | 9 | 5 hrs | 804 | DH/BP | E | mid-July | 3 |
| 28. Pioneer Basin | 20 | 2–3 days | 2,581 in, 2,000 out | BP | D | mid-July | 3 |
| 29. Gable Lakes | 9 | 7 hrs | 3,220 | DH/BP | D | late July | 3 |
| 30. Moon Lake | 22 | 2–4 days | 4,010 | BP | D | mid-July | 3 |
| 31. Lake Italy | 24 | 2–4 days | 4,850 in, 1,160 out | BP | D | August | 3 |
| 32. Sabrina Basin | 14 | 7 hrs | 2,020 | DH/BP | M | mid-July | 3 |
| 33. Humphreys Basin | 16.8 | 2–3 days | 2,103 | BP | D | mid-July | 3 |
| 34. Evolution Valley | 53 | 5–7 days | 8,958 | BP | D | August | 3 |
| 35. Dusy Basin | 16 | 2– 3 days | 2,180 in, 600 out | BP | M | mid-July | 3 |

| | MILEAGE | HIKING TIME | ELEVATION (FEET) | HIKE TYPE | DIFFICULTY | TRAIL OPEN | PERMITS |
|---|---|---|---|---|---|---|---|
| 36. South Lake to Whitney Portal | 92.8 | 10–12 days | 20,353 | BP | D* | August | 3 |
| 37. Big Pine Lakes Basin | 16 | 2 days | 3,160 | BP | D | mid-July | 3 |
| 38. Brainard Lake | 12 | 7 hrs | 2,900 | DH/BP | D | mid-July | 3 |
| 39. Sawmill Lake | 16 | 2 days | 5,400 | BP | D* | mid-June | 3 |
| 40. Kearsarge Lakes Trail | 13 | 8 hrs | 2,623 in, 923 out | DH/BP | D | mid-June | 3 |
| 41. Meysan Lake | 10 | 8 hrs | 3,960 | DH/BP | D | mid-June | 3 |
| 42. Mount Whitney | 21.4 | 12–15 hrs | 6,131 | DH/BP | D* | mid-July | 3 |
| 43. New Army Pass Loop | 19.7 | 2–4 days | 2,920 | BP | D | August | 3 |
| 44. Rocky Basin Lakes | 26 | 2–4 days | 2,200 in, 1,160 out | BP | M | July | 3 |
| 45. Cobalt and Crystal Lakes | 9.8 | 6 hrs | 2,988 | DH/BP | D | mid-July | 4 |
| 46. Five Lakes, Little and Big | 28.4 | 3–4 days | 9,310 | BP | D | mid-July | 4 |
| 47. Franklin Lakes | 10.8 | 6 hrs | 2,527 | DH/BP | M | mid-July | 4 |
| 48. Eagle Crest | 8 | 4 hrs | 2,180 | DH/BP | M | mid-July | 4 |
| 49. Giant Forest Loop | 9.5 | 6 hrs | 960 | DH | E | May | † |
| 50. Alta Meadow | 11.4 | 6 hrs | 2,060 | DH/BP | M | mid-June | 4 |
| 50. Alta Peak | 13.8 | 8 hrs | 3,936 | DH/BP | D | July | 4 |
| 51. Pear Lake | 13.4 | 8 hrs | 2,290 | DH/BP | M | June | 4 |
| 52. Twin Lakes | 13.6 | 8 hrs | 2,975 | DH/BP | D | June | 4 |
| 53. Jennie Lake | 14 | 7 hrs | 1,774 | DH/BP | M | mid-June | †† |
| 54. Redwood Canyon Loop | 9.5 | 5 hrs | 1,240 | DH/BP | E | mid-May | 4 |
| 55. East Kennedy Lake | 23 | 2–4 days | 6,100 | BP | D | mid-July | 4 |
| 56. Granite Lake and Granite Pass | 21 | 2–4 days | 5,392 | BP | D | mid-July | 4 |
| 57. Rae Lakes Loop | 46 | 4–5 days | 6,943 | BP | D | August | 4 |
| 58. Wood Chuck Lake | 18 | 2–3 days | 3,380 | BP | D | mid-July | 5 |

† no camping on this loop

†† no wilderness permit required; fire permit needed

| | MILEAGE | HIKING TIME | ELEVATION (FEET) | HIKE TYPE | DIFFICULTY | TRAIL OPEN | PERMITS |
|---|---|---|---|---|---|---|---|
| 59. Disappointment Lake | 27 | 3–4 days | 3,020 | BP | D | mid-July | 5 |
| 60. Dinkey Lakes | 9 | 5 hrs | 1,250 | DH/BP | E | July | 5 |
| 61. Kaiser Loop Trail | 15 | 9 hrs | 3,110 | DH/BP | D | late June | 5 |
| 62. George Lake | 9.6 | 5 hrs | 1,460 in, 480 out | DH/BP | M | mid-June | 5 |
| 63. Blayney Meadows Hot Springs | 18 | 2–3 days | 780 | BP | M | mid-August | 5 |
| 64. Devils Bathtub | 10 | 6 hrs | 1,327 | DH/BP | M | July | 5 |
| 65. Silver Divide Loop | 27.2 | 3–4 days | 4,527 | BP | D | August | 5 |
| 66. Post Peak Loop | 25.1 | 3–4 days | 4,040 | BP | D | mid-July | 5 |
| 67. Chain Lakes | 13.8 | 8 hrs | 2,100 | DH/BP | M | July | 5 |
| 68. Buena Vista Lakes Loop | 28.1 | 3–4 days | 2,400 | BP | D | July | 6 |
| 69. Ostrander Lake | 12.4 | 7 hrs | 1,560 | DH/BP | M | mid-July | 6 |
| 69. Hart Lake | 15.4 | 9 hrs | 2,000 | DH/BP | D | August | 6 |
| 70. Yosemite Point | 8.4 | 6 hrs | 3,040 | DH/BP | D | mid-June | 6 |
| 71. Half Dome | 16.4 | 9 hrs | 4,870 | DH/BP | D | July | 6 |
| 72. Merced Lake | 27.4 | 3–4 days | 3,181 | BP | D | mid-June | 6 |
| 73. Rancheria Falls | 13 | 6 hrs | 1,800 | DH/BP | D | May | 6 |
| 74. Grand Canyon of the Tuolumne | 48.8 | 4–6 days | 6,935 | BP | D | July | 6 |
| 75. Ten Lakes | 12.6 | 7 hrs | 2,190 in, 750 out | DH/BP | M | July | 6 |
| 76. Clouds Rest | 14 | 8 hrs | 2,300 | DH/BP | D | July | 6 |
| 77. Lower Cathedral Lake | 7 | 4 hrs | 1,010 | DH/BP | E | July | 6 |
| 77. Sunrise High Sierra Camp | 12.8 | 7 hrs | 1,760 | DH/BP | M | July | 6 |
| 78. Vogelsang Loop | 20.9 | 2–4 days | 2,300 | BP | M | July | 6 |
| 79. Young Lakes | 12.9 | 7 hrs | 1,620 | DH/BP | M | mid-July | 6 |
| 80. Glen Aulin | 11 | 6 hrs | 770 | DH/BP | E | July | 6 |
| 80. McCabe Lakes | 29 | 3–4 days | 2,060 | BP | M | mid-July | 6 |
| 81. Mono Pass | 9 | 5 hrs | 902 | DH/BP | E | mid-July | 6 |

| | MILEAGE | HIKING TIME | ELEVATION (FEET) | HIKE TYPE | DIFFICULTY | TRAIL OPEN | PERMITS |
|---|---|---|---|---|---|---|---|
| 82. 20 Lakes Basin | 8.4 | 4 hrs | 523 | DH/BP | E | mid-July | 7 |
| 83. Peters Creek Grove | 12 | 7 hrs | 1,040 in, 760 out | DH/BP | M | year-round | 8 |
| 84. Skyline to the Sea Trail | 32.5 | 2–4 days | 673 | BP | M | year-round | 9 |
| 85. Berry Creek Falls Loop | 11 | 6 hrs | 1,300 | DH/BP | M | year-round | 9 |
| 86. North Rim Trail | 13.5 | 7 hrs | 1,282 | DH/BP | M | year-round | 9 |
| 87. Pine Valley | 12 | 8 hrs | 300 in, 1,500 out | DH/BP | M | April | 10 |
| 88. Mount Carmel | 9 | 5 hrs | 2,580 | DH/BP | M | March | 10 |
| 89. Manuel Peak | 9 | 5 hrs | 3,039 | DH | D | year-round | 10 |
| 90. Sykes Camp | 19.5 | 2–4 days | 2,100 | BP | M | April | 10 |
| 91. Santa Lucia Trail | 12 | 7 hrs | 3,540 | DH | D | April | 10 |
| 92. Arroyo Seco | 10 | 5 hrs | 2,320 | DH/BP | M | mid-March | 10 |
| 92. Cook Camp | 12 | 6 hrs | 2,600 | DH/BP | D | mid-March | 10 |
| 93. Lost Valley | 11 | 6 hrs | 1,372 in, 760 out | DH/BP | M | April | 10 |
| 94. North Chalone Peak | 8 | 4 hrs | 2,004 | DH | M | year-round | 11 |
| 95. High Peaks Loop | 9.3 | 5 hrs | 1,580 | DH | M | year-round | 11 |
| 96. North Wilderness Loop | 9.9 | 7 hrs | 983 | DH | M | year-round | 11 |
| 97. Wilson Peak | 7.4 | 5 hrs | 1,830 | DH/BP | M | year-round | 12 |
| 98. Kelly Lake | 9.4 | 6 hrs | 1,550 in, 550 out | DH/BP | M | year-round | 12 |
| 98. Coit Lake | 11.6 | 7 hrs | 2,036 in, 650 | DH/BP | M | year-round | 12 |
| 99. Poverty Flat Loop | 10 | 6 hrs | 2,300 | DH/BP | M | year-round | 12 |
| 100. China Hole | 9.8 | 5 hrs | 1,480 | DH/BP | M | March | 12 |

# INTRODUCTION

## BEFORE YOU LEAVE HOME
### A Guide to the Guidebook

If you have never used this type of guidebook before, here are some quick suggestions on how to find a hike suited to your needs and interests.

To start, check the **location map** found on page 9 to determine which hikes in this book are in the area you wish to visit. Next, take a look at the list of summary information at the top of each hike you are interested in doing. You will want to start off by considering the **round trip** or **loop trip** mileage. That is the total number of miles you will need to walk to complete the hike. Because most of the hikes in this book are in the High Sierra, you should also pay attention to the trail's total **elevation** gain and to the elevation of the **high point** reached. Trips that start at, or climb above, an altitude of 7,000 feet require an acclimation period before you set out—please carefully read the "Hiking at High Elevation" section of the "Safety Considerations and Hazards" section in this Introduction so that you fully understand the ramifications of hiking at high elevation.

Once you have determined the number of miles to be hiked and the elevation gained, take a look at the **hiking time**. This is the length of time the average hiker (acclimated to the elevation) will spend walking to and from the destination. If you are driving up from sea level and starting your hike the same day, figure a much slower pace, averaging just a little better than 1 mile per hour. The hiking time does not include rest stops, view-gazing stops, or lunch breaks.

Finally, check the section that tells you when the trail is **hikable** on an average year. This listing does not mean that the trail will be snowfree or that all the rivers will be low enough to hop across with your boots on. Hikable means the trail should be snowfree enough and the rivers low enough for an average hiker to reach the given destination on an average year. If you are planning just one hike for the summer, check with the Forest Service or Park Service agency that manages the area and find out when they think the trail will be at its best for the year you are planning your hike; August and September are usually safe bets.

**Maps** are very important. The artist's renditions of the trails in this book are not sufficient for navigation and are not designed to be an aid if you get into difficulties along the way. Always carry a map of the area in which you are hiking, with the contours clearly shown. See the "Maps" section in the Introduction for more information.

The **permits** section is there to guide you to the Wilderness Permits, Regulations, and Quotas section of the Appendix, which has detailed information for each hike. Please note that as of 2003, wilderness permits were not required for day use on hikes described in this book except on the

Mount Whitney Trail, starting from Whitney Portal. Only overnight hikes require a permit.

Also included is a **difficulty** rating for each trail. (This is required by the publishers, but is not something any reasonable person will want to pay attention to.) The most variable and the most potentially hazardous factors cannot be included in a two-dimensional rating system. These factors include, but are not limited to: the physical condition of you, the hiker, and how well you acclimate to the elevation; and the previous winter's weather, which determines the amount of snow in the mountains during the summer. The amount of snow will in turn determine the amount of flooding in the rivers, which in turn will affect the relative safety of the river crossings.

Other hazards created by a heavier than normal snow pack include snow-covered trails at the higher elevations. Lingering patches of snow in the passes will be ice hard until warmed by the midday sun and, in some cases, they may fail to soften at all. Serious injuries have resulted from people slipping when crossing or descending these hard snow patches on what otherwise is normally an easy-to-hike trail.

There is also a long list of daily variables, such as heat and thunderstorms, that can create a multitude of problems, including heat exhaustion, lightning, or hail storms.

*Hiker's camp at Elba Lake in John Muir Wilderness (Hike 30)*

In consideration of the possible problems, all trails are given a rating for their *potential* to be an easy, moderate, or difficult hike. **Potentially easy** trails have less than 1,000 feet elevation gain and any fast-moving water encountered along the trail is crossed by a bridge or sturdy footlog. The potential difficulties found on these trails include, but are not limited to, problems associated with hiking at high elevations, heat, storms, slippery trails, and lingering snowfields. On a **potentially moderate** trail, elevation gain ranges from 1,000 feet to 2,500 feet. Some fords may be encountered; however, after the spring melt, the water in the river crossings should be slow moving without strong ebbs or currents. Hikers on potentially moderate trails should carry an extra pair of shoes for water crossings. Unexpected storms or a lingering snow pack will cause the rating of the trail to immediately increase to difficult. **Potentially difficult** trails may have one of the following problems: over 2,500 feet of elevation gain, a high-elevation pass where snow lingers until late in the summer, or fast-moving water to cross. The final category is for the unequivocally difficult trails. These trails are physically demanding and should be attempted only by strong and well-conditioned hikers who are experienced with high elevations, crossing fast moving water, and dealing with crossing or avoiding steep snow slopes.

Finally, the text below the information section will guide you to your destination and give you an idea of what you can expect to find along the way.

## Current Information

Despite best intentions, maps and guidebooks cannot keep current with the constant changes effected by man and by nature on forest roads and trails. When looking for the most up-to-date information, you should contact the agency that manages the area, as listed in the Reservations and Information section of each hike and in the Appendix at the back of the book.

## Maps

The map of the area in which you plan to hike is one of your most basic and essential pieces of equipment, and you are ill prepared without it. Experienced hikers usually carry at least two maps covering the same area. One of the maps—such as a Forest Map or a Wilderness Area Map—will give a large overview of the area; the second will be a detailed topographic map, preferably an up-to-date U.S. Geological Survey (USGS) 7.5-minute quadrangle.

Forest Maps show roads and trailhead access for individual forests. The U.S. Forest Service (USFS) also has a series of maps that cover individual wildernesses, showing topography and trails. These maps are sufficient for navigation as long as you travel only on primary trails in well-signed areas. For further information on where and how to obtain the maps you need, see the Appendix.

## Wilderness Permits

Wilderness permits are required for all overnight trips in national parks and designated national forest wilderness areas (except for sections of the Ventana and the Toiyabe). At the time of this writing, day hikers are required to have permits only on the Mount Whitney hike. The remaining day hikes are legal without permit as long as you are back to the trailhead the same day you started the hike. Backpackers in the national forest outside of the wilderness areas are not required to have a wilderness permit; however, a fire permit must be carried. See the Appendix for details.

## Parking Permits

Hikers and all other visitors using California's state parks are expected to pay a day use fee when parking a vehicle in the park. Day use fees are levied only on cars parked within the park. In 2003, the fees were not levied on park users arriving on foot or in vehicles that were registered at a state park campsite. These fees are fairly nominal at this time but may increase if budget shortfalls remain the norm.

National parks and monuments charge an entrance fee. Every vehicle and pedestrian entering the park on a road, as opposed to a trail, will be required to pay a fee. The entrance fee covers multiple park entries for up to a week. Annual passes can be purchased that offer savings to those planning multiple visits to the same park. Golden Eagle Passes are available if you are planning to hike in more than one national park or monument throughout the year.

In 2003, the only national forest area requiring parking permits was the Los Padres National Forest. The required Adventure Pass must be displayed in all vehicles at trailhead parking areas throughout the forest. These permits may be purchased for a single day or for an entire year. Adventure Passes are available from Forest Service offices and a long list of commercial vendors. For a complete list, check the Los Padres National Forest website at *www.r5.fs.fed.us/lospadres/*. Permits are also available from Los Padres National Forest, 6755 Hollister Avenue, Suite 150, Goleta, CA 93117. The Forest Service also accepts Golden Eagle Passes (the annual pass purchased for entry to national parks) as well as Adventure Passes as valid parking permits.

A guidebook is not the proper forum for discussing pros and cons of the volatile issue of the Forest Service levying fees for public access to public lands. If you are concerned with this trend, get involved. Learn the issues and alternatives and then write to your public officials.

## Clothing and Equipment

Weather in the central section of the High Sierra is some of the best found in any major mountain range in the world. During the summer, daytime temperatures generally range from a comfortable 60 degrees to 80 degrees Fahrenheit. At night, temperatures are in the 30- to 40-degree range, although it can get much colder. By September, be prepared for nighttime temperatures in the frigid twenties or the bone-chilling teens.

This ideal weather makes us all a little careless when packing. You tend to forget that the afternoon thunderstorm, which usually passes over in 20 minutes, can last for 8 hours. Rain showers can turn to miserable hailstorms or unanticipated snowstorms. Even though you can hike for years and never encounter anything but ideal conditions, you need to be prepared for the worst by carrying winter clothing, a full set of rain gear, and a shelter to crawl into.

Always pack a full set (tops and bottoms) of long underwear. Synthetic long underwear is best; cotton is useless when wet, and wool, which will keep you very warm, is known to cause a lot of itching and scratching. You should also be sure to keep a hat and a pair of gloves in your pack at all times. Because gloves and hats are easy to forget or misplace, it is best to have a spare set that stays in your pack between trips.

Footwear is a real problem. Since lightweight, relatively inexpensive boots have come onto the market, many people have been seduced by their comfort to the point of jeopardizing their safety. Lightweight boots have their place on day hikes when the trail is in good condition. They do not belong on extended trips in the High Sierra, where rocky trails climb over passes that may be snow bound for most of the summer. Heavy boots are essential when carrying a heavy pack. They strengthen the ankles and help to prevent accidents when descending a tilting slab of granite or crossing a snow slope. The stiffer soles of heavy boots allow you to kick steps into snow and retain your footing once your step is set. When you think about the discomfort of an accident and the expense of a rescue, the cost and extra weight of a heavy boot does not seem so excessive.

Never leave the trailhead without the Ten Essentials tucked into your pack, be it a day pack or a backpack. This list of essentials has been developed by people with years of hiking experience and those who rescue lost and injured hikers.

### Ten Essentials

1. **Navigation (map and compass):** Before leaving home, check to be sure that your map covers the entire area of the hike and is packed in a protective waterproof bag. Along with the map, you should carry a compass or a GPS or both. These are essential tools for navigation when walking through a cloud in the High Sierra or if you should loose the trail when crossing a snow-covered pass. When using a compass, be sure to check the declination of the area before taking a reading.

2. **Sun protection (sunglasses and sunscreen):** This is an absolute necessity at high elevations. Sunglasses help to prevent the eyes from becoming sunburned. Always wear sunglasses when on snow and consider wearing them even on cloudy days. Sunscreen is

extremely important in protecting skin from sun burn, especially at high elevations. Be especially liberal when applying sunscreen to the ears, nose, neck, shoulders, and behind the knees. Many long-anticipated High Sierra trips have been spoiled by a failure to use sunscreen on the first day out. Sunscreen will also help to prevent long-term skin damage from solar radiation.

3. **Insulation (extra clothing):** Carry more than you think you will possibly need. Lightweight layers are ideal, such as several warm tops, long underwear bottoms, and a feather-weight pair of wind pants, which can be pulled over the clothes you are wearing if the weather takes a dramatic turn for the worst or if you have to spend an unexpected night out with a party member who sprains an ankle along the trail.

4. **Illumination (headlamp or flashlight):** Always carry an extra bulb and extra batteries.

5. **First-aid supplies:** It is not enough to just buy a prepackaged first-aid kit and throw it into your pack. You need to be familiar with the contents and know how to use them. Excellent first-aid classes are given by the American Red Cross.

6. **Fire (fire starter plus matches or lighter):** The High Sierra is not the best place in the world to try to build an emergency fire. Wood is nonexistent in the higher elevations. If you are stranded in the wilderness in bad weather, you will have to plan to descend to between 9,000 and 10,000 feet to find fuel. And, frankly, unless a fire will save someone's life, the use of wood at that elevation is criminal. In place of fire, carry chemical hand-warmers and emergency shelters.

   When hiking below 6,000 feet, carry matches in a waterproof container. You should also carry candle stubs and chemical paste for starting fires on really wet days.

7. **Repair kit and tools (including knife):** A repair kit can be as simple as you like. A favorite item in every kit is Duct tape. This gray tape holds the world together. It can hold tent poles, backpacks, hiking boots, or even your shorts together in an emergency. Take a 4-inch dowel and wind a foot or two of this miracle tape around it for storage. (It also makes wonderful splints and is a great wrap for sprained ankles.)

   In addition to Duct tape, a good repair kit includes a multipurpose knife, a thin hank of parachute cord 50 to 100 feet long for hanging food or packs out of reach of animals or for tying things together, an extra shoelace, and a needle and thread so you don't have walk around with your shirt tied around your waist when you rip your only pair of shorts.

8. **Nutrition (extra food):** You should end your trip with something left over to eat on the way home.

9. **Hydration (extra water):** Never leave the car without at least a quart of water in your pack. If you drink a lot, carry two quarts. No matter how lightweight you are trying to go, never skimp on water in the High Sierra. Dehydration at high elevations leads directly to heat exhaustion and death.

10. **Emergency shelter:** Always carry an emergency shelter when you hike. This does not have to be anything expensive or fancy. For a day hike, one or two garbage bags are all that is needed. For overnight hikes, a lightweight tarp can be shaped into a one-night survival shelter if needed. Just be certain that whatever you carry is big enough for you to crawl in or under in case you have to weather out an extended thunderstorm above timberline.

## ON THE TRAIL
### Camping

The fragile nature of the High Sierran meadows and lakeshores cannot be overstated. At high elevation, plants must deal with the stresses of a short growing season, warm days, cold nights, strong winds, rain that falls in thundering torrents or not at all, and shallow soil. The addition of further stress from trampling feet or being crushed by a tent will kill most alpine plants. If several parties camp in the same fragile location, such as a meadow, a bald spot of compacted earth will form and vegetation may not return for many years.

Plan carefully when you set up your camp. If possible, select an already established campsite and avoid creating another. Do not dig trenches around your tent, remove any vegetation, or move rocks. Always camp at least 200 feet away from water. Never camp on vegetation no matter how soft it looks (that vegetation is going to send out an army of mosquitoes in the evening anyway).

When possible, pitch your tent on a slab of level granite or a sandy bench. Self-standing tents are best for this purpose because they can be pitched anywhere. Carry a foam pad to cushion your tired bones from the hard rocks.

Once you have found your campsite, exchange those heavy boots for a pair of soft-soled camp shoes. Your feet will thank you and so will the soil and delicate plants around camp. Numerous trips to the creek or lake for water can cause harm to delicate vegetation along the way, so carry a collapsible water bag and make only one trip for water instead of five.

### Water

Polluted streams and lakes in the backcountry are examples of why hikers must limit their use of soaps and be extremely diligent about following all required procedures for keeping a clean camp in the wilderness. Thirty years ago, hikers routinely dipped their cups in streams and enjoyed a drink of cold mountain water whenever they were thirsty. As more hikers began to enjoy the wilderness, creeks and lakes became fouled with parasites, and nowadays no water can be assumed safe to drink unless it has been treated.

The most publicized parasite is *Giardia lamblia,* which can cause diarrhea and other flulike symptoms about two weeks after drinking the contaminated water. There are other less-notorious bugs that cause similar problems, sometimes within a few hours of ingesting the water. The most effective way of treating water is to bring it to a rolling boil for at least 5 minutes. Mechanical water purifiers—pumps or drip bags—are also effective but are prone to breakdowns. When added to water, chemicals such as iodine will kill all parasites; however, there is some debate as to their effect on humans.

### Garbage and Sanitation

There is no magic that will make your little campfire hot enough to consume aluminum foil or heavy plastics. That may sound like an obvious statement, but there is something about a campfire in the backcountry that makes even the most intelligent people forget what will burn and what will not. Maybe the elevation does something to our fire savvy; someone should study this phenomenon. Think about this the next time you walk by a fire pit and see some aluminum poking out. Better still, stop and fish it out. If you choose to burn your garbage in the campfire, make fishing out the leftovers a morning ritual.

Except for the fire pits, hikers are doing a great job of keeping trails and camp areas clean. We can all pat ourselves on the back, because the improvement over the last twenty years has been astounding. There are still a few Neanderthals who are burying their garbage. Please do not follow suit; that stuff has a way of popping up again in a few years.

If you carried a package of food into the wilderness, you can certainly carry the empty packaging back out. Better still, plan ahead and eliminate all excess packaging before you leave home by taking food out of one or more layers of its bulky wrappings.

Do not wash dishes or your body in or even near a lake or a stream. Carry the water needed back to your camp and do your washing there. Avoid using any type of soap or detergent, including so-called biodegradable soaps, near water. Neither food scraps nor soaps are good for the water. When cleaning fish, do not throw the entrails into the water. You should bury the entrails in a deep hole away from the camp area to discourage bears and rodents from wandering through camp looking for tasty fish snacks.

Human waste is one of the most pervasive problems in the backcountry. As more people become addicted to the beauty of the wilderness, the problem is compounded by those who foul the water and continue the cycle of parasite regeneration. Always carry a small plastic trowel and dig a hole for your excrement 8 to 10 inches deep and at least 200 feet from any water, campsites, or trails. Carry your used toilet paper out in a plastic bag.

## Bears

I don't know if it is the food, elevation, wonderful scenery, or just natural inclination, but the bears of California are some of the smartest in the country. Bears in Yosemite National Park have learned how to remove windows out of cars to get at the food left inside. Some bear families have been known to specialize in breaking into certain makes of cars. These bears have no trouble finding backpackers' food. You can use all the procedures that have successfully fooled bears in other parts of the country—such as hanging food bags 20 feet off the ground, suspended on skinny tree branches, or counterbalancing food with no accessible ropes—and California bears will be chewing on your gorp and beef jerky before someone in the neighboring tent has time to start snoring.

There are few things that can spoil a carefully planned backpack trip faster than watching a bear run off with all your food. And thanks to the availability of human food, the number of bears in the wilderness areas of California is increasing. These bears are intelligent and are following hikers to their favorite campsites, living and traveling at elevations where they must rely on human food for survival.

The best way to eliminate the bear problem and ensure the success of your trip is proper food storage. On most trails in Sequoia, Kings Canyon, and Yosemite National Parks, hikers are required to store all their food in bear-resistant canisters. These heavy, bulky tubes are a real headache. Not only do they take up a large chunk of space in your backpack, they are also very hard to pack. The most widely used canister is 12 inches long and $8\frac{1}{4}$ inches wide, and has a $5\frac{3}{4}$-inch diameter access hole in the top.

Packing the canisters is a challenge. Before you leave home, repackage all your food into small bags that will fit easily into the hole. Large group meals will need to be broken down into small parts in order to fit in the small hole at the top of the canister. Replace bulky foods, such as macaroni and bread rolls, with compact equivalents such as dried potato flakes or rice and hard tack or tortillas. Remember, if starting your hike in the morning, your first two meals, a lunch and a dinner, can be carried outside of the canister.

Toiletries such as toothpaste, sunscreen, and bug repellent also need to fit into the bear canister. The best method to achieve this is to repackage these items into lightweight plastic containers before you leave home.

Bear-resistant food canisters are an undeniable pain. However, there are some positive aspects to them: They make great backcountry camp seats and tables.

In areas where bear-resistant canisters are not required, all food and toiletries should be hung at night and during the day when you are away from your camp. Counter-balancing is the recommended method. The equipment required is a 15-foot piece of rope, two equally weighted food bags, a sturdy tree with its first branch at least 18 feet off the ground, and a long stick for balancing the food bags and retrieving them later. (If you do not understand this technique, ask for some explanatory literature with a diagram when you pick up your wilderness permit.)

If you find yourself above timberline without a food canister, you should suspend your food over an overhanging cliff or, as a last resort, bury your food under a pile of rocks as far from camp as possible and hope for the best.

Some of the most popular campsites in the national parks have food-storage boxes. When boxes are available, you are advised to join the crowds and camp near them. Bears that continually fail to find food will move on, hopefully to search for natural foods.

If a bear comes around your camp, yell, bang cooking pots, and wave jackets in the air. If the bear does not leave, you should. Although the bear is interested only in your food, it is a dangerous animal. Never approach a bear or try to get your food back from it. Leave cubs alone at all times.

## The Sacred Rite of the Campfire

Fires are an ancient ritual used to ward off evil and give warmth in the night. Unfortunately, this comforting tradition of spending an evening watching shapes and colors dance through the flames is denuding the mountains of wood. The nightly fire requires a lot of fuel, a resource that is slow to replenish in the high country. When you strip the forest floor of dead wood, you are destroying a microhabitat important to the survival of many small plants and animals, which in turn are important to the survival of the entire ecosystem. In the high meadows, a single night's campfire can consume the equivalent of one to two small, sturdy trees. This resource will renew itself—in 70 to 100 years.

Simply stated, there are too many hikers for each of us to have a campfire in the wilderness. Dead wood and other available fuel have been used up in the high country, and it will be years before the trees can generate a new crop. The soil in which these trees must grow is now lacking nutrients because wood has been removed and burned, rather than decaying, making regeneration that much more difficult. It is a vicious cycle.

*Backpackers using camp stove to prepare a gourmet wilderness feast*

To protect the high country, fires are prohibited in most areas above 9,000 feet. In areas that receive heavy use, the restrictions may extend to lower elevations. Where fires are allowed, build them only in an existing fire ring in an established campsite. For your fire, use only dead wood picked up off the forest floor well away from your campsite. Do not break dead-looking branches off trees or snags. And never cut green wood.

Always carry a small camp stove for your cooking, or eat your food cold. For warmth, you should rely exclusively on your food and shelter and not on a campfire. Spend your evenings looking at the stars and moon rather than blinding your eyes to the beauty of the night by staring into the fire.

### Group Size

To reduce the impact of hikers on the wilderness, Forest Service and Park Service rules limit group size to fifteen people. In the national parks and a few high-use areas in the wilderness, group size is limited to eight. This rule was designed for the welfare of the wilderness. Please respect it.

### Pets

Pets are not allowed on trails in the national parks or in the California big-horn sheep zoological areas. Check your map before you start hiking with your pet to be sure your trail does not pass through any restricted areas.

When on the trail with your pet, you must keep it under voice control or physical restraint at all times. Pets are not allowed to harass wildlife or hikers. Treat your pet's feces the same way you treat your own: Bury it in a hole 8 to 10 inches deep and at least 200 feet away from all water, campsites, and trails.

The first time you hike with your pet, do not make the mistake of believing voice control is sufficient to restrain your animal. At home, your pet may understand where the boundaries are, but the trail will be a new experience for both of you. The dog will be exposed to a whole new world of smells from people and wild animals. Weather and altitude can also affect your pet. Dogs often become possessive of the trail you are walking on or an entire camp area. When dogs meet other dogs and fight for dominance in the middle of a peaceful meadow, you may find yourself in an embarrassing and potentially dangerous situation. Always have the leash handy.

### Horses and Packers

Horse packers may be found at nearly every popular trailhead in the Sierra. These are some of the most knowledgeable, friendly, and almost always helpful ambassadors of equestrian rights found anywhere in the world. Their services are popular. For a price, they will pack you in to a high lake, or you can have your gear packed in while you walk. You can even arrange to be fully taken care of at one of the High Sierra camps. If you have an accident, need directions, or want information concerning the condition of the trail, talk to the horse packers.

When a hiker sees a horse and rider approaching, it is the hiker's responsibility to move off the trail and let the horse pass. If possible, move off on the downhill side of the trail; however, never endanger yourself to do so. When you see a horse approaching, call out a greeting and let the horse and rider know you are there to avoid spooking the horse. If you are on a narrow section of trail, retreat to a safe place to let the horses pass. When in doubt, discuss the situation with the riders and let them tell you what they can do.

Why do you have to follow these rules? Why do horses get the right-of-way on a trail? The answer is simple: Horses may be pretty, but they are much larger and a whole lot dumber than you. No matter how you feel about horses, the trail is not the place to make your point. A little thoughtless action on the part of a hiker could endanger the life of the rider, the horse, and even the hiker. Clients of the horse packers are especially at risk as many are novice riders.

### Theft

Although not a problem at every trailhead, break-ins do occur in some areas. To reduce your risk of a break-in, leave the fancy car at home and drive the old beater to the trailhead. Use a steering-wheel locking device and make sure your car appears empty of personal possessions when you leave. Lock all extra clothes in the trunk and take any valuables with you.

In the Mineral King area of Sequoia National Park, marmots have learned to be proficient trailhead vandals. They chew on hoses, tires, and wires. The only protection against these destructive rodents is to rap a fine wire mesh around the outside of your car. If you do not carry wire, be sure to have plenty of duct tape in your repair kit to patch holes in frayed wires and rubber tubes.

## SAFETY CONSIDERATIONS AND HAZARDS
### Weather and Storms

Thunderstorms are the main weather hazard during the summer months in the High Sierra. Storms come up quickly and hikers must be prepared. Think ahead and plan to be in a safe place when a storm arrives. If storms have been building up at a certain time of day, for several days in a row, plan your day's activities accordingly. When a storm hits, the safest place to be is in a forested area away from the tallest tree. Open mountains and ridge tops are the most hazardous places to be in a storm. Other places to avoid are open meadows, caves, edges or bases of cliffs, and anywhere near water.

If a storm catches you in the open, remove your pack and any other metal objects you may be carrying. Put your sleeping pad on a rock that is just big enough to sit on, place only your feet and posterior on the material, and wait the storm out. Do not attempt to quickly put the tent up; the poles may attract lightning.

## Snow

Early season hikers should arm themselves with ice axes (and know how to use them), wear stiff-soled leather boots for traction, and cover the tops of their boots with gaiters to keep the snow out. They should also be proficient map readers and know how to navigate with a compass and/or GPS when the trail disappears under the snow for miles on end. If you do not have all these skills and the required equipment, wait until the snow melts before you head to the high elevations.

By midsummer you will still find lingering snowfields at the higher passes. When at all possible, walk around the snow rather than over it. Old snow can be a tricky thing, with hidden air pockets where you will suddenly and unexpectedly break through. Old snow is often hard and difficult to kick steps into. A slip on old, icy snow will result in a few abrasions at best; at worst, you may take a bone-breaking slide to the bottom.

## Falling Rocks

Falling rocks are a constant hazard on steep mountain slopes. Most falling rocks are random occurrences. When you hear a rock falling down the hillside above you, look for protection and yell "rock" to warn anyone else in the vicinity of the danger. If you need to cross a rock-fall area, go one at a time, quickly and quietly. Do not rest or camp in old rock fall areas. If you should have the misfortune of kicking loose a rock on a trail, yell "rock" to warn hikers below, even if you don't think anyone is there.

## River Crossings

In order to preserve your wilderness experience, the Forest Service has chosen to leave many creeks unbridged. As a result, trails are usually designed to ford creeks at an area considered suitable for a horse to cross. Hikers are left to enjoy their wilderness anyway they can get across it.

Obviously, you are not a horse, so you must set about looking for alternative crossings. In many areas a bit of searching will reveal a sturdy log over the water or a wider point where the water is not flowing as fast. If you should slip off the log on the way across, attempt to fall downstream rather than up so you are not washed into the log.

Before you cross that sturdy log or wade that creek, look around for a long stick that could help you stabilize as you cross. Next, loosen the shoulder straps and unbuckle the hip belt of your pack so you can quickly shed your load if you slip.

Plan all crossings of major unbridged streams for the early morning, when the water flow tends to be lower. When crossing deep, fast-moving water, leave your boots on for the best possible traction and wear gaiters to keep from getting too waterlogged. However, these crossings should be rare and are best avoided. Wet boots are an invitation to blisters later. Most crossings can be handled by removing your boots and wearing a pair of water shoes. You should also arm yourself with a heavy stick for balance.

Keep the stick on the upstream side to avoid being pulled downstream.

Never tie a rope to someone who is crossing a creek. Ropes have a frustrating tendency to drag people under and a rope may even act as an anchor if it gets caught under a rock. If some members of your party, such as children, have trouble fording a creek, send one person ahead to tie a rope on the far side and set up a hand-line.

Some river crossings should not be attempted until late summer or early fall. If you have questions about a certain crossing, make inquiries when you pick up your wilderness permit. If the person issuing the permit cannot give you an answer, have that person call someone who is familiar with the crossing in question. Remember, river crossings have resulted in the loss of lives in the wilderness.

### Hiking at High Elevations

Hiking in the High Sierra demands a lot more of your body than a low-elevation trip in the Coast Range. If you simply jump out of your car at the trailhead and head up the trail, chances are you will find yourself moving rather slowly, covering much less ground than you hoped.

It is especially important to figure in the effect of the elevation when you are planning an extended hike through the high country. Do not plan to cover long distances for the first couple of days of your trip. A slow, easy start gives your body time to adjust to the weight of the pack and to the elevation. If the hike begins at a high elevation, 7,000 feet or above, spend one or more days near the trailhead acclimating. This is a good time to explore the area with a couple of day hikes before heading out on a long trek.

### Exhaustion and Altitude Sickness

Hikers who head straight from their low-elevation homes to the High Sierran trailheads know that their bodies need time to adjust. Breathing becomes rapid as your lungs try to extract the customary amount of oxygen from the thinner air. Given time, your blood increases the proportion of oxygen-carrying corpuscles to compensate for the lack of oxygen. If you do not give your body enough time to make the necessary adjustment, you can expect to feel fatigue, nausea, weakness, and shortness of breath. These symptoms should be regarded with concern, as they may be the early signs of high-altitude pulmonary edema or cerebral edema and can culminate in loss of life.

If you find yourself suffering from even the slightest symptoms of exhaustion or altitude sickness, slow down, drink more fluids, and eat a high-energy snack. If you wait until you are sick to do something about it, you have simply compounded the problem. Even if you do not feel any symptoms on the first day of a hike, make a special effort to drink plenty of liquids.

If the symptoms do not improve after a night's rest or if you notice dizziness, shortness of breath, rapid pulse, confusion, loss of memory, or persistent coughing, you should descend to a lower elevation as rapidly as possible. If you have a large party, send someone ahead to alert the police or park rangers that there is a medical emergency in your party.

### Snakes

Rattlesnakes are found throughout California and should be a matter of constant concern below 7,000 feet. Along the trail, always check for snakes before you sit down or set your pack down. Make a thorough area inspection before you set up your tent. Never stick your hand into a crack in a rock or under a log or rock without carefully visually inspecting it first.

Snakes tend to strike low, at the foot or ankle level. Protect yourself by wearing boots and long, loose pants. Do not walk around camp barefoot in a snake-infested area. In the evening when going for water or firewood, always wear shoes. If camping in a snake area, use a tent and keep the door closed to avoid having one of these warmth-loving reptiles decide to share your sleeping bag with you.

Snakes do not want to see you any more than you want to see them. They will avoid contact with people whenever possible. When contact is unavoidable, the snake usually will announce its presence with an aggressive rattle, which means it is time for you to move away because the snake cannot.

If someone in your party is bitten by a rattlesnake, the best treatment is to immobilize the victim and then transport this person to the nearest hospital or clinic for treatment. The victim should move as little as possible.

Like all other living creatures, rattlesnakes are protected by law in national parks. The snakes are a natural part of the wilderness and should be respected.

### Ticks

In the coastal regions, ticks appear after the first good rains of November or December and are annoyingly in evidence until the end of June. In the higher mountains, the season varies with the snowmelt, beginning in March. They hang on the ends of grass and bushes and wait for a critter, human or otherwise, to come along and brush them off.

Ticks do not dig in immediately; they usually crawl around a bit to find a warm place before attaching themselves. If you feel something crawling under your clothes, stop and check it out. Ticks are hard to get off once they have burrowed under your skin.

Ticks prefer tender skin, so check under the band of your pants, underwear, collar, and socks frequently. At night do a thorough tick check, which means running your hand through your hair, exploring armpits, and checking out all the other "you know where" places that can't be mentioned by name in a family book.

*Western black-legged tick*

Ticks are less in evidence during the middle of the day. The eager-beaver early risers will get the most ticks on the trail. Late starters will find that many of the ticks have been brushed off already. Hikers who are first on the trail may find a tick-stick to be a handy piece of equipment. A tick-stick is simply a walking stick or a dead branch picked up along the trail that can be used to beat any overhanging brush as you walk.

Clothing such as long-sleeved shirts and long pants with cuffs or gaiters can help protect you from ticks. Insect repellent that has a heavy dosage of N, N-diethyl-meta-toluamide (DEET) is also effective.

Because ticks are known carriers of Lyme disease and Rocky Mountain spotted fever, it is important to remove all ticks as soon as you find them. If the tick has imbedded itself, cover it with heavy oil (carry some in your first-aid kit for this purpose). The oil will close up the tick's breathing pores, forcing it to withdraw. Wait for half an hour; if the tick has not backed out, you must unscrew it by pulling counterclockwise with tweezers. If you cannot remove the tick or if part of the tick remains behind after you have unscrewed it, you must see a doctor.

### Poison Ivy and Poison Oak

You should be aware of poison ivy and poison oak when hiking in the coastal regions and in some low-elevation sections of Sequoia, Kings Canyon, and Yosemite National Parks.

Poison ivy and poison oak grow leaves in distinctive groups of three. Watch for these plants along creeks and in wooded areas. In the fall the leaves turn bright red. The poison from these plants are found in an oil that is carried in the sap and may be picked up by brushing the leaves with your legs as you walk by or by handling the twigs and wood. If you burn these shrubs, the toxins become airborne and are very dangerous to breathe.

The best defense against poison ivy and poison oak is not to touch it. Wear protective clothing when hiking and then take them off before you get into your tent at night. Handle your clothing with care. If your skin should accidentally brush up against the poison oak or ivy, wash the affected area thoroughly with soap and water. Be very careful not to get it on your hands and spread it to other parts of your body.

### Mosquitoes

In the Sierra, mosquitoes can descend on you like a thunderstorm on a peaceful day. That beautiful green meadow, that inviting creek, that peaceful lake, that lovely green forest are all home to hoards of mosquitoes in midsummer.

Without a little preparation, your carefully planned hike to one of the most beautiful lakes in the entire Sierra can turn into a mosquito-swatting march in Hell. You must be prepared to either don a covering layer of clothing or dose your exposed skin and some of your unexposed skin with mosquito repellent. A hat with face netting can be convenient around camp.

### Sun

Sunglasses and sunblock lotions are essential equipment for hiking in the High Sierra, where the atmosphere lacks the ingredients that block out the harmful effects of the sun. Without them, a simple overnight hike can result in a tremendous sunburn and blisters. An extended trip can be ruined by a bad sunburn on the first day out. Over time, continual exposure will cause wrinkles and brown spots at best and may eventually lead to skin cancer and melanoma.

Wear protective clothing, including a hat, and apply sunscreen with an SPF factor of 15 or greater many times during the day. Don't miss the ears, nose, cheeks, and neck.

### A Final Word

A safe trip is a trip that has been well thought out and prepared for. Experienced hikers should accompany the inexperienced. Mountain first-aid classes should be taken by all. An accident can turn a pleasant trip into an instant nightmare. If you are the only one trained in first aid, it does not do you any good if you are the one who gets hurt.

Let someone responsible know where you are going and when you will return. It is also a good idea to tell this person when it is okay to start worrying and call for help. Pack the Ten Essentials and be prepared for the worst, even if it means carrying a few extra pounds in your pack. Always remember: The mountains do not care if you come back dead or alive. So plan ahead, be prepared, and then relax and enjoy your hike.

### A NOTE ABOUT SAFETY

Safety is an important concern in all outdoor activities. No guide-book can alert you to every hazard or anticipate the limitations of every reader. Therefore, the descriptions of roads, trails, routes, and natural features in this book are not representations that a particular place or excursion will be safe for your party. When you follow any of the routes described in this book, you assume responsibility for your own safety. Under normal conditions, such excursions require the usual attention to traffic, road and trail conditions, weather, terrain, the capabilities of your party, and other factors. Keeping informed on current conditions and exercising common sense are the keys to a safe, enjoyable outing.

*The Mountaineers Books*

# 1 | COLE CREEK LAKES

**Round trip: 28 miles**
**Hiking time:** 2–4 days
**High point:** 8,280 feet
**Elevation gain:** 3,400 feet in; 1,740 feet out
**Difficulty:** Potentially difficult
**Hikable:** Mid-July through September

**Driving directions:** Drive Highway 88 to the Bear River Lake turnoff, located 30.5 miles east of Jackson, and descend 2 miles toward the lake. When the road divides, stay right, following the signs for Cole Creek Campground. After 2.4 miles the road divides again; go left on Road 8N14 for 5.8 miles. Just before Cole Creek Campground take a left, still on Road 8N14, and continue for another 3.4 miles to an intersection. Tanglefoot Trailhead is located to the left, 0.4 mile on Road 8N14E (6,640 feet). If the final section does not look passable for your vehicle, park at the intersection and walk.
**Maps:** USFS Mokelumne Wilderness; USGS Bear River Reservoir and Mokelumne Peak
**Permits:** Amador Ranger Station and Carson Pass Information Center (Case 1)

Surprising vistas, pleasant lakes, and scenic campsites are the rewards for this long and difficult trek up the Tanglefoot Trail to Cole Creek Lakes. Despite an off-highway vehicle (OHV) road that allows back-door access from the Silver Lake area, early season visitors who do not mind tramping through a bit of snow will find complete solitude. (No campfires are permitted above 8,000 feet.)

**THE HIKE.** From the parking area, the dusty trail ascends gradually through the forest. At the end of 1.5 miles, the trail divides (6,800 feet). Most of your fellow hikers will leave you here, taking the left fork to Shriner Lake. Your trail then descends into Tanglefoot Canyon, where the small creek is crossed without much difficulty.

Now you begin a meandering ascent of the east side of Tanglefoot Canyon, to reach, at 4.5 miles, Moraine Lake (7,105 feet), a pleasantly shaded campsite and the last certain water for the next 7.5 miles.

Beyond Moraine Lake the trail heads north through forest, skirting flower-covered meadows while ascending to a view over the granite maze of Tanglefoot Canyon from an 8,240-foot shoulder of Mokelumne Peak. With your goal in view to the north, the trail makes a heart-breaking descent. After dropping 800 feet, cross two seasonal creeks, pass a couple of small campsites, and then begin to climb. The trail, which has been excellent up to this point, heads steeply up the hillside and virtually disappears in the forest. Follow the blazes on the trees with care.

At 10 miles, reach an open meadow with an old signpost at the center. The trail divides here. Straight ahead is the unmaintained Long Lake Trail, which, if you do not get lost, can save a mile of walking and several hundred feet of climbing. The safer choice is the Munson Meadow Trail, located at the upper left corner of the meadow. This trail also has its obscure moments and must be followed with care as it climbs over the forested hillside to a ridge.

*Cole Creek drainage*

From the ridge, descend left to reach tiny, sloping Munson Meadow at 12 miles. There is an intersection here: Water is located to the right; Long Lake and Cole Creek Lakes are to the left. From the meadow, climb briefly then descend to a four-way intersection at 13 miles (7,800 feet). Long Lake and several forested campsites are located 0.5 mile to the right. To the left is the unmaintained Long Lake Trail. Continue straight

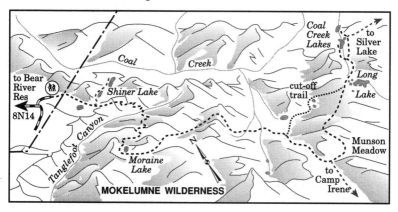

33

to reach the first of the three Cole Creek Lakes, at 14 miles (8,040 feet).

The first Cole Creek Lake is small and forested. Leave the main trail before it crosses the outlet and follow an unsigned path along the left shore to the second and most scenic of the lakes. Small, secluded campsites with views of Mokelumne Peak may be found along the southwest side of the lake, tucked into folds of the granite hillside.

## 2 | EMIGRANT LAKE

**Round trip: 8 miles**
**Hiking time:** 4 hours
**High point:** 8,600 feet
**Elevation gain:** 810 feet
**Difficulty:** Potentially easy
**Hikable:** Mid-July through September

**Driving directions:** Drive Highway 88 west for 0.8 mile from Caples Lake Resort. Park just below Caples Lake Dam (7,790 feet).
**Maps:** USGS Mokelumne Wilderness; USGS Caples Lake
**Permits:** Amador Ranger Station and Carson Pass Information Center (Case 1)

Emigrant Lake lies on the dividing line between forest and high alpine meadows. At the north end of the lake, a few hardy trees provide sheltered campsites, while the remainder of the lake is surrounded by steep cliffs and flower-covered meadows. Easy access makes this a popular destination in midsummer, so plan to arrive early to secure a good campsite.

Snow lingers on the forested hillsides below Emigrant Lake long after it has melted from the open slopes above. Early season visitors should be prepared with good footwear for crossing steep, icy snow slopes and for fording flooded creeks.

**THE HIKE.** The trail begins at the upper right side of the parking area and heads straight up the steep hillside to the top of the dam, where it enters the Mokelumne Wilderness. The broad and nearly level trail parallels the lakeshore, a popular fishing area. After the first 0.2 mile, you will pass from forest to meadows then back into forest. At the 1-mile point, the Old Emigrant Road Trail branches off on the right. Continue straight ahead on a trail that becomes progressively rougher.

The trail leaves Caples Lake at 1.7 miles and heads up a forested valley, paralleling Emigrant Creek. At 2 miles, you will pass a spur trail to Kirkwood Ski Area on the right, then begin a steady climb. The trail crosses a seasonal stream and then Emigrant Creek. Above Emigrant Creek, a switchback brings you up the granite-strewn hillside to meadows where

*Emigrant Lake*

boot-beaten paths to campsites branch off in every direction. Continue straight across the meadow and through a narrow band of trees to Emigrant Lake (8,600 feet).

The lake is in a deep cirque with Covered Wagon Peak towering over the southwest side and a shoulder of Fourth of July Peak dominating the

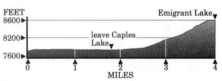

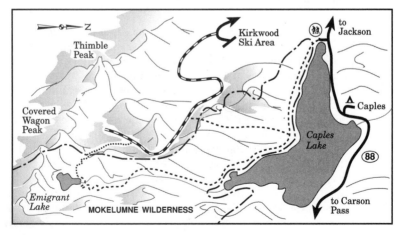

eastern skyline. Campsites must be at least 300 feet from the lakeshore. No campfires are allowed at the lake.

Fourth of July Peak and Covered Wagon Peak are easy cross-country destinations from Emigrant Lake for hikers with off-trail experience and a good map. Experienced routefinders may make a loop on the return trip by contouring cross-country from Emigrant Lake west to the ski area and then following the Old Emigrant Trail back to Caples Lake. The trail is nearly invisible in the vicinity of the Kirkwood ski runs. The best course is to traverse the basin to the first chairlift and descend. Find the ski area service road and follow it 0.5 mile to a well-marked trail on the right. Head down to rejoin the Emigrant Lake Trail on the shores of Caples Lake.

## 3 | SHOWERS LAKE

**Round trip: 9 miles**
**Hiking time:** 5 hours
**High point:** 8,800 feet
**Elevation gain:** 720 feet in; 400 feet out
**Difficulty:** Potentially moderate
**Hikable:** Late June through September

**Driving directions:** Drive Highway 88 toward Carson Pass. At 0.2 mile west of the summit, turn north into a large parking area (8,480 feet). A parking fee is charged from June through September.
**Maps:** USFS Mokelumne Wilderness; USGS Caples Lake, Carson Pass, Echo Lake
**Permits:** Lake Tahoe Basin Management Unit and Carson Pass Information Center (Case 1)

Meandering meadows, glowing with brilliant masses of alpine blooms: lupine, scarlet gilia, mountain pennyroyal, several shades of paintbrush, and vibrant yellow mule ears. Showers Lake lies within the wildflower garden of the Sierra Nevada and is at its best in early summer.

Wildflowers are not the only reason to hike here. Showers Lake is an ideal destination with numerous campsites and wonderful boulders for picnicking. As an added incentive, there is an alternate, scenic loop route that may be followed on the way back.

**THE HIKE.** Walk north from the parking lot on the Pacific Crest Trail (PCT). The trail skirts a grove of stately Jeffery Pines and at 0.5 mile crosses a small seasonal creek, which marks the beginning of the climb.

At 1 mile, pass a junction with the Old Meiss Trail on the left. Stay right, following the PCT as it climbs steadily for another 0.5 mile to the open ridge crest and small pond at Meiss Pass (8,760 feet). The view demands

*Showers Lake*

attention. To the south are Elephants Back, Round Top, The Sisters, Thimble Peak, Black Butte, and Caples Lakes. On a clear day, Lake Tahoe is visible to the north.

Follow the trail across Meiss Pass then descend, dropping 400 feet to the broad, open Upper Truckee River valley. The trail crosses the creek three times; the second and third crossings will be wet and potentially difficult in early season.

At 2.6 miles, a spur trail heads left to the reconstructed Meiss Cabin and barn (a skiers' hut in the winter). A few feet beyond lies an intersection with the Tahoe Rim Trail. Stay left and continue down the nearly level valley on the PCT.

At 3.1 miles, the trail crosses the Upper Truckee

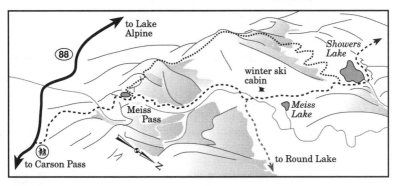

River for the final time. Shortly after, pass an unmarked trail on the left, to Schneider Camp. Stay right and descend to a marshy, bug-breeding meadow above Meiss Lake. The trail begins a gradual climb, which soon steepens into a full-scale assault on the hillside. After crossing several colorful flower fields, the trail reaches an 8,800-foot ridge crest overlooking Showers Lake. Pass a second, unsigned intersection to Schneider Camp and descend a final 0.1 mile to the forested lakeshore at 4.5 miles.

For hikers looking for a challenge and views, on the return trip there is a high-route loop option. Snow lingers on these hillsides, so wait until August to attempt this route unless you are carrying an ice ax. From Showers Lake, follow the PCT back up the first hill and go right on the unmarked Schneider Camp trail. Climb steeply to the 9,100-foot ridge crest. At this point, leave the trail and head south on a boot-beaten track along the crest. The path frequently disappears in the rocky soil, but the route is obvious. The ridge crest is followed to a 9,452-foot high point before you descend back to the rejoin the PCT at Meiss Pass.

## 4 | FOURTH OF JULY LAKE

**Round trip: 10 miles**
**Hiking time:** 6 hours
**High point:** 9,360 feet
**Elevation gain:** 787 feet in; 1,196 feet out
**Difficulty:** Potentially moderate
**Hikable:** Mid-July through September

**Driving directions:** Drive Highway 88 to the summit of Carson Pass and park at the Information Station (8,573 feet). A parking fee is charged.
**Maps:** USFS Mokelumne Wilderness, USGS Caples Lake and Carson Pass
**Permits:** Carson Pass Information Station (Case 1)

Four bright lakes in sturdy granite cups, dazzling vistas, and nature's finest flower gardens combine in this not-to-be-missed excursion into the Mokelumne Wilderness. This is a perfect area with wide trails traversing broad, meadow-covered benches. There are even a couple of optional, difficult, cross-country excursions. Unfortunately, like so many perfect areas, this one has been nearly loved to death.

As part of the healing regimen prescribed by forest managers for this over-loved area, camping is restricted to specified sites. Campsite permits must be obtained from the Carson Pass Information Station before starting the hike. No campfires are permitted.

**THE HIKE.** From the Information Station, follow the Pacific Crest Trail

*Round Top Lake*

(PCT) south into the forest. The trail descends briefly then leads up the hillside, entering the Mokelumne Wilderness at the end of the first 0.5 mile.

After a steady climb, the trail passes to the right of 8,810-foot Frog Lake. This pretty lake is a popular stopping point for many hikers. The main trail continues climbing for another 0.1 mile to a major intersection. The

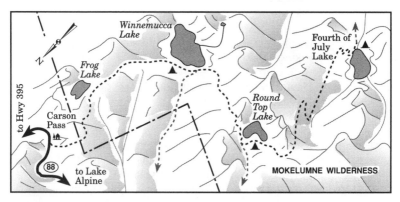

PCT goes left. Stay right, traversing flower-covered hillsides below Elephants Back and enjoying views of Caples Lake and the Meiss Pass area to the west and north.

At 2.5 miles, the trail crosses a low saddle and descends to Winnemucca Lake (9,060 feet). Here the trail splinters and hikers are left to choose the best trail. Go straight, passing a spur trail to Woods Lake and then crossing the outlet creek on a couple of shaky logs.

Beyond Winnemucca Lake, the trail ascends an open hillside. On the left, note the boot-beaten path to the top of 10,381-foot Round Top, a highly recommended but very difficult and challenging off-trail side trip. At 3.5 miles, the trail crosses another ridge, then descends to 9,220-foot Round Top Lake. After splashing your feet in the water, continue west. Stay left at a second intersection with a trail to Woods Lake and descend gradually through broad meadows around the sides of The Sisters.

The rate of descent increases until the trail reaches a wind-blown saddle overlooking a steeply sloping basin. Fourth of July Lake lies 1,000 feet below. The trail down is nicely graded though somewhat narrow and rocky. Hikers who brave the descent will find the lake a pleasant destination with considerably more solitude than found at the lakes above.

If the final descent to Fourth of July Lake is not to your liking, consider an easy ascent of Fourth of July Peak, accessed by a boot-beaten path from the saddle overlooking the lake.

# 5 | GRANITE AND GROUSE LAKES

**Round trip to Granite Lake: 4 miles**
**Hiking time:** 2 hours
**High point:** 8,700 feet
**Elevation gain:** 580 feet
**Difficulty:** Potentially easy
**Hikable:** Mid-July through September

**Round trip to Grouse Lake: 12 miles**
**Hiking time:** 7 hours
**High point:** 9,260 feet
**Elevation gain:** 1,324 feet in; 900 feet out
**Difficulty:** Potentially easy
**Hikable:** August through September

**Driving directions:** Drive Highway 88 east from Carson Pass 6.4 miles and then turn right on Blue Lake Road. (From the east, the turnoff is located 2.5 miles west of the Lake Tahoe intersection.) Follow Blue Lake Road for 11.9 miles (of which 7.2 are on pavement) to an intersection at

Lower Blue Lake. Go right on a signed PG&E road for 1.7 miles to find a parking area at the base of Upper Blue Lake Dam. The hike begins from the left side of the parking area (8,136 feet).
**Maps:** USFS Mokelumne Wilderness; USGS Pacific Valley, Carson Pass, Caples Lake, and Mokelumne Peak (trail not noted)
**Permits:** Amador Ranger Station, Carson Ranger Station, Carson Pass Information Station, and Markleeville Guard Station (Case 1)

This is a magnificent High Sierran ramble through verdant meadows and across rocky ridges to the shores of a small subalpine tarn cupped in a granite basin. The relatively minor elevation gain makes this hike superb for beginning backpackers or an excellent day trip for ambitious walkers. Campsites can be found at several points along the trail; however, by midsummer the only certain water is at Granite and Grouse Lakes. No campfires are allowed.

**THE HIKE.** The trail begins by crossing the overflow channel of Upper Blue Lake. If the water happens to be flowing, cross on the dam and walk back down the opposite side of the channel to reach the trail. After heading through forest for 1,000 feet, traverse a small creek and then pass the first of two spur trails from Middle Creek Campground before beginning a gradual but steady climb. At the 1-mile point, you will arrive at an unmarked intersection. Continue straight and enter the Mokelumne Wilderness.

The meandering climb continues. The trail passes a small lake at 1.3 miles and reaches aptly named Granite Lake at 2 miles (8,700 feet). Traverse along the shore to the southwest corner of the lake, then go left and cross a low saddle. The trail then descends into the first and the prettiest of three basins.

At 2.5 miles reach the lower end of the first basin, where the trail abruptly heads uphill

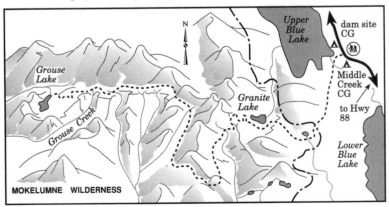

MOKELUMNE WILDERNESS

*Grouse Lake Trail*

on a steep rib of granite. The well-defined tread disappears here and you must follow the tree blazes and ducks (small piles of rocks) to keep on course. The climb is followed by a traverse to the west on a steep hillside overlooking Meadow Lake and then a descent through a second basin. The trail climbs steeply before descending into the third basin.

Cross the third basin and ascend west to a rocky ridge with an excellent view over the Mokelumne Wilderness. The trail heads north along the open ridge crest to reach the trip's 9,260-foot high point, then begins a descending traverse. At the 5-mile point Grouse Lake comes into view, and the trail suddenly plunges downhill, dropping 800 feet in the next mile as it descends a steep gully to a small bench above the lake. Contour right through grass, brush, and then forest to reach Grouse Lake (8,400 feet) at 6 miles. The trail ends at the lakeshore. Campsites are located to the right and left.

# 6 | BULL RUN LAKE

**Round trip: 7.4 miles**
**Hiking time:** 4 hours
**High point:** 8,400 feet
**Elevation gain:** 860 feet in; 560 feet out
**Difficulty:** Potentially easy
**Hikable:** July through September

**Driving directions:** Drive Highway 4 to Mosquito Lakes Trailhead, located 8.2 miles west of Ebbetts Pass. The trailhead is located at the west end of the lakes (elevation 8,050 feet).

**Maps:** USFS Carson–Iceberg Wilderness, USGS Pacific Valley and Spicer Meadows Res.
**Permits:** Alpine Station (Case 1)

The focal point for hot and tired hikers arriving at Bull Run Lake is an inviting granite island, which attracts swimmers like flies. Unless you are completely unselfconscious, pack a bathing suit for yourself, life vests for the nonswimmers, and fishing poles for everyone, then plan to spend a long day at this delightfully accessible lake.

Bull Run Lake is reached by a relatively short 3.7-mile trail, making it an ideal day trip. The lake is also a relaxing backpacking destination with spacious campsites. On weekends the lake can be very crowded.

Ambitious hikers can take the basic hike and turn it into a loop as described below.

**THE HIKE.** Two trails start from the trailhead sign. The trail to Bull Run Lake heads into the forest, contouring south around the end of Mosquito Lakes. The second is the old Emigrant Trail, which descends steeply to the west, paralleling the road. (The Emigrant Trail is the first leg of the loop route.)

The trail to Bull Run Lake climbs the ridge overlooking Mosquito Lakes and then continues south along the rolling hillcrest. After 0.4 mile reach the boundary of the Carson–Iceberg Wilderness. The trail then rolls along the ridge crest, descending and then climbing several times before reaching the Heiser Lake junction at 1.5 miles (8,320 feet). Heiser Lake is located 0.4 mile up the left-hand trail. It is a small and rather long lake, studded with granite islets. The shoreline is grassy, with several campsites.

The trail to Bull Run Lake heads to the right from the Heiser Lake junction, plunging down the rocky hillside with a minimum of switchbacks. At 2.7 miles reach the Bull Run junction (7,840 feet). Go left, descending

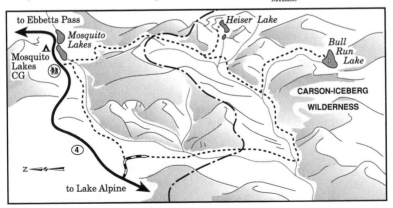

*Island in center of Bull Run Lake*

briefly then climbing up a series of giant granite steps. Watch the trail carefully; it is easy to wander off-route on the granite.

Arrive at Bull Run Lake at 3.7 miles (8,350 feet). Campsites are located all around the lake under the stately pines. Please do not trample the fragile meadows.

If you would like to turn this trip into a loop, start at Mosquito Lakes and descend on the old Emigrant Trail along the embryonic Stanislaus River. The trail receives little maintenance and fades in and out. At 1.3 miles reach an abandoned road. Go left and follow the old road around a fenced-in field to find the Stanislaus Meadow Trailhead road. Stay left and walk to the end of the road, then follow a well-maintained trail for 2 miles to the Bull Run Lake junction. After a visit to Bull Run Lake, follow the trail on uphill to the Mosquito Lakes trailhead to complete the loop.

# 7 | PARADISE VALLEY LOOP

**Loop trip: 15 miles**
**Hiking time:** 2 days
**High point:** 9,340 feet
**Elevation gain:** 2170 feet
**Difficulty:** Potentially moderate
**Hikable:** Mid-July through September

**Driving directions:** Drive Highway 4 to the Highland Lakes Road turn-off, located 1.3 miles west of the Ebbetts Pass summit. Follow the steep Highland Lakes Road south for 5.1 miles. Turn left just before the first lake and park at Gardner Meadow Trailhead (8,575 feet).
**Maps:** USFS Carson–Iceberg Wilderness; USGS Dardanelles Cone and Disaster Peak
**Permits:** Hathaway Pines Ranger Station and Alpine Lake Ranger Station (Case 1)

The rugged mountains of the Carson–Iceberg and Emigrant Wildernesses form a dramatic backdrop for the miles of rich green meadows traversed on this scenic loop. Your route follows the Pacific Crest Trail (PCT) south along the ridge crests, followed by a descent through the beautiful meadows of Paradise Valley to Adams Camp. The final leg of the loop climbs gradually through alternating forest and meadows to end with a stroll across the enchanting Upper Gardner Meadow.

This hike is at its best be-

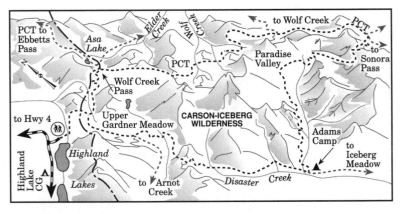

*Upper Gardner Meadow*

tween mid-July and early August, when snow still lingers on the trail. The snow may make walking harder but it keeps the cattle out and the seasonal creeks still flow with vigor, providing numerous campsites with water.

**THE HIKE.** The loop begins on a broad trail that crosses (with a long jump) an active little creek, then winds around a steep hillside. At 0.5 mile the trail divides; stay left, following the signs to Wolf Creek Pass. The right-hand trail is the return leg of your loop.

The well-used trail weaves across several small, soggy, and very over-grazed meadows to reach an intersection at 1.7 miles (8,400 feet). Take the right fork and head south on the PCT, toward Sonora Pass.

The PCT climbs steadily to an 8,720-foot forested divide and then descends into upper Wolf Creek basin. After crossing the creek, the trail climbs around the shoulder of a meadow-covered ridge to reach the Murray Canyon Trail intersection at 5.5 miles. About 500 feet beyond, pass the base of a hill composed of columnar basalt, then cross a forested saddle. The trail rolls along the hillside, passing an excellent campsite at the head-waters of Murray Canyon.

At 7 miles, the trail crosses a saddle and enters a vast sagebrush-covered amphitheater surrounded by rows of peaks, including Stanislaus, Sonora, and White Mountain. From the saddle, descend for 0.6 mile to a four-way intersection, where the loop route leaves the PCT and turns right on Disaster Creek Trail.

Head up the Disaster Creek Trail for 300 feet, until it disappears on the dry hillside. Go right and walk straight up the slope to find the trail in the trees. The trail remains well defined as it climbs to the 9,340-foot crest of a broad ridge. At 8 miles, head down into Paradise Valley, plunging through rich meadows and passing by several campsites. The trail parallels tumbling and cascading Paradise Creek throughout the 3-mile descent.

At 11 miles cross Paradise Creek, usually on a log, and enter the popular Adams Camp (7,720 feet). Go right, recross Paradise Creek, and follow Disaster Creek up-valley through a series of well-grazed meadows for the next 2.5 miles. At 13.5 miles, pass the Arnot Creek Trail turnoff and continue straight into the nearly level Upper Gardner Meadow. At 14.5 miles your trail intersects the Wolf Creek Pass Trail; go left for the final 0.5 mile back to the Gardner Meadow Trailhead.

# 8 | NOBLE AND ASA LAKES

**Round trip to Noble Lake: 9 miles**
**Hiking time:** 5 hours
**High point:** 8,700 feet
**Elevation gain:** 400 feet
**Difficulty:** Potentially easy
**Hikable:** Mid-July through September

**Round trip to Asa Lake: 14 miles**
**Hiking time:** 8 hours
**High point:** 9,350 feet
**Elevation gain:** 950 feet
**Difficulty:** Potentially easy
**Hikable:** Mid-July through September

**Driving directions:** Drive Highway 4 for 0.4 mile east of the Ebbetts Pass summit to the large Forest Service Ebbetts Pass trailhead for the Pacific Crest Trail (PCT), located on the south side of the road (8,700 feet). The trailhead has a rest room but no running water.
**Maps:** USFS Carson–Iceberg Wilderness; USGS Ebbetts Pass
**Permits:** Self-registration at the trailhead (Case 1)

Noble and Asa Lakes are popular day-hike destinations. This is such a scenic area that it is lucky the lakes are there; otherwise, it would be hard to know when to stop walking on this spectacular stretch of trail.

Snow lingers on the steep hillsides in the Ebbetts Pass area, often through mid-July. Early season hikers should carry an ice ax.

**THE HIKE.** From the upper end of the parking area, follow the trail as it climbs at a gradual pace through the forest for 0.2 mile to intersect the PCT. Go left on the PCT South and continue the well-graded ascent to a saddle

*Pacific Crest Trail south of Ebbetts Pass*

between two rounded knolls. Views of weathered ridge crests and a host of unnamed summits can be found by taking a short side trip to the crest of one or both knolls.

The trail descends, losing 100 feet of elevation, then contours a sloping meadow and crosses a seasonal stream. At 1.2 miles begin a longer descent, which starts with a switchback down a forested hillside then continues as a sloping traverse over a meadow-covered slope overlooking Noble Canyon. To the east lies a magnificent wall of rocky summits dominated by Silver and Highland Peaks. At 2.7 miles, shortly after passing the Noble Canyon Trail on the left, the descent ends and the trail resumes its climb.

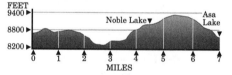

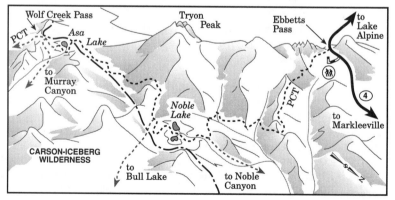

At 3.2 miles, cross Noble Creek and then switchback up a hillside covered with volcanic boulders. A broad and somewhat overused meadow below Tryon Peak is reached at 4.5 miles. Shortly after entering the meadow, Noble Lake (8,700 feet) comes into view. Campsites are located in the trees surrounding the meadows west of the lake.

To reach Asa Lake, pass Noble Lake and continue up the broad, open basin. The trail passes the Bull Lake Trail intersection to reach a 9,350-foot saddle at 5.3 miles, with views over Bear Tree Meadow and the Highland Lakes. Descend gradually for 1.7 miles to the Asa Lake intersection. Go right and head steeply uphill for 500 feet to the small, forested lake at 7 miles (8,580 feet).

# 9 | RAYMOND LAKE

**Round trip: 21.2 miles**
**Hiking time:** 2–3 days
**High point:** 9,000 feet
**Elevation gain:** 1,200 feet
**Difficulty:** Potentially moderate
**Hikable:** August through September

**Driving directions:** Drive Highway 4 to the large Forest Service PCT parking area 0.4 mile east of the Ebbetts Pass summit (8,700 feet).
**Maps:** USFS Mokelumne Wilderness; USGS Ebbetts Pass
**Permits:** Trailhead registration (Case 1)

Keeping your eyes on the trail rather than glued to the scenery is the most difficult challenge when hiking this extraordinary section of the Pacific Crest Trail (PCT). The trail wanders over a meadow-covered plateau skirting the base of weathered ridges and colorful hillsides while passing jagged rock pillars and oddly rounded domes. The objective, Raymond Lake, is an alpine beauty tucked in a rock-bound cirque at the base of Raymond Peak.

**THE HIKE.** The trail begins with a gradual climb of a forested hillside to intersect the PCT at 0.2 mile. Continue straight, following the PCT North. At 0.5 mile, carefully cross the Ebbetts Pass Highway and then climb, with an easy switchback, to the crest of a granitic saddle for the first of many sweeping vistas, this one overlooking the highway and Kinney Reservoir. The trail traverses north around Ebbetts Peak, descends, and climbs, passing several ponds and little Sherrold Lake. At 2.2 miles pass a spur trail to Upper and Lower Kinney Lakes.

The trail follows a high route around Upper Kinney Lake then begins one of the most exotic traverses on the entire PCT. At this point you leave the granitic landscape behind and enter Raymond Meadows, which lies at

*Rocky ridge crest north of Eagle Creek*

the southern end of a broad, meadow-covered bench. On the hills above, volcanic pillars make up the fantastic ramparts of Reynolds Peak.

The trail crosses a seasonal creek and climbs around an open hill before descending to cross Raymond Meadows Creek at 4.5 miles. You then

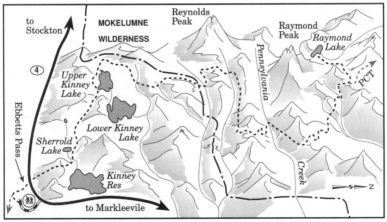

climb a low hill and descend to Eagle Creek at 5.6 miles. Following the creek, the trail heads down-valley for 0.2 mile then turns uphill, winding its way among rocky pillars to an 8,500-foot pass before switchbacking down to Pennsylvania Creek and a small campsite at 7.4 miles. The trail then gains over 600 feet in the next mile, to the crest of a sage-covered saddle.

The trail descends 300 feet into deeply gullied Raymond Canyon and then climbs to the crest of the next ridge. Shortly beyond is the Raymond Lake Trail intersection, at 9.9 miles (8,660 feet). Go left and spend a final 0.7 mile on a gradual ascent to a well-earned rest at the lake. In order to protect this fragile area, campsites must be located 0.2 mile away from the lake.

# 10 | CRABTREE TRAIL

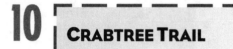

**Loop trip: 13 miles**
**Hiking time:** 6 hours
**High point:** 7,900 feet
**Elevation gain:** 1,030 feet
**Difficulty:** Potentially moderate
**Hikable:** July through September

**Driving directions:** Drive east from Sonora on Highway 108 for 29 miles to the Summit District Ranger Station at the Pinecrest Lake turnoff. Go east on Pinecrest Lake Road 0.3 mile to an intersection and then turn right and head uphill toward the Dodge Ridge Ski Area for 3.1 miles. Where the road divides, stay right, following signs to Aspen Meadow for 0.5 mile. At a T intersection, turn left. After 1.6 miles this road divides; continue straight on Road 4N26 and go through Aspen Meadow. The next section of road is gravel, rough, and washboarded. After 2.8 slow miles, the Crabtree Trailhead spur road leaves the main line and descends to a huge paved parking area with a vault toilet and no water. One-night camping is permitted here (7,180 feet).
**Maps:** USFS Emigrant Wilderness; USGS Pinecrest and Cooper Peak
**Permits:** Summit Ranger Station at Pinecrest (Case 1)

Day hikes, easy weekend backpack trips, and extended adventures are all possible along this unique trail system at the northwest corner of the Emigrant Wilderness. The scenery—from the rounded granitic domes and rock-walled canyons to the sparkling lakes and flower-covered meadows—is addicting, enticing you to explore farther into the wilderness.

Two main trails, a ridge route and a valley route, provide the main legs of any loop in this area. The two main trails are joined by several connectors ideally located for custom tailoring a trip to fit your time and energy.

*Granite stairway on Crabtree Trail*

**THE HIKE.** From the parking lot, cross Bell Creek on a wide bridge and then pass the Lake Valley Trail. Stay on the Crabtree Trail as it heads up through forest. At 1.3 miles note the Pine Valley Trail on the right; this is the return leg of the loop. For now, stay left and continue on to Camp Lake (campsites are located south of the lake on the ridge and have a one-night limit). Pass the 1-mile spur trail to overused Bear Lake and then descend to cross a little creek, hopefully on a log. The trail then climbs to the crest of a large hump,

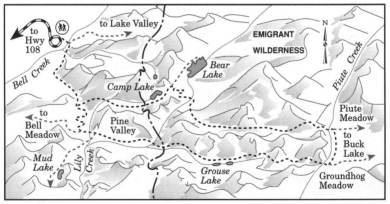

where it levels off and passes a series of small puddles and larger, lily-covered mosquito hatcheries. A steep descent off the hump brings you to Piute Meadow at 6.3 miles.

Carefully cross Piute Creek and continue about 200 feet to an intersection. At this point the described loop turns right on Groundhog Meadow Trail and descends 0.5 mile to the lower end of Groundhog Meadow. For campsites, go left to the meadow. The loop route heads right (west) and recrosses Piute Creek, then descends a narrow, scenic canyon to reach Grouse Lake at 8.7 miles. Campsites are located to the right of the trail at the edge of the cliffs.

At 9.8 miles, scout around to find a log to cross Bear Creek and then head through the forest. The Mud Lake intersection is passed at 10.5 miles and 1,000 feet beyond, pass the Pine Valley Connector trail on the right. Head uphill past a group of anomalous basaltic towers to reach the Crabtree Trail at 11.5 miles. Go left to complete your 13-mile loop.

For other, longer trips, consider continuing east from Piute Meadow to Gem Lake for a 19.5-mile loop or to Deer Lake for a 21.6-mile loop. If you continue on all the way to Buck Lake, you will have a 24-mile loop adventure.

## 11 | WHITESIDES MEADOW

**Round trip: 12 miles**
**Hiking time:** 6 hours
**High point:** 9,160 feet
**Elevation gain:** 1,280 feet in; 880 feet out
**Difficulty:** Potentially moderate
**Hikable:** August through September

**Driving directions:** Drive east from Sonora on Highway 108 for 29 miles to the Summit District Ranger Station at the Pinecrest Lake turnoff. Go east on Pinecrest Lake Road 0.3 mile to an intersection and then turn right and head uphill toward the Dodge Ridge Ski Area for 3.1 miles. Where the road divides, stay right, following signs to Aspen Meadow for 0.5 mile. At a T intersection, turn left. After 1.6 miles this road divides; continue straight on Road 4N26 and go through Aspen Meadow. Pass the Crabtree Trailhead turnoff at 2.8 miles and continue straight on Road 4N27 for 4.1 miles, to the Gianelli Cabin Trailhead at the top of the ridge (8,570 feet).
**Maps:** USFS Emigrant Wilderness; USGS Pinecrest and Cooper Peak
**Permits:** Summit Ranger Station at Pinecrest (Case 1)

This is a wonderful ridge-top ramble to the vast meadows at the northwest corner of Emigrant Wilderness. Whitesides Meadow is just one of many

*Small lake in Whitesides Meadow*

possible destinations for this hike and is an ideal location for a base camp for further exploration. (*Please note:* Cattle are authorized to graze the meadows from mid-July through late September. Until the U.S. government provides the funds to buy out the grazing rights, hikers will have to be prepared to put up with a bit of a mess.)

**THE HIKE.** The trail starts out with an easy grade, heading north to the edge of a ridge overlooking the South Fork Stanislaus River canyon. The trail then begins a switchbacking

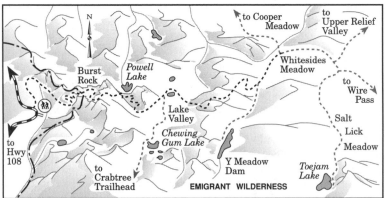

ascent of the forested hillside. At the ridge crest the route takes you over the open summit of Burst Rock (9,161 feet) to views of Castle Rock, the Three Chimneys, and The Dardanelles. A sign tells the story of the emigrants who brought their wagons over the trail you will be hiking—something to think about as you head up the next steep hill.

From Burst Rock, descend to a broad saddle and the popular Powell Lake, where you will leave most of your fellow hikers. Beyond the lake, the trail climbs up and over a granite-capped ridge and then descends steeply to the upper end of a grassy meadow where, at the 3-mile point, the Lake Valley Trail branches off to the right. Continue straight, climbing up the next ridge to reach the hike's 9,160-foot high point. As you descend the east side of this ridge you will see Hay Meadow to the northeast and massive Granite Dome to the east.

The trail dips to a saddle and a junction with the Y Meadow Dam Trail and then begins a gradual ascent past several small ponds and a small creek. A dam at 5.3 miles signals your entrance into Whitesides Meadow (8,830 feet). Campsites may be found across the dam or at the upper (north-eastern) end of the meadow along the Cooper Meadow Trail.

For day excursions from a base camp at Whitesides Meadow, try a 6-mile round trip to Cooper Meadow and its historic cabins, a 5-mile round trip to Upper Relief Meadow, a 4-mile round trip to Toejam Lake, or a 7-mile round trip to Wire Lake or Long Lake.

## 12 | KENNEDY LAKE

**Round trip: 15 miles**
**Hiking time:** 8 hours
**High point:** 7,830 feet
**Elevation gain:** 1,450 feet
**Difficulty:** Potentially moderate
**Hikable:** July through September

**Driving directions:** Drive State Route 108 for 9.4 miles west of Sonora Pass summit to Kennedy Meadows Road. Head south for 0.6 mile and turn left to the large trailhead parking area (6,380 feet).
**Maps:** USFS Emigrant Wilderness; USGS Sonora Pass (High Trail not noted)
**Permits:** Summit Ranger Station at Pinecrest or Groveland Ranger Station (Case 1)

The beautiful alpine valley at the end of this relatively easy hike to Kennedy Lake is not the place to go in search of solitude. This delightful area attracts a multitude of hikers and horse packers. Adding to the mess

*Cows, permanent summer residents at Kennedy Lake*

and congestion, a large herd of cows resides at the lake throughout the summer.

**THE HIKE.** Your trip to a beautiful backcountry valley begins with a very mundane, 0.5-mile walk up a paved road from the overnight parking area to Kennedy Meadows Resort. Walk past the resort and around a gate and continue up-valley on a busy dirt road.

After a mile, the road ends and the route jogs left onto a wide, rocky trail. At 1.2 miles, cross a sturdy bridge and then head up a narrow canyon along the edge of a roaring creek. The climb along the spectacular creek is on a steep trail blasted into the perpendicular hillside. At 1.5 miles Kennedy Creek comes into view, thundering down the hillside in an impressive waterfall. When the trail divides, stay to the right; you'll rejoin the horse path a little farther up.

At 2.7 miles (7,230 feet), go left on the Kennedy Lake Trail and continue the steep climb for another 0.5 mile. The climb eases at 3.2 miles where the trail crosses Kennedy Creek on a horse bridge and enters the Kennedy Creek valley. Head

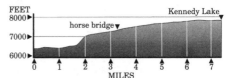

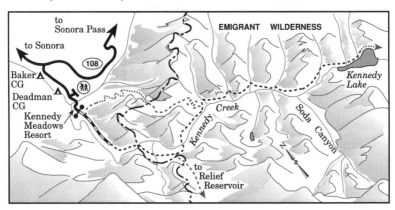

up-valley on a wide and very dusty trail. At 4 miles pass an unsigned intersection with the Night Cap Peak Trail. At this point most of the climbing is over and the trail rolls along the nearly level glacier-carved valley floor, with views of Soda Canyon and the wide cirque below Relief Peak. As forest gives way to meadows, look for the first of many campsites.

A cattle fence denotes the close proximity of Kennedy Lake. Head around the gate and then across a meadow that gets progressively damper as you go. Pass an old cabin, then walk to the next bend of the creek, where you will find a shaky log crossing to the large campsites on the opposite side.

To continue to the lake, go left, uphill, to drier meadows, where a well-beaten route heads to the lake. Several small campsites are located along the shore. If time and energy allow, the Night Cap Peak Trail offers a challenging alternative return route. This trail receives only occasional use, requires a good map, and entails some extra climbing. The rewards are solitude and delightful views south over Relief Reservoir.

# 13 | EMIGRANT WILDERNESS LOOP

**Round trip: 39.5 miles**
**Hiking time:** 4–6 days
**High point:** 9,720 feet
**Elevation gain:** 4,460 feet
**Difficulty:** Difficult (very)
**Hikable:** Mid-August through September

**Driving directions:** Drive State Route 108 west 9.4 miles from Sonora Pass summit to Kennedy Meadows Road. Head south for 0.6 mile and then turn left to the large Forest Service trailhead parking area (6,380 feet). (You may wish to drive the remaining 0.5 mile to the end of the road, at Kennedy Meadows Resort, and drop off your packs.)
**Maps:** USFS Emigrant Wilderness; USGS Sonora Pass, Emigrant Lake, and Copper Peak
**Permits:** Summit Ranger Station at Pinecrest (Case 1)

This loop travels from forested valleys to spectacular lakes and broad meadows nestled among the rugged peaks of the Emigrant Wilderness. Challenges abound. The trails are in poor condition, often nothing more than deep, rocky trenches churned by years of stock abuse. In some areas the trails disappear and routefinding skills are required; in other areas the trails are quagmires where cattle hooves have sunk deeply into the soft soil. However, the greatest difficulties are the numerous, occasionally hazardous, fords.

**THE HIKE.** Your trip begins with a very unexciting paved-road walk from the parking area up-valley for 0.5 mile to Kennedy Meadows Resort. Walk around a gate and continue on a dirt road, used by vehicles accessing private campsites up-valley. The road climbs gradually, skirts around the edge of Kennedy Meadow, and ends 1 mile from the resort. Head left onto a wide, rocky trail, which enters the wilderness and then crosses the Stanislaus River at 1.7 miles.

Beyond the bridge, the trail is blasted into the sides of the cliff as it climbs a narrow canyon. At 2 miles Kennedy Creek comes into view, thundering down the hillside in an impressive waterfall. The trail crosses the river a second time, then climbs to an intersection with the Kennedy Lake Trail at 3.2 miles (7,230 feet). Shortly beyond, pass the PG&E control cabin for Relief Dam. The trail leaves the wilderness at the power company development, then reenters soon after.

Proceeding another mile brings you to a viewpoint over Relief Reservoir. The trail traverses above the east shore of the reservoir, then descends to ford Grouse Creek at 4.2 miles. Water and some scenic campsites are passed before you begin a series of switchbacks that bring you to the Y junction that marks the start of the loop portion of your hike, at 6.2 miles (7,670 feet). You will return by the trail on the right. For now, stay left and head up Summit Creek toward Brown Bear Pass and Emigrant Lake.

The trail climbs over a low hill then heads into Saucer Meadow. Before long you are paralleling Summit Creek and passing several inviting campsites. The going is slow

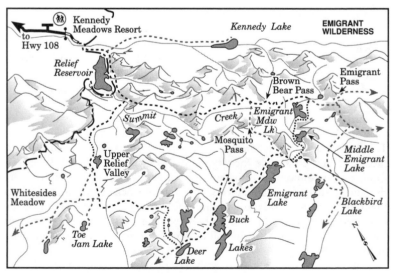

*Duckwall Memorial commemorates those who first traveled this trail.*

as you continue your ascent of the narrow valley on a dusty, boulder-strewn trail that has been pulverized by years of stock overuse. A steep climb leads to Sheep Camp at 10 miles. The trail then heads up to Lunch Meadow to reach an intersection with the Mosquito Pass Trail at 11.5 miles (9,420 feet). Go straight, toward Brown Bear Pass.

Most of the stock heads for Mosquito Pass, so the condition of the trail improves significantly after the intersection. The climb to the pass is gradual and is enlivened by views of Granite Dome and Relief Peak. Brown Bear Pass summit is reached at 12.7 miles (9,720 feet). After taking in the view, descend a mile to a large basin, where you will find Emigrant Meadow Lake and campsites. Cross the lake's inlet and in 0.2 mile, go left and head southwest down Cherry Creek valley. The trail leads you across a low ridge and then through a ford of Cherry Creek before reaching Middle Emigrant Lake after 1.2 miles. The trail becomes sporadic as you traverse around the west shore of the lake and make your way down-valley. Eventually the faint tread just disappears in the meadow. When the creek switches from the south to the north side of the valley, ford it and continue down the south side to reach Blackbird Lake at 16.5 miles (9,000 feet).

From Blackbird Lake, head northwest on a good trail for 0.5 mile to intersect the Mosquito Pass Trail, then go left to reach Emigrant Lake at 17.5 miles. Good campsites may be found near the lake's inlet and outlet. (No campfires allowed within 0.5 mile of the lake.)

Once more you are on stock trail. The tread becomes progressively worse as you traverse the north shore of Emigrant Lake. You must climb over a low ridge and then descend to ford Buck Meadow Creek before arriving at Buck Lakes at 20.5 miles (8,300 feet). There are plenty of campsites and lots of people here, many of whom were brought in by horse packers.

Proceeding to Deer Lake, you will once again lose the trail among the rocks and verdant, wet meadows. After fording the outlet creek from Long Lake, reach an intersection at 22 miles and go right (north) toward Upper Relief Meadow. The trail is rough to Spring Creek, where there is another creek to wade. At 26.2 miles, near the upper end of Salt Lick Meadow, the trail divides (8,600 feet). Go right and head northeast for a mile to Upper Relief Valley. This is a marshy area and campsites are best established along the drier edges of the valley.

From Upper Relief Valley to Lower Relief Valley the trail is badly eroded and cut by washouts, making the steep descent very challenging. Lower Relief Valley (8,122 feet) has less water than the upper valley and a lot more camping opportunities. Unfortunately, the cows also seem to prefer this valley, and cow pies decorate the landscape.

From Lower Relief Valley the descent is brisk. The trail parallels Relief Creek for a while and then fords it. This is a very dangerous crossing and is not recommended during snowmelt or after a storm. The water runs swift and deep. If you are carrying a stout cord, a hand line can be very helpful for shorter members of the group to hang on to. You should wear your boots.

From the ford, the trail heads northeast for 0.3 mile to intersect the Relief Reservoir Trail at 33.3 miles. Go left for the final 6.2 miles back to the trailhead. (The resort offers showers. Frogs in the shower stalls are complimentary.)

*Brown Bear Pass*

# 14  LATOPIE LAKE

**Round trip: 9 miles**
**Hiking time:** 5 hours
**High point:** 10,800 feet
**Elevation gain:** 1,576 feet
**Difficulty:** Potentially moderate
**Hikable:** Late-July through September

**Driving directions:** Drive Highway 108 to Sonora Pass. The trailhead parking lot is located a short 0.1 mile west of the summit (9,624 feet).
**Maps:** USFS Emigrant Wilderness; USGS Sonora Pass
**Permits:** Brightman Flat Information Station and Summit Ranger Station (Case 1)

For a quick dash into the alpine world of the High Sierra, the Pacific Crest Trail (PCT) out of Sonora Pass is hard to beat. From the 9,624-foot starting point, the trail climbs into a rare and exquisite land where tiny flowers bloom in profusion and the rocks are arranged with an artistic flare.

Latopie Lake and its neighbor, Koening Lake, stand out like dazzling oases in this world of rock. The lakes are ideally located for spending a lazy couple of hours watching the clouds drift over the surrounding peaks.

**THE HIKE.** From the parking lot, walk the ridge crest south to Sonora Pass. Cross Highway 108 and head up the hill on the PCT. Within a few feet the trail splinters; stay right, passing sturdy whitebark and lodgepole pines as you ascend to the crest of a small hill. If you are already out of breath and think every bit of elevation gain is precious, you will not be happy to see the trail descending to a small creek.

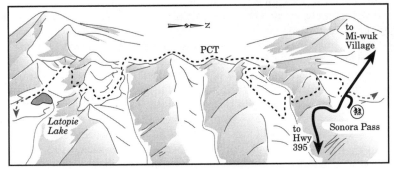

*Latopie Lake*

After crossing the creek, the trail winds across a basin full of Brewer's lupine, mule ears, alpine buckwheat, and mountain helenium. Near the creek beds are blazing displays of yellow monkeyflowers.

The trail makes a sweeping climb, contouring across walls of the basin. The ascent seems slow and the trail grade is very gradual; however, as you near the 10,000-foot mark and your breath comes in gasps, the slow climb seems quite reasonable.

At 2.3 miles the trail takes you to a ridge crest with expansive views over the Middle Fork Stanislaus River valley. The ridge crest is followed for the next 0.2 mile until you cross a 10,800-foot saddle and begin a 1.2-mile-long traverse above Blue Canyon. Twisted and weathered rocks offer mute testimony to the area's volcanic origins while flowers add spots of color to the rocky slopes.

At 3.7 miles the trail crosses an exposed saddle with a view of Deadmans Lake, to the south. You then descend 400 feet to a small basin on the east side of the crest before climbing to a 10,800-foot col at 4 miles. Latopie Lake now lies directly below your feet and is reached by an easy descent from the col. However, if your feet would prefer to wander, continue south on the PCT for another 3 miles to the Leavitt Lake intersection before turning back.

*Note:* The trail is usually snow-covered until late July or early August. Snow slopes are steep and should only be crossed with an ice ax in hand. Always carry a wind jacket and be alert for sudden changes in the weather.

# 15 | CINKO LAKE

**Round trip: 30 miles**
**Hiking time:** 2–4 days
**High point:** 9,400 feet
**Elevation gain:** 2,200 feet
**Difficulty:** Potentially difficult
**Hikable:** Mid-July through September

**Driving directions:** Drive east on Highway 108 for 7.9 miles from Sonora Pass, or west 7 miles from the Highway 395 intersection, to the Leavitt Trailhead parking area (7,200 feet). The parking area has running water, toilets, and garbage cans.
**Maps:** USFS Hoover Wilderness; USGS Pickle Meadow and Tower Peak
**Permits:** Bridgeport Ranger Station and Leavitt Trailhead (Case 2)

Wander from lake to lake through verdant meadows and along thundering creeks to awesome views of the beautiful West Walker River Basin. Cinko Lake, located on the flanks of the snow- and ice-clad peaks of the Sierra Crest, is the perfect destination for an idyllic hike.

**THE HIKE.** From the parking area, walk east on Highway 108 for 200 yards to Leavitt Meadow Campground. Descend through the camp area, staying left where the road divides, to reach the trailhead and day-use parking area at the river's edge.

The trail begins by crossing the West Walker River on a bridge and then heading up the dry hillside to a bench and an intersection. Go right

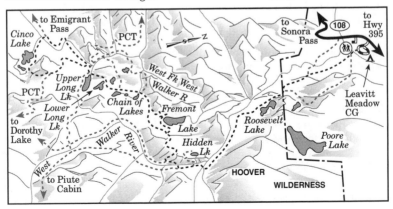

*Roosevelt Lake*

and walk through Leavitt Meadow to Roosevelt Lake. (The Secret Lake Trail, to the left, rejoins your route up-valley, adding an extra mile to the total.)

Pass two unsigned trails from the horse-packer station on the right in the Leavitt Meadow area, then climb a low ridge to intersect the Secret Lake Trail at 2.5 miles. Continue ahead and descend to Roosevelt Lake, at 3 miles (7,290 feet). The campsites here and at adjoining Lane Lake are very over-used. Beyond Lane Lake you will gain elevation at a steady rate. Pass a good campsite at 4.4 miles, where the trail brushes the edge of the West Walker River. At this point the climb becomes serious, pushing up to the crest of a knoll. Enjoy the view from the top, then plunge down to the Hidden Lake Trail junction and campsite at 5.5 miles.

The terrain is exceedingly scenic as the trail traverses granite cliffs along the very edge of the rushing river. At 6.7 miles the trail divides. Your trail fords the river. If the hikers' log is in place, go ahead and cross. If not, take the left fork and continue up-river until you find a safe crossing. Do not try to wade the deep and swift river.

At 7.2 miles the trail divides (7,900 feet). Go right, and head up a dusty hillside for 0.8 mile to Fremont Lake (8,220 feet), which has good, though often crowded, campsites. To continue, return to the saddle above Fremont Lake and head toward the Chain of Lakes. This scenic trail climbs to a forested saddle and then descends into a delightful mosquito habitat at the lakes. Stay left at a signed junction to Walker Meadows and left again at an unsigned junction, to Fremont Canyon. Descend to the largest lake in the chain, then climb over a granite rib to Lower and Upper Long Lakes and more campsites.

From Upper Long Lake, go right (north) for 0.2 mile to intersect the Pacific Crest Trail (PCT) at 11.7 miles (8,960 feet), at the West Fork West Walker River bridge. Go left and walk south on the PCT, following signs to Cinko Lake. After 0.2 mile the trail divides. Cinko Lake can be reached by either trail. The Emigrant Pass Trail approach is a mile shorter, with one unavoidably wet creek crossing. If you prefer to stay dry, go left and follow the PCT for 2 miles, to the second Cinko Lake intersection. From here it is only a 1-mile climb past Bills Lake to reach Cinko Lake (9,230 feet), at 15 miles.

Cinko Lake is a small subalpine gem cupped between Grizzly Peak and a pink granite dome. Campsites are numerous around the lake and among the benches above.

# 16 | TAMARACK LAKE

**Round trip: 9 miles**
**Hiking time:** 5 hours
**High point:** 9,660 feet
**Elevation gain:** 2,560 feet
**Difficulty:** Potentially moderate
**Hikable:** Mid-July through September

**Driving directions:** Drive Highway 395 to Bridgeport. At the north end of town find Twin Lakes Road and follow it southwest for 10.3 miles. Pass a self-service laundry and showers on the right, then take the first road on the left, signed "National Forest Campgrounds." Follow this road for 0.6 mile to the Day Use Area, with rest rooms (7,100 feet).
**Maps:** USFS Hoover Wilderness; USGS Twin Lakes
**Permits:** Bridgeport Ranger Station (Case 2)

Nestled beneath the steep walls of Monument Ridge and Crater Crest is a rocky basin carpeted with high alpine meadows and highlighted with hardy trees. In that basin lies Tamarack Lake, a true subalpine masterpiece. This is a peaceful place, receiving only a fraction of the number of hikers that throng Barney Lake (Hike 17). The trail, however, is steep and can be rather discouraging under the midday sun. Start your hike early and carry plenty of water.

**THE HIKE.** Walk back down the road 400 feet to the start of the trail. The trail begins by climbing steeply. After ascending 200 feet, cross the

*View of Monument Ridge from meadow near Tamarack Lake*

powerline road and continue steeply up an old moraine. Before long you will have a view of Lower Twin Lakes, Robinson Creek valley, Sawmill Ridge, and Sawtooth Ridge.

After climbing over two false summits, the trail reaches the 7,930-foot moraine crest and an un-signed intersection at 0.7 mile. Go right and head gradually up along the moraine. To the east lies Upper Summer Meadows, a rich pasture and

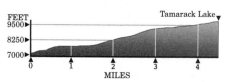

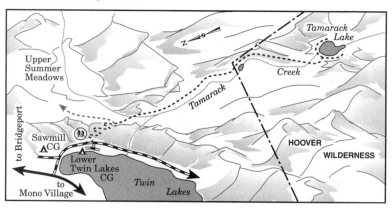

home to many sheep. After a relatively easy 0.5-mile traverse, the climb resumes up flower- and sage-speckled slopes to Tamarack Creek; cross it with an Olympian long jump.

With the exception of one small grove of aspen trees, the climb is exposed to the hot sun. Watch to the north and east as views of Bridgeport, the reservoir, and the Sweetwater Mountains unfold.

At 3.6 miles the trail reaches the entrance of Tamarack Valley (9,200 feet) and the steep climb subsides a bit. The trail bends left, contouring around an expanding swamp before it can continue up-valley. After a short climb, pass to the left of a lush meadow and reach an unmarked intersection. Go right and cross a small, marshy creek, then head across the wet meadow, using tree limbs to guide you over the mud and back onto the well-marked path. The trail heads up through a band of trees to reach Tamarack Lake (9,660 feet) at 4.5 miles. Campsites are spread around the lake; take your pick.

Unlike the steep and impenetrable granitic mountains to the west, the area around Tamarack Lake is of volcanic origin and invites exploration. The cross-country hiker may continue on from the end of the trail at Tamarack Lake for another mile to two other lakes or to an 11,100-foot saddle on the Crater Crest.

# 17 | CROWN POINT LOOP

**Loop trip: 22.5 miles**
**Hiking time:** 3 days
**High point:** 10,150 feet
**Elevation gain:** 3,340 feet
**Difficulty:** Potentially difficult
**Hikable:** August through September

**Driving directions:** Drive Highway 395 to the ranger station located 1 mile south of Bridgeport and pick up your wilderness permit. Head north to the center of town and turn west on Twin Lakes Road. Continue 14 miles to road's end, at Mono Village Resort (7,070 feet). Day hikers may park for free. Backpackers need to pay a fee at the campground entrance before heading out.
**Maps:** USFS Hoover Wilderness; USGS Buckeye Ridge and Matterhorn Peak
**Permits:** Bridgeport Ranger Station (Case 2)

Lingering snowfields and a difficult river crossing make it advisable to wait until August before setting out on this elegant loop through the Hoover Wilderness to a remote corner of Yosemite National Park. The suggested itinerary allows 3 days for the hike, with overnight camps at Crown and Peeler Lakes.

Start your hike at the north side of the marina store. Go left and walk as straight as possible through the crowded campground. At the upper end of the camp area, skirt a gate and then follow the road up-valley. Where the road bends left to cross the river, continue straight on a trail. Before long the trees give way to open meadows, with Victoria Peak to the right and the incredible Sawtooth Ridge to the left. At 2.9 miles the trail begins to climb with a series of long, lazy switchbacks.

After hopping a couple of creeks, reach Barney Lake (8,300 feet) at 4 miles. Several campsites and a million mosquitoes may be found near the outlet. The trail continues up-valley, heading toward Crown Point, climbing and then descending granite slopes along the lakeshore.

At 4.5 miles you must cross Robinson Creek. The unavoidable ford is fairly deep but not extremely fast. The trail then heads steeply up the forested hillside for 0.3 mile and fords the creek again. Here the water is deep, fast, and dangerous. Take time to find a good log crossing.

Beyond the fords, the trail zigzags up the granite hillside to an intersection at 6.7 miles (9,100 feet), which marks the start of the loop portion of the hike. Go left and traverse a lake-studded bench below Crown Point to reach Crown Lake (9,030 feet) at 8.2 miles. Tent sites on the granite ledges above the lake have views of Slide Mountain, Kettle Peak, and Sawtooth Ridge.

Beyond Crown Lake the trail climbs 0.7 mile to an intersection with the Mule Pass Trail. Stay right and continue up the open valley, passing Snow Lake to reach Rock Island Pass (10,150 feet) at 10.2 miles.

From the pass, head down a faint and poorly marked trail into Yosemite National Park. At 12.3 miles, cross Rancheria Creek (usually a dry crossing) and then go left for 100 feet to intersect the Kerrick Meadow Trail (9,300 feet).

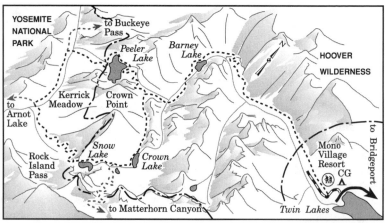

*Rock Island Pass*

Head to the right and hike up through a classic Sierra meadow, where granite boulders pop up like mushrooms in a velvet sea of green. The meadow is wet and the trail crosses numerous little creeks. Reach the next intersection at 13.8 miles, 5.5 miles from Crown Lake. Take the right fork and head toward Peeler and Twin Lakes.

Peeler Lake (9,500 feet), reached at 14.4 miles, has two outlets, one to the east and one to the west. Campsites may be found near the east outlet or halfway around the lake.

From Peeler Lake the trail climbs 100 feet out of the basin and then descends briskly for a mile to close the loop portion of the hike at the Crown Lake intersection. Retrace your steps for the final 6.7 miles back to Twin Lakes.

# 18 | HOOVER LAKES

**Round trip to Hoover Lakes: 13 miles**
**Hiking time:** 7 hours
**High point:** 9,860 feet
**Elevation gain:** 1,780 feet
**Difficulty:** Potentially moderate
**Hikable:** Mid-July through September

**Driving directions:** To reach the Green Creek Trailhead, drive south on Highway 395 for 3.9 miles from the Bridgeport Ranger Station. Go right on gravel-surfaced Green Creek Road for 3.5 miles to the intersection

with Virginia Lakes Road. Turn sharply right and continue another 5.2 miles to a large trailhead with a toilet, running water, and garbage cans (8,080 feet).
**Maps:** USFS Hoover Wilderness; USGS Dunderberg Peak
**Permits:** Bridgeport Ranger Station (Case 2)

Except for several difficult creek crossings, the Green Creek Trail to Hoover Lakes is ideal for relaxed backpacking. The numerous lakes, excellent scenery, and low-mileage days make this the kind of hike where you spend more time enjoying the scenery than nursing sore feet up the trail.

**THE HIKE.** Your trip begins with a stroll along a forested ridge above Green Creek Campground. After 0.5 mile the trail intersects a gated road; go right and follow the road up-valley for 0.3 mile, to the road's end.

The ascent is steady as the trail heads up-valley through beautiful wildflower gardens along Green Creek. Climb over two granite humps with views up Glines Canyon to Virginia Peak, and at 2.7 miles pass an intersection with the West Lake Trail (an excellent 3-mile side trip). The main trail stays to the left and continues up-valley for 0.3 mile to Green Lake (8,945 feet). Here you must cross the creek, either on the dam or, when the water is high, on a log.

From the forested shores of Green Lake, the trail climbs south, making two creek crossings before reaching East Lake (9,458 feet) at 4.5 miles and another creek crossing. If the creek is high, cross on the dam. Campsites are located all around this subalpine lake.

The trail heads around the east side of the lake, then passes little Nutter Lake and more campsites. At 5.5 miles a spur trail branches left to very scenic Gilman Lake, located in a basin below Dunderberg Peak. Beyond the intersection the

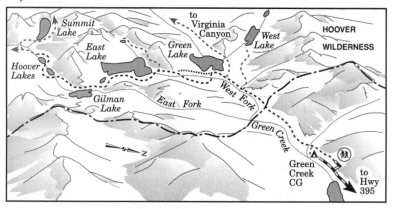

*East Lake*

trail ascends again, passing a couple of small lakelets before making a mandatory and moderately difficult ford of East Green Creek. At 6.5 miles you will pass through a narrow canyon that soon opens up to a broad 9,819-foot bench and the first Hoover Lake. The trail threads its way between the first and second lakes, fording the creek again. Campsites around these high alpine lakes are open, exposed, and scenic.

# 19 | KOIP PEAK PASS TRAVERSE

**One-way trip: 23.7 miles**
**Hiking time:** 3–4 days
**High point:** 12,263 feet
**Elevation gain:** 3,743 feet
**Difficulty:** Potentially difficult
**Hikable:** August through September

**Driving directions:** Drive south from Lee Vining to the northern June Lake Loop turnoff and go right for 1.5 miles. At the Parker Lake–Walker Lake sign, go right on a dusty road and then take an immediate left. At 0.4 mile stay right, following the Walker Lake signs. At 1.3 miles from the June Lake Road, take a left on a rough and narrow road for 1.9 miles

to a small trailhead parking area (8,360 feet). Leave your second vehicle at the Rush Creek Trailhead, 7 miles beyond the Walker Lake turnoff.
**Maps:** USFS Ansel Adams Wilderness; USGS Koip Peak
**Permits:** Lee Vining and Mammoth Lakes Ranger Stations (Case 3)

This scenic High Sierran traverse crosses four passes, parallels the shores of five alpine lakes, traverses numerous flower-covered meadows, and passes so many high vistas you will feel like you are walking on top of the world. This extremely scenic traverse with steep and rocky trails, lingering snowfields, and high elevations is recommended for strong hikers who have taken the time to acclimate before starting.

**THE HIKE.** Your traverse begins with a steep climb, gaining what feels like a lot more than the 160 feet of elevation that the map shows. Cross a forested ridge, then plunge down the far side toward Walker Lake (7,940 feet). At 0.5 mile the trail divides; stay left. The trail gradually levels and then heads around the top of the lake, where you cross Walker Creek on a log jam and battle mosquitoes to reach an intersection at 0.8 mile. Go left and begin the hardest, and hottest, climb of the traverse as you ascend Bloody Canyon to Sardine Lakes. The trail is steep, designed for hardy hikers rather than horses. At 3.5 miles pass Sardine Lake (9,880 feet). Continue up the amazingly steep trail, which takes only 0.5 mile to climb the next 500 feet. At the top of the hill, pass a small tarn. Leave the trail and go left to good campsites at Upper Sardine Lake (10,360 feet).

From Upper Sardine Lake

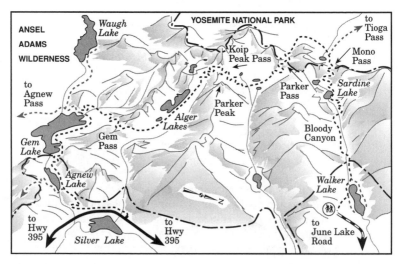

*Campsite near Alger Lakes*

it is an easy 0.5-mile stroll to Mono Pass (10,840 feet). Follow the trail 0.1 mile north from the pass, then go left on the poorly signed and all-but-invisible Parker Pass Trail. Cross the meadow to a well-defined trail on the far hillside. The trail climbs up the low ridge and then heads south into breathtaking views.

At 6.7 miles the trail crests 11,050-foot Parker Pass, then descends past a couple of small tarns with mediocre campsites. The lowest tarn is at 10,810 feet; beyond this point the trail begins its climb to Koip Peak Pass. The trail is steep and switchbacks relentlessly, with unexcelled views east over Mono Lake. Allow at least 3 hours to reach the 12,263-foot pass. (Consider the possibility of electrical storms before you start up.)

The descent from Koip Peak Pass is rapid and relatively easy to Alger Lakes (10,620 feet), reached at the 13.5-mile mark of the traverse. Campsites are located on the peninsula between the two lakes.

From Alger Lakes, the trail climbs briefly past a couple of meadow-fringed tarns, then traverses southeast to forested Gem Pass (10,410 feet) at 15 miles. From this point it is a 4-mile descent to Gem Lake (9,045 feet) and the Rush Creek Trail. Campsites are located at the intersection and to the east along the lakeshore. Go left for the final 4.7 miles of scenic walking along Gem Lake, then Agnew Lake. The traverse ends with a breathtaking descent down the cliffs to the Rush Creek Trailhead at Silver Lake.

# 20 | ISLAND PASS LOOP

**Loop trip: 21 miles**
**Hiking time:** 3 days
**High point:** 10,200 feet
**Elevation gain:** 3,477 feet
**Difficulty:** Potentially difficult
**Hikable:** Mid-July through September

**Driving directions:** Drive south from Lee Vining on Highway 395 to the first June Lake Loop Road turnoff, then go west on Highway 158 for 8.5 miles to the Rush Creek Trailhead (7,223 feet).
**Maps:** USFS Ansel Adams Wilderness; USGS Koip Peak and Mt. Ritter
**Permits:** Mono Lake and Mammoth Lakes Visitor Center (Case 3)

An endless stream of summer visitors make the long trek up Rush Creek to fish or sit by the shore of one of four large, sparkling lakes and contemplate the rugged peaks reflecting in their crystalline waters. Apply for your backpacking permit in early March if you wish to ensure a date for hiking this popular loop route.

**THE HIKE.** The trail crosses Alger Creek on a log bridge and then skirts an RV park before switchbacking up the cliffs on the hillside above Silver Lake. You will cross the Cal Edison funicular railroad twice before the concrete edifice of the Agnew Lake Dam comes into view. As soon as you spot the dam,

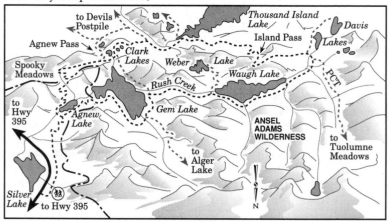

*Banner Peak dominates the skyline above a small tarn at Island Pass.*

look left for the unsigned Spooky Meadow Trail, which is the return route for your loop.

Walk past Agnew Lake (8,508 feet) and continue the climb to a second dam, which holds the waters of beautiful Gem Lake (9,045 feet). The trail makes an up-and-down traverse around the north side of the lake, passing numerous campsites. At 4.7 miles, pass the Alger Lakes Trail intersection and the last of the lakeshore campsites. At this point the trail leaves the lake and heads over a ridge to forested Rush Creek and the Agnew Pass–Clark Lakes Trail intersection. Continue straight, paralleling Rush Creek and passing several large campsites while ascending gradually to the dammed outlet of Waugh Lake (9,424 feet) at 6.5 miles. Pass a spur trail to Weber Lake, then continue straight around Waugh Lake to find campsites at 7 miles. More campsites are located on an unmarked spur trail at the upper end of the lake.

Beyond Waugh Lake the trail climbs gradually to cross Rush Creek (look for a good log), then heads south to intersect the combined John Muir Trail/Pacific Crest Trail (JMT/PCT) at 8.5 miles (9,680 feet). Go left (south) and ford three forks of Rush Creek (wet in early season) in the next 0.4 mile. Shortly beyond the third crossing is the sometimes-obscure Davis Lake Trail intersection. The 1-mile side trip into the open Davis Lake basin leads to scenic campsites away from the crowds.

At 9.9 miles reach the crest of 10,200-foot Island Pass. Pass a couple of small ponds with outstanding views of Banner Peak and several secluded campsites. Descend to Thousand Island Lake (9,834 feet) at 11.4 miles, where the JMT and PCT split. All camping here must be done at least 0.2 mile away from the outlet.

The loop route follows the PCT south for 1.7 miles to the Clark Lakes Trail. Go left and cross the ridge at an unnamed 9,900-foot saddle, passing several small and rocky lakelets before arriving at the parklike Clark Lakes and several large, shaded campsites. Continue descending to reach a three-way junction at 14.8 miles. To the left a well-graded trail descends back to the Rush Creek Trail near Gem Lake. If your knees are not strong or the soles of your shoes are a bit slick, that is the trail to take. The loop route goes to the right, ascending to a small tarn, then descends steeply through Spooky Meadow. Below the meadows the trail switchbacks down a slope of loose scree and then crosses Rush Creek just below the Agnew Lake Dam. This ends the loop portion of the hike. Go right for your final descent back to Silver Lake on the Rush Creek Trail.

## 21 | THOUSAND ISLAND LAKE LOOP

**Loop trip: 18.9 miles**
**Hiking time:** 2–4 days
**High point:** 10,160 feet
**Elevation gain:** 2,760 feet
**Difficulty:** Potentially difficult
**Hikable:** Mid-July through September

**Driving directions:** From the Mammoth Lakes Visitor Center, drive up through town on Highway 203. After 1.2 miles, go right on Minaret Road (Highway 203). Head up for another 4.2 miles to the Mammoth Mountain Ski Area, then take the shuttle bus to Agnew Meadows. From the bus stop, walk the dirt road 0.3 mile to the second trailhead parking lot (8,320 feet). The bus ride is mandatory between the hours of 7:30 A.M. and 7:00 P.M.; if arriving before or after these hours, you may drive to the trailhead after paying a per-person entrance fee. You are also allowed to drive to the trailhead if you are spending the night before the start of your hike at one of the valley's campgrounds. Reservations are recommended if you are planning on securing one of these highly sought-after campsites. See Case 6 for more shuttle-bus information.

**Maps:** USFS Ansel Adams Wilderness; USGS Mammoth Mountain and Mt. Ritter
**Permits:** Mammoth Lakes Visitor Center (Case 3)

The stunningly scenic Middle Fork of the San Joaquin River Valley has a richly deserved reputation as an excellent hiking area. There are three trails up the Middle Fork Valley that converge near Thousand Island Lake, creating several loops. This hike follows the High Trail, with its exceptional views of the Minarets and the Ritter Range north to Thousand Island Lake, then returns south along the base of the Ritter Range via the John Muir and River Trails.

**THE HIKE.** Start your loop by following the High Trail north from the first of the two parking areas. After several hundred feet, cross an unsigned trail from the pack station. Go straight and begin a series of switchbacks that will take you 500 feet above the valley floor to meadows and views of Mammoth Mountain, then head northeast on a long, ascending traverse. At 2.7 miles pass an eye-catching viewpoint of Shadow Lake, the Minarets,

*Thousand Island Lake*

and Mount Ritter. Beyond the viewpoint, the trail begins a scenic 4.5-mile traverse over open meadows covered with waist-high lupine and corn lilies. The first of three trails to Clark Lakes and Agnew Pass branches off to the right at 5.2 miles. One mile beyond, go straight at a four-way intersection with a trail to Agnew Pass on the right and a connector to the River Trail on the left. Contour around the head of the valley, passing the swampy Badger Lakes at 6.3 miles. Campsites are located at the largest Badger Lake, 0.2 mile to the southeast. The High Trail and River Trail join at 6.8 miles. Continue straight for 1 more mile to Thousand Island Lake (9,840 feet). No camping is allowed within a 0.2-mile radius of the lake's outlet. Good campsites may be found by heading along the north or south shores of the lake.

From Thousand Island Lake, head south on the John Muir Trail (JMT), which climbs to Emerald Lake and then to Ruby Lake. Campsites may be found at either of these two jewels. The trail then climbs to a 10,160-foot pass before descending to Garnet Lake (9,700 feet) at 10.3 miles. With snow-speckled Banner Peak piercing the sky at the upper end, Garnet Lake is the undeniable gem of this loop. Find your campsite along the north shore, at least 0.2 mile away from the outlet.

Cross the Garnet Lake outlet and pass an unmarked junction with a River Trail lateral. Head around the lake for another 0.2 mile and then climb with lazy switchbacks to a 10,160-foot saddle. The descent down the south side of the saddle is rocky, and before long the trail enters the forest. At 14.5 miles the JMT intersects the Shadow Creek Trail and goes left, down-valley.

At 15.3 miles leave the JMT and go straight, on the Shadow Lake Trail. Weave your way around the day hikers near the lake, then descend along the cascading Shadow Creek to cross the Middle Fork San Joaquin

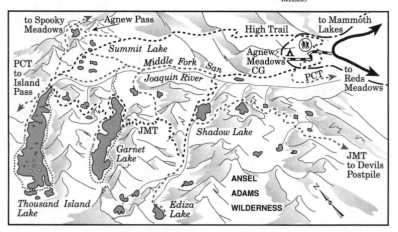

River on a sturdy bridge (8,000 feet). At 17.3 miles, go right on the River Trail and climb the 320 feet required to bring you back out of the valley. At 18.4 miles the River Trail ends. Go left on the PCT, following signs to Agnew Meadows. A few feet beyond the intersection, the trail divides; stay right for the final 0.5 mile back to the trailhead parking area.

## 22 | SHADOW OF THE MINARETS

**Round trip to Ediza Lake: 20 miles**
**Hiking time:** 2–4 days
**High point:** 9,630 feet
**Elevation gain:** 2,620 feet
**Difficulty:** Potentially difficult
**Hikable:** Mid-July through September

**One-way traverse: 16.2 miles**
**Hiking time:** 3–4 days
**High point:** 10,300 feet
**Elevation gain:** 3,580 feet
**Difficulty:** Difficult
**Hikable:** August through September

**Driving directions:** From the Mammoth Lakes Visitor Center, drive up through town on Highway 203. After 1.2 miles, go right on Minaret Road (Highway 203). Head up for another 4.2 miles to the Mammoth Mountain Ski Area, then take the shuttle bus to Agnew Meadows. From the bus stop, walk the dirt road 0.3 mile to the first of two trailhead parking lots (8,320 feet). The bus ride is mandatory between the hours of 7:30 A.M. and 7:00 P.M.; if arriving before or after these hours, you may drive to the trailhead after paying a per-person entrance fee. You are also allowed to drive to the trailhead if you are spending the night before the start of your hike at one of the valley's campgrounds. Reservations are recommended if you are planning on securing one of these highly sought-after campsites. See Case 6 for more shuttle-bus information.
**Maps:** USFS Ansel Adams Wilderness; USGS Mammoth Mountain, Mt. Ritter, and Crystal Crag
**Permits:** Mammoth Lakes Visitor Center (Case 3)

Let your own abilities determine which of these two hikes you will take into the spectacular country around the base of Mount Ritter and the Minarets. The Ediza Lake hike follows excellent trails to a beautiful destination. The traverse hike—which continues from Ediza Lake on a steep and sketchy route to Iceberg, Cecile, and Minaret Lakes—requires routefinding skills, a bit of easy scrambling, and, for much of the summer, an ice ax for crossing the icy slopes around Iceberg Lake. At Minaret Lake, the traverse route rejoins well-maintained trails for the descent to Devils Postpile National Monument.

**THE HIKE.** From the parking area, walk south on the Pacific Crest Trail (PCT), following signs to Shadow Lake. The trail crosses Agnew Meadows, then traverses the forest. At 0.5 mile, pass an unmarked spur trail to the campground on the right. Continue straight to a major intersection, where you will leave the PCT and head right, on the River Trail.

The River Trail descends to the San Joaquin River and then heads up-valley. At 1.5 miles, leave the River Trail and go left on the Shadow Lake Trail, which crosses the San Joaquin on a sturdy bridge. The trail then climbs, switchbacking up an open hillside along cascading Shadow Creek to Shadow Lake (8,789 feet) and the first close-up view of the Minarets.

Follow the trail around the north shore to the upper end of Shadow Lake, where you will join the John Muir Trail (JMT) at 4.2 miles. To continue on to Ediza Lake, go straight, following the JMT north up the forested valley, paralleling Shadow Creek. At 5 miles leave the JMT as it turns north toward Garnet Lake. Continue up the delightfully scenic valley to reach Ediza Lake (9,340 feet) at 7 miles. No camping near the lakeshore. Campsites are located on the benches high above the lake.

Ediza Lake is a true alpine beauty and a satisfying destination for any trip. It can be used as a base camp for day hikes to the lakes

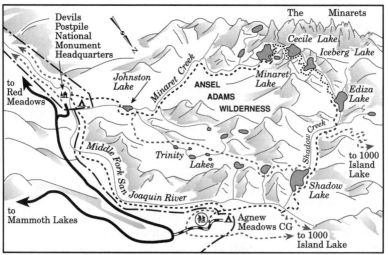

*View of steep descent route from Cecile and Minaret Lakes*

above or as an overnight stop before attempting the next stage of the very difficult traverse.

The official trail ends at the north end of Ediza Lake; however, a well-defined path heads around the lake. At the south end, stop and look ahead at your route to Iceberg Lake. The lake is located south of Ediza Lake, at the base of the Ritter Range. Look up and spot a granite hump. The good-size creek that descends from a low saddle on the left side of the hump is the outlet from Iceberg Lake, your destination.

As you start up, the trail fractures into a multitude of boot paths. You need to find the well-used trail that parallels the creek and then climb up and over the saddle to Iceberg Lake (9,840 feet).

Iceberg Lake sits in a sheltered granite basin and is the receptacle for the large masses of snow that slides off the sheer wall of the Minarets throughout the winter and spring. The snow lingers around the lake for most of the summer, and the next stage of your hike to Cecile Lake often requires traversing or climbing icy snow slopes. Campsites that are both comfortable and legal are difficult to find at Iceberg Lake.

Once again, stop and scope out your route before continuing on from Iceberg to Cecile Lake. Look south across the lake to the waterfall descending from a low saddle 500 feet above. The top of the waterfall is your goal.

Traverse around the left (east) side of Iceberg Lake, then, keeping your goal in sight, ascend the rocky slope on the left side of the waterfall. The final 75 feet are very steep, requiring both hands to hang onto the rocky slope. Cecile Lake (10,300 feet), at the top of the waterfall, has several comfortable and very scenic campsites at either end. The lake is nestled right at the base of Clyde Minaret and the feeling of high-mountain wilderness is all pervasive.

The next stage of your traverse is a boulder hop around the east side (shorter but more difficult) or west side (longer and slightly easier) of Cecile Lake to a spectacular view of the Ritter Range. Then you must head down the steep, cliffy hillside to idyllic Minaret Lake, in the basin below. There is no easy way down. From the southeast corner of the lake, walk to the trees at the end of the moraine and locate a rugged gully that descends in giant steps. Head down using both hands at the start. Descend slowly and use a great deal of caution.

Minaret Lake (9,820 feet) is reached after an incredibly hard and time-consuming 3-mile hike from Ediza Lake. Excellent campsites are located around the lake on all but the north.

Once you reach the base of the cliff below Cecile Lake, you will be on a good trail for the remainder of the traverse. The trail heads around the east shore of Minaret Lake to the outlet, where you should take a last look at the Minarets before descending steeply on well-worn tread to intersect the JMT opposite the marshy shores of Johnston Lake (8,120 feet) 4.5 miles from Minaret Lake (14.5 miles from the Agnew Meadows Trailhead).

After 0.2 mile, cross Minaret Creek to reach the Beck Lakes Trail intersection. Continue straight on the JMT and shortly after, begin to descend into the San Joaquin River valley on a wide and very dusty trail. Your goal is now the headquarters of the Devils Postpile National Monument. Near the floor of the valley, cross the PCT and follow the signs to the monument headquarters on the JMT, which will take you around the meadows to a sturdy bridge over the river. Leave the JMT and go left, heading back up-valley for 0.1 mile to reach the headquarters and road at 16.2 miles (7,600 feet). From here you simply wait for a shuttle bus for the free ride back to your car.

## 23 | MAMMOTH CREST TRAVERSE

**One-way trip: 12 miles**
**Hiking time:** 7 hours
**High point:** 11,230 feet
**Elevation gain:** 810 feet
**Difficulty:** Potentially difficult
**Hikable:** July through September

**Driving directions:** From the Mammoth Lakes intersection on Highway 395, follow Highway 203 for 3.7 miles to the Lake Mary Road. Continue straight for another 3.7 miles, then turn left on Forest Road 4S09, signed for Lake Mary and Cold Water Campground. After 0.6 mile, go

left again and follow Forest Road 4S25 through the campground for 0.6 mile. Park at the second trailhead (9,120 feet).
**Maps:** USFS John Muir Wilderness (North Section); USGS Bloody Mountain (meters) and Crystal Crag; Ansel Adams Wilderness Map
**Permits:** Mammoth Lakes Visitor Center (Case 3)

From the popular Mammoth Lakes Recreation Area, the Mammoth Crest appears as a solid wall of impenetrable cliffs, so it may come as a surprise to find that the moderately sloping southwest side of the crest is an excellent place for a scenic hike. Views from the crest are expansive, spanning the High Sierra from Silver Divide, over Fish Valley, across the John Muir Wilderness, down into the Devils Postpile area, then north across the Ansel Adams Wilderness to the Minarets and Mount Ritter.

This traverse is almost a loop, beginning at Cold Water Campground and ending 2.2 miles northwest at Lake George. Two miles of this traverse, between Duck Pass and Deer Lakes, are actually more like a route than a trail, as you follow a sketchy path over high meadows. (*Note:* The connection between Duck Pass and Deer Lakes is not shown on the John Muir Wilderness map and is marked incorrectly on the Ansel Adams Wilderness Map.)

**THE HIKE.** The first 4 miles of your traverse are spent hiking up the wide and well-traveled Duck Pass Trail, which begins with a moderate climb into an upper valley and then levels off to pass Arrowhead Lake, Skeleton Lake, and Barney Lake.

From Barney Lake the trail switchbacks up a steep wall to the 10,800-foot summit of Duck Pass. Go 100 feet beyond the crest of the pass and then head up the hill on the right. Walk through a grove of hardy trees and then over meadows, staying just a bit to the right of the ridge crest. Once you reach the meadows, watch for a well-worn boot path that heads steadily west to an 11,230-foot divide. The path crosses the

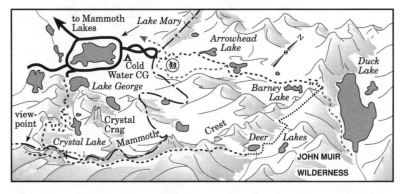

divide and then descends across a grassy basin to a view of upper Deer Lake.

At the lower end of the basin the trail makes one switchback down a band of rocks and then disappears. Stay to the left and continue down by clambering over the rubble. At the base of the rocks you will find a path that contours around the right side of Upper Deer Lake and then crosses a low saddle before descending along the left side of Middle Deer Lake (10,560 feet). At the base of the middle lake you will pass several large campsites and then meet the Mammoth Crest Trail.

The Mammoth Crest Trail climbs steeply to an 11,180-foot point just below the crest and then heads northwest in a rolling traverse. At one point the trail divides; the two paths rejoin shortly after. Before long you will descend to an open plateau sprinkled with lupine. Cross this open area, then walk along the ridge until you reach a point where the soil turns red. The trail divides here. For the best views, stay left and follow the unofficial trail along the ridge crest for 0.5 mile, then go right to rejoin the official route, which spends the next 2.5 miles in a switchbacking descent. At 11 miles, pass the spur trail to Crystal Lake and at 12 miles arrive at the busy Lake George parking area. If you did not come prepared with a shuttle car, you now have a 2-mile road walk back to the Duck Pass Trailhead.

*Duck Lake at Duck Pass*

# 24 | VALENTINE LAKE

**Round trip: 10 miles**
**Hiking time:** 5 hours
**High point:** 9,702 feet
**Elevation gain:** 1,840 feet
**Difficulty:** Potentially moderate
**Hikable:** July through September

**Driving directions:** From Highway 395, take the Mammoth Lakes exit and drive west on Highway 203 to Mammoth Lakes Visitor Center and Ranger Station. Continue past the ranger station for 0.3 mile and go left at the stoplight on Old Mammoth Road. After 0.8 mile take another left on Sherwin Creek Road and follow it for 1.4 miles. (The pavement ends after the museum turnoff, then reappears farther down the road.) Turn right on a road signed to Sherwin Lakes Trailhead. In 0.3 mile the road divides; stay left for the final 0.1 mile to the trailhead (7,820 feet).
**Maps:** USFS John Muir Wilderness (North Section); USGS Bloody Mountain
**Permits:** Mammoth Lakes Visitor Center (Case 3)

An early start is recommended for this popular hike near the town of Mammoth Lakes. The midday sun can be fierce on the dusty switchbacks, which lead hikers from the sage-covered valley floor to the dramatic subalpine basin where Valentine Lake lies sandwiched between rugged walls of granite.

**THE HIKE.** The trail heads across the high prairie, climbing briefly and then descending to cross Sherwin Creek on a sturdy bridge. The climb intensifies as the trail heads into a series of well-graded switchbacks. Views of Mammoth Mountain as well as of the bourgeoning town of Mammoth

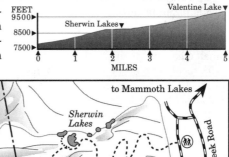

*Sherwin Lake*

Lakes help to keep interest high as you ascend the sun-baked hillside.

At 2.2 miles, the trail crosses the crest of the hill and levels off. Soon after, a trail branches right, heading to the first of the two largest Sherwin Lakes (8,674 feet). Many hikers stop here, satisfied with the dramatic view up the Sherwin Creek valley. However, unbelievable as it may seem, the best is still ahead. After a short rest, continue on up the main trail.

At 2.5 miles pass the official Sherwin Lakes junction. To the right, a trail heads 0.2 mile through the forest, past a small waterfall, to the upper Sherwin Lake.

The Valentine Lake trail continues its well-graded ascent, crossing a small creek and then heading up through a wondrous rock garden dotted with regal old Sierra junipers with massive, twisted trunks.

At 3.3 miles, the Sherwin Lakes Trail meets the Valentine Lake Trail (8,829 feet). In 2003, this was an unsigned junction. The trail joining on the left climbs up from the YMCA camp in the valley below and has a bad habit of looking like the official trail on the way back down, so make a mental note of it as you go by.

The trail enters the John Muir Wilderness, crosses a marshy hillside, and then skims below a massive boulder field. After passing a small, marshy pond at 4.5 miles, the final 0.5 mile is spent switchbacking up a steep slope to reach trail's end at 9,702-foot Valentine Lake. Cross Sherwin Creek on a couple of logs, then wander along the west shore of the lake to find your preferred picnicking or camping site.

# 25 | MCGEE CREEK

**Round trip to Steelhead Lake: 11 miles**
**Hiking time:** 6 hours
**High point:** 10,350 feet
**Elevation gain:** 2,150 feet
**Difficulty:** Potentially difficult
**Hikable:** Mid-July through September

**Round trip to Big McGee Lake: 14 miles**
**Hiking time:** 8 hours
**High point:** 10,480
**Elevation gain:** 2,280 feet
**Difficulty:** Potentially difficult
**Hikable:** Mid-July through September

**Driving directions:** Drive Highway 395 to McGee Creek Road, located 6.5 miles north of Tom's Place and 8.5 miles south of Mammoth Junction, and go west. Cross Crowley Lake Road, then head up Forest Road 6. Pavement ends at 2.3 miles and the road ends at 3.3 miles, at a large parking area with rest rooms (8,200 feet).
**Maps:** USFS John Muir Wilderness (North Section); USGS Convict Lake and Mt. Abbot
**Permits:** White Mountain Ranger Station and Mammoth Lakes Visitor Center (Case 3)

Brilliant displays of red, crimson, blue, and gold flowers contrasting with the blue-grays of the peaks that rise straight up from green meadows to the deep blue sky are the first clues of the visual euphoria awaiting those who hike in the McGee Creek Valley. The two destinations listed above are both worth a visit. Steelhead Lake is reached by a side trail off McGee Creek and is a great destination for anyone carrying a fishing pole. The second destination, Big McGee Lake, lies at the base of colorful Red and White Mountain and is fringed with delicate meadows.

Expect lots of dust, horse deposits, and very hazardous creek crossings. The lower valley has little shade, so plan an early start to avoid the heat.

**THE HIKE.** From the trailhead sign you may follow either the trail or the old road up-valley. After an easy mile the road and trail join at the wilderness boundary. Continue up the open valley on the old mining road, traversing sage-covered meadows vibrantly highlighted with wildflowers. A couple of seasonal streams are crossed before you reach the first ford of McGee Creek, at 2.7 miles.

At 3.2 miles pass a side trail, which descends to a grassy meadow and

*The trail crosses several high alpine meadows just below Big McGee Lake.*

the first of many campsites. Continuing up-valley, a second, and potentially dangerous, crossing of McGee Creek is reached at 3.5 miles. A single
log has been placed for hikers' use just above the ford.

The road and trail part company soon after the second ford. Stay on the
trail and climb steadily through forest to reach the Steelhead Lake intersection, at 4.3 miles. If heading
to Steelhead Lake, cross
rushing McGee Creek on a
log; do not attempt to ford.
On the south side of the

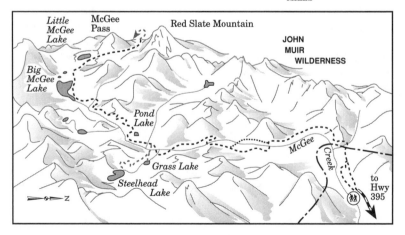

creek, the rocky trail climbs steeply past the turnoff to forested Grass Lake, then on to reach the rocky basin that cradles Steelhead Lake (10,350 feet) at 5.5 miles. Campsites are numerous.

Beyond the Steelhead Lake intersection, the McGee Creek Trail switchbacks over a granite hump, passes Round Lake, and then climbs into alpine meadows where it levels a bit before reaching Big McGee Lake (10,480 feet) at 7 miles. The campsites around the lake are small but very scenic.

If you have time to explore, continue on up the trail to Little McGee Lake, then climb steeply to the crest of 11,900-foot McGee Pass at 9 miles. Be prepared to walk over snow, as the pass is rarely clear until September. On the west side of the pass, the trail switchbacks down to more lakes.

# 26 | TAMARACK LAKES

**Round trip: 9.5 miles**
**Hiking time:** 5 hours
**High point:** 11,600 feet
**Elevation gain:** 1,900 feet
**Difficulty:** Potentially moderate
**Hikable:** Mid-July through September

**Driving directions:** Drive Highway 395 south 15.1 miles from the Mammoth Lakes intersection or 24.2 miles north from the White Mountain Ranger Station in Bishop. Turn west at Tom's Place and follow the Rock Creek Road 8.9 miles to the Rock Creek Lake Campground turnoff. Go left and follow the road to the campground, where it divides. Hikers' parking is to the left (9,700 feet).
**Maps:** USFS John Muir Wilderness (North Section); USGS Mt. Morgan
**Permits:** White Mountain Ranger Station and Mammoth Lakes Visitor Center (Case 3)

Beneath the rugged ramparts of Broken Finger Peak lie the starkly beautiful Tamarack Lakes. The trail to the lakes is one of the lesser known in the Rock Creek area and you can, at times, find enough solitude for a quiet contemplation of the High Sierran scene. The low number of visitors stems in part from the almost total lack of comfortable campsites around the rocky, sloping shores of the lakes. Backpackers are advised to camp at one of the lakes below and day hike up to the Tamaracks.

**THE HIKE.** The trail starts at the end of the second parking bay and heads steeply uphill. At 0.2 mile is an intersection with a trail from Mosquito Flat. Continue straight ahead on a now much wider trail, which climbs for a bit and then levels off on a broad bench at 10,170 feet. At 1 mile the trail divides. The left fork goes to Wheeler Crest. Take the right fork

*Tamarack Lakes Trail*

and head up a trail that climbs in short, steep spurts, interspersed with level strolls across green meadows.

Francis Lake Trail branches off on the right at 1.7 miles, and shortly beyond you will pass Kenneth Lake (10,360 feet) and good campsites. At 2.4 miles the trail divides again. The left fork meanders east for 0.5 mile to the marshy shores of Dorothy Lake and more campsites. Stay right and climb over a moraine, then descend into the East Fork Creek Valley, where you will cross broad meadows and pass a marshy pond. At 3 miles the trail begins a steep, rough climb up to the rocky world of the High Sierra.

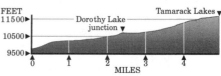

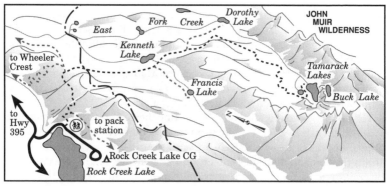

The trail follows the creek up a narrowing valley and then, at 11,000 feet, arrives at a marshy meadow beneath a wall of cliffs. Follow a narrow band of vegetation up-valley and then head to your right to avoid the steepest sections of the headwall. At 4.3 miles the climb ends, and the final 0.2 mile is an easy and very scenic traverse along the crest of the headwall to the two Tamarack Lakes. The first lake is tiny. The second lake is much larger, and its rich green waters are home to an active population of fish. A rough trail, made more of imagination than form, continues a short 0.2 mile to tiny Buck Lake.

# 27 | LITTLE LAKES VALLEY

**Round trip to Lower Morgan Lake: 9 miles**
**Hiking time:** 5 hours
**High point:** 11,104 feet
**Elevation gain:** 804 feet
**Difficulty:** Potentially the easiest hike in the book
**Hikable:** Mid-July through September

**Driving directions:** Drive Highway 395 south 15.1 miles from the Mammoth Lakes intersection or north 24.2 miles from the White Mountain Ranger Station in Bishop. Turn west at Tom's Place and follow Rock Creek Road until it divides at 9.7 miles. Stay left on a single-lane road for the final 1.2 miles to the road's end, at the Mosquito Flat Trailhead (10,300 feet).
**Maps:** USFS John Muir Wilderness (North Section); USGS Mt. Morgan and Mt. Abbot
**Permits:** White Mountain Ranger Station and Mammoth Lakes Visitor Center (Case 3)

You only need to walk a few feet up the Little Lakes Valley to see that this is a very special place. It is also one of the rare High Sierran hikes where it is not absolutely necessary to acclimate before you begin your trip, as the relatively low elevation gain makes it an ideal first hike at high elevation or a great weekend outing for the family.

**THE HIKE.** Following signs to Mono and Morgan Passes, head up the Little Lakes Valley, paralleling Rock Creek on an old road. At 0.2 mile is a short, steep climb, which should be taken slowly at this elevation. The trail divides at 0.5 mile, with the Mono Pass Trail to Pioneer Basin heading to the right (Hike 28). Stay to the left, following signs to Morgan Pass.

The beautiful scenery crosses over into the realm of the spectacular as the trail traverses an open meadow, with views of four snow- and ice-clad peaks whose shear walls and serrated ridges tower above the 13,000-foot

*Morgan Pass*

mark. Watch for climbers with ropes and ice axes heading up the side valleys to scale the summits.

At 0.7 mile, walk past Mack Lake, somewhat hidden on the left, then head past Heart Lake, then Box Lake, to reach Long Lake and the first good campsites at 2 miles. At Long Lake the trail follows the route of an old mining road along the lakeshore and then climbs steadily to the Chickenfoot Lake intersection at 2.7 miles. Chickenfoot Lake (10,789 feet) is located 0.2 mile left of the main trail and has excellent camping.

The trail continues its gradual climb through green meadows, spotted in August with paintbrush and elephant's-head. At 3.2 miles, pass the Gem Lakes spur trail on the right, which leads to a couple of small lakes jammed into a small valley at the toe of the magnificent Bear Creek Spire. Scenic but small campsites can be found around the lakes.

The trail climbs steeply to cross 11,104-foot Morgan

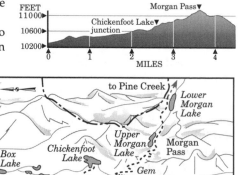

Pass at 3.5 miles. Walk between huge chunks of granite, then descend to Upper Morgan Lake (10,940 feet) at 4 miles. The only camping around this boulder-strewn lake is directly below the pass. The trail, which shows signs of use by 1930s miners, contours around the upper lake and then drops to Lower Morgan Lake (10,700 feet) at 4.5 miles. This is a friendly lake, lacking the beauty of the Little Lakes Valley but with plenty of large, protected campsites. Beyond the lower lake, the trail descends through an unpleasant mess of mining roads and talus to Pine Creek.

## 28 | PIONEER BASIN

**Round trip: 20 miles**
**Hiking time:** 2–3 days
**High point:** 12,000 feet
**Elevation gain:** 2,581 feet in; 2,000 feet out
**Difficulty:** Potentially difficult
**Hikable:** Mid-July through September

**Driving directions:** Drive Highway 395 for 25 miles north from Bishop to the Tom's Place exit. Go west on Rock Creek Road for 10.3 miles to its end at the Mosquito Flat Trailhead (10,300 feet). Parking is a problem; if there are no slots available, you must go back 0.3 mile and find an available space at the picnic area.
**Maps:** USFS John Muir Wilderness (North Section); USGS Mt. Morgan and Mt. Abbot
**Permits:** White Mountain Ranger Station and Mammoth Lakes Visitor Center (Case 3)

Pioneer Basin is one of those places that should be on every hiker's "must do" list. This outstanding hike begins in the beautiful Little Lakes Valley and crosses scenic, 12,000-foot Mono Pass before reaching one of the most enchanting basins in the Sierra.

Your wilderness permit entitles you to one free night at the walk-in campground at the 10,300-foot trailhead, to acclimate to the thin air. The only water available is from the creek; however, you may pick up water at one of the many campgrounds on your drive up. Hikers who do not overnight at the trailhead to acclimate should plan on hiking only a short distance the first day.

**THE HIKE.** The trail parallels Rock Creek as you walk up the Little Lakes Valley toward a wall of 13,000-foot summits. Within a few feet of the trailhead you will pass the walk-in campground. Continue up-valley until the trail divides, at 0.5 mile. Stay right, following signs to Mono Pass.

At 0.7 mile, pass the spur trail from the pack station and then continue,

*Snowfields linger for most of the summer on open slopes near Mono Pass and Summit Lake.*

climbing through stunted white bark pines, passing several memorable viewpoints over Little Lakes Valley. At 2 miles, the trail to Ruby Lake branches off to the left (11,300 feet). The lake is 0.3 mile to the west and is well worth the side trip if you are looking for a scenic picnic spot or campsite.

Beyond the Ruby Lake intersection every step is uphill, and with each step the scenery becomes more spectacular. The trail climbs above Ruby Lake with steep switchbacks.

At 3.7 miles you will arrive at the crest of 12,000-foot Mono Pass. This is breathtaking High Sierra

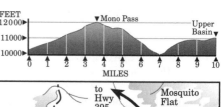

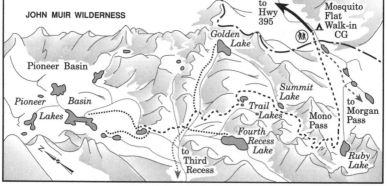

country, requiring a mandatory sit-down to catch your breath and enjoy the exhilaration of the high elevation before descending to barren Summit Lake (11,910 feet) at 4.4 miles. The rate of descent increases as the trail nears Trail Lakes at 5.4 miles (11,210 feet). Here you will find the first campsites below the pass, as well as a backcountry ranger station. Needle Lake, located 0.4 mile south of Trail Lakes on a cross-country route, offers a bit more seclusion.

From Trail Lakes, descend steadily for 1.2 miles to ford Golden Creek at 6.6 miles (10,400 feet). The trail parallels the creek as it descends another 0.4 mile to the reach the Pioneer Basin Trail intersection at 10,000 feet. Go right and follow the trail on a steady ascent for the next 2 miles into the basin.

The basin has over twenty lakes, with numerous campsites, plentiful views, and an abundance of mosquitoes. At 9 miles you will arrive at Lower Basin Lake and the end of the official trail (10,881 feet). Proceed around either side of the lake and continue to climb until you reach the Upper Basin, where you will find some solitude on the lower slopes of Mount Hopkins, Mount Crocker, and Mount Stanford.

If you have several days to spend, plan to take excursions to Golden Lake and the beautiful Fourth Recess Lake.

# 29 | GABLE LAKES

**Round trip: 9 miles**
**Hiking time:** 7 hours
**High point:** 10,740 feet
**Elevation gain:** 3,220 feet
**Difficulty:** Potentially difficult
**Hikable:** Late July through September

**Driving directions:** Drive Highway 395 north from the White Mountain Ranger Station in Bishop 10.4 miles or south from Tom's Place 13.9 miles. Turn west on Pine Creek Road and continue for 9.7 miles, then go left into a large dirt parking lot at Pine Creek Pack Station (7,520 feet).
**Maps:** USFS John Muir Wilderness (North Section); USGS Gable Lakes
**Permits:** White Mountain Ranger Station and Mammoth Lakes Visitor Center (Case 3)

The four Gable Lakes, in a rocky basin below Four Gables Mountain, are the scenic objective of this difficult hike. Few people make the trek to these relatively unknown lakes, and those who do will find solitude, fishing, and many photographic opportunities around the old mines and rocky lakeshores.

**THE HIKE.** To find the Gable Lakes Trail, walk to the archway at the

*The second of the Gable Lakes*

entrance to the Pine Creek Pack Station, then go left and head up through the employees' living area. After 100 feet the road divides; stay left. Where the road bends sharply left, leave it and continue straight on a well-defined trail.

After climbing a few feet, the trail begins to switchback.

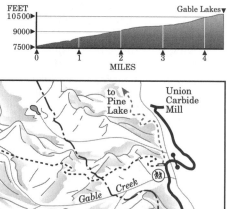

At switchback number ten, the trail heads into a slightly descending traverse toward the deep Gable Creek Gorge. By switchback number sixteen, you will have climbed to an excellent view over the beautiful Pine Creek Valley as well as the pack station and the messy Tungsten Mine with its large settling pond. At the nineteenth switchback, pass a couple of old tramway towers and an old phone box (without phone) left by miners. After one more switchback, the climb abates at 8,380 feet and the trail heads up-valley on a long ascending traverse. Near the 2-mile point, pass a spur trail heading off to the left, which crosses the valley and climbs to an abandoned mine on the east side.

A second group of switchbacks signals a change of pace. These moderately graded switchbacks climb to the crest of a 9,420-foot bench. The trail then descends to the West Fork Gable Creek and becomes indistinct in the tall grass. It then reappears as it heads into the rocks at the upper end of the meadow. The trail again becomes difficult to follow as it crosses a second meadow, where it has been badly eroded by two streams. Once you reach the cliffy slopes beyond, you will have well-defined switchbacks to follow.

From the summit of the hill descend to the creek, a raging torrent in this area. A couple of mining shacks can be seen on the far side. Do not cross here unless the creek is nearly dry. Most of the summer it is best to stay on the right side of the creek and head uphill on a narrow, boot-beaten path. Climb to a band of rocks and parallel them for 200 feet until you intersect a well-graded trail. To the right, the trail climbs over a rocky knoll to the second Gable Lake and several small campsites. To the left, the trail descends to the lowest Gable Lake (9,940 feet) and a relatively easy creek crossing at the outlet. A steep trail then climbs past an immense amount of mining debris to the third Gable Lake (10,740 feet). The fourth Gable Lake is reached by an easy 0.3-mile cross-country hike from the third lake.

# 30 | MOON LAKE

**Round trip: 22 miles**
**Hiking time:** 2–4 days
**High point:** 11,120 feet
**Elevation gain:** 4,010 feet
**Difficulty:** Potentially difficult
**Hikable:** Mid-July through September

**Driving directions:** Drive Highway 395 north 10.4 miles from the White Mountain Ranger Station in Bishop or south 13.9 miles from Tom's Place. Turn west on Pine Creek Road and continue for 9.7 miles, then go left into a large dirt parking lot at Pine Creek Pack Station (7,520 feet).

**Maps:** USFS John Muir Wilderness (North Section); USGS Mount Tom
**Permits:** White Mountain Ranger Station and Mammoth Lakes Visitor
Center (Case 3)

Ascend to a high, lake-dotted plateau and find a small tent site to be your temporary home. The view from this new address is a showcase of nature's best work. Creeks lace this area, tripping from lake to lake with spirited little waterfalls. All this scenery makes returning to a more permanent address rather difficult.

Try to start your hike in the early morning to avoid the heat, which turns the lower portions of the trail into an oven by midday.

**THE HIKE.** Walk through the pack station, passing the horse corral and tack rack to locate the trailhead on the far side. Shift your body into low gear and start the long grind up past a large mining operation.

After the first mile the trail ends and you continue your climb with long, hot switchbacks on an old mining road. The trail returns at the base of the old Brownstone Mine and heads over a steep, rocky slope overlooking the Pine Creek waterfalls. By 3.3 miles the trail has gained the crest of the hill and enters the cool shade of the upper valley forests, where it crosses Pine Creek on a sturdy footbridge. At 4.8 miles from the valley floor, the trail arrives at Pine Lake (9,942 feet).

Head around Pine Lake then up a small rise to Upper Pine Lake and the first of many campsites. The trail contours around the lake and then fords the creek from Honeymoon Lake (a wet crossing until midsummer). Continue to climb through thinning forest to reach an intersection at 6 miles (10,440 feet). Just 0.1 mile to the right are excellent campsites overlooking Honeymoon Lake. Stay left on the Pine Creek Trail and climb past several small, seasonal ponds.

At 8 miles, the trail reaches the crest of 11,120-foot Pine Creek Pass. Snow lingers here; however, horse packers

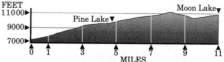

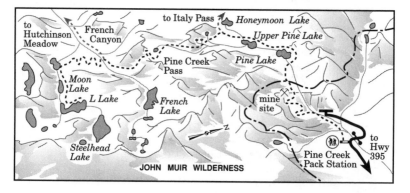

*Pine Creek Pass*

usually create a safe path by midsummer.

Descend gradually into a wide valley for 1.5 miles to an intersection at the head of French Canyon (10,640 feet). Go left on a boot path that crosses a small creek and then climbs past small Elba Lake.

From Elba Lake, follow the inlet stream up to Moon Lake (10,998 feet), reached at 11 miles from the pack station. Campsites are located along the south and east sides of this high alpine lake.

The larger L Lake is located just 0.5 mile away on an upper bench. The trail ends there; however, it is easy to continue over this open landscape to explore the eight other lakes spread around the basin. Views are excellent, topped with a thundering waterfall across the valley descending from Royce Lake.

# 31 | LAKE ITALY

**Round trip: 24 miles**
**Hiking time:** 2–4 days
**High point:** 12,350 feet
**Elevation gain:** 4,850 feet in; 1,160 feet out
**Difficulty:** Potentially difficult
**Hikable:** August through September

**Driving directions:** Drive Highway 395 north 10.4 miles from the White Mountain Ranger Station in Bishop or south 13.9 miles from Tom's Place. Turn west on Pine Creek Road and continue for 9.7 miles, then go left into a large dirt parking lot at Pine Creek Pack Station (7,520 feet).

**Maps:** USFS John Muir Wilderness; USGS Mount Tom and Mt. Hilgard
**Permits:** White Mountain Ranger Station and Mammoth Lakes Visitor Center (Case 3)

Adventure and beautiful scenery await all who make this difficult trek from the Pine Creek Trailhead to Lake Italy. The adventure comes while navigating the frequently traveled but only vaguely marked route from Honeymoon Lake up and over the granite-strewn slopes of Italy Pass to Lake Italy. Beautiful scenery surrounds you from start to finish, varying from knife-edged ridges and thundering waterfalls to exquisite alpine lakes and lush green meadows.

This is not a hike for everyone. The well-maintained trail to Honeymoon Lake is rough and very steep. Beyond the lake the trail gradually disappears. In theory, the route is marked by ducks; in reality, the ducks are nearly impossible to follow and you must rely on your instincts and your map. Carry a compass, and wear stout boots in anticipation of encountering snow.

**THE HIKE.** Follow the Pine Creek Trail for 6 miles to an intersection marked by a large rock cairn, located 0.2 mile above Upper Pine Lake (see Hike 30 for details). Go right and walk a few feet to Honeymoon Lake (10,350 feet). Paths, which branch off in every direction, lead to campsites.

At Honeymoon Lake you leave the dust, the horse manure, and the good trail behind. From the lakeshore, climb straight up sloping granite slabs and then hop a creek near the top to reach an improved trail that climbs to a beautiful meadow. Here you must cross another creek before continuing the steep climb. At the crest of a rocky rib, the trail perversely descends to ford yet another creek. Once across, head uphill, crossing and recrossing the same creek two more times. (If you stay on the

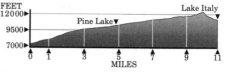

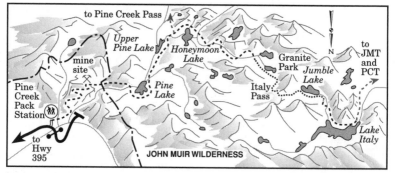

west side of the creek to avoid the next two crossings, be prepared for a bit of scrambling on a steep slope.)

The trail now disappears as it climbs over slabs of rock into an area of little vegetation and numerous lakes (more than the map shows) called Granite Park. Watch closely for the ducks and lines of pebbles defining the route.

At the lower end of Granite Park the trail splinters. Stay low, paralleling the shores of the lower two lakes. At the head of the second large lake, the trail crosses a creek then climbs out of the meadows and into the moonscape atmosphere of the upper valley. If you lose the trail now, simply stay to the right side of the valley and hike northwest toward a low divide at the head of the rocky cirque. The 12,350-foot summit of Italy Pass is reached 4 miles from Honeymoon Lake.

From the pass, head down on a trail that is even less established than the one you came up on. Stay just a little north of center and descend the rocky basin to a small, grassy bench overlooking Jumble Lake, where you should locate a defined trail. The hillsides surrounding this deep blue lake are dotted with a jumble of boulders. Campsites are limited to small spaces between the large rocks.

The trail contours north above Jumble Lake and then drops steeply to Lake Italy (11,202 feet). Campsites are located on the south shore to the right of the trail and near the outlet. The lack of vegetation around the lake allows for a wealth of views of 13,000-foot peaks. Feast your eyes on Mount Hilgard, Mount Gabb, Mount Abbott, Mount Dade, Bear Creek Spire, and Mount Julius Caesar—a lineup that could keep a mountain climber busy for a week.

*Tarn in Granite Park*

# 32 | SABRINA BASIN

**Round trip to Hungry Packer Lake: 14 miles**
**Hiking time:** 7 hours
**High point:** 11,100 feet
**Elevation gain:** 2,020 feet
**Difficulty:** Potentially moderate
**Hikable:** Mid-July through September

**Driving directions:** From the center of Bishop, drive west on Highway 168, following signs to Sabrina and South Lakes for 15.4 miles to a Y intersection; take the right fork and continue to Lake Sabrina. The backpackers' parking area is located at the North Lake turnoff, 18.5 miles from Bishop. Day hikers may continue another 0.7 mile and park near the trailhead or at the north side of the dam (9,080 feet).
**Maps:** USFS John Muir Wilderness (Central Section); USGS Mt. Thompson and Mt. Darwin
**Permits:** White Mountain Ranger Station (Case 3)

Sabrina Basin is dotted with lakes—large and small, blue, aqua, green, and gray. The lakes are nestled below massive granite peaks with cliffs and sloping granitic blocks forming the shorelines. If you are not lucky enough to obtain a wilderness permit for an overnight stay, plan to day hike this trail. The beauty of this area is worth the price of sore toes and tired legs.

The trail into the basin is not without its challenges. From its high-elevation start, the trail climbs to even thinner air, making for slow going on

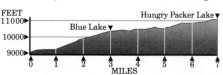

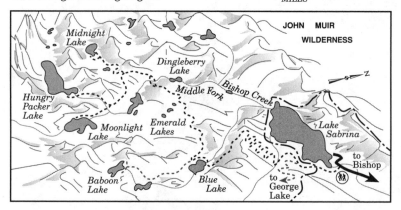

*Mount Wallace and Hungry Packer Lake*

the steep and rocky ground. When crossing granite slabs, the trail disappears and some routefinding skills are required. Streams must be forded, which is a wet proposition in early summer.

**THE HIKE.** The trail climbs above the dam and then traverses open slopes above the southeast shore of Lake Sabrina. At 1.2 miles a lateral trail to George Lake climbs steeply off to the left; continue straight. Shortly after this intersection, cross two creeks where, if you are very lucky, you may be able to keep your feet dry. The trail then heads into the trees and makes several dusty, dry, horse-churned switchbacks to an overlook of the valley and ruby-colored Mount Emerson. Up-valley, Mount Wallace, Mount Haeckel, and a roaring falls of the Middle Fork Bishop Creek dominate the scene.

The climb is steady as the trail bends into a side valley to reach extremely popular Blue Lake (10,390 feet) at 3 miles. Campsites and mosquitoes may be found on granite benches all around this rocky lake.

To continue on, you must make a challenging crossing of the deep outlet creek on skinny logs. The trail then heads around the west side of the lake for 0.2 mile to an intersection. Go right on the Dingleberry Lake Trail.

Following the trail, work your way around a series of granite ridges and pass the marshy Emerald Lakes at 4 miles. At 5 miles, descend to the attractive Dingleberry Lake and more campsites (10,480 feet).

Shortly after Dingleberry Lake the trail divides. Stay right and walk over a granite slab to a ford of Middle Fork Bishop Creek. Stepping stones help to keep feet dry in the late season; however, early season hikers are advised to take their boots off and wade.

The horse and hiker trails rejoin after the ford and cross a meadow before climbing more granite. At 5.7 miles a 1-mile spur trail branches right to Midnight Lake (11,060 feet) and several nice campsites. At 6.2 miles the trail bends to the right and follows the outlet creek 0.7 mile to Hungry Packer Lake and campsites (11,100 feet). Hikers heading to Moonlight Lake need to head cross the granite slabs, passing Sailor Lake and then follow one of the faint paths up the rib to the lakeshore (11,070 feet).

## 33 | HUMPHREYS BASIN

**Round trip: 16.8 miles**
**Hiking time:** 2–3 days
**High point:** 11,423 feet
**Elevation gain:** 2,103 feet
**Difficulty:** Potentially difficult
**Hikable:** Mid-July through September

**Driving directions:** From Highway 395 in Bishop, turn west on Highway 168 (called Line Street) and follow it toward Lake Sabrina. At 15.2 miles the road divides; stay right for 3.2 miles before turning right again on North Lake Road. Head up for 2.1 miles to North Lake Campground, where you will want to drop your packs before driving back down-valley 0.7 mile to the hikers' parking area (9,360 feet).
**Maps:** USFS John Muir Wilderness (North Section); USGS Mt. Darwin and Mount Tom
**Permits:** White Mountain Ranger Station (Case 3)

Reserve your wilderness permits early for a trek to this popular High Sierran basin. Part of the hike is on the busy Piute Pass Trail and part of the hike is on sketchy boot-beaten paths or unmarked cross-country routes over the open hills. Walk softly, staying on rocks whenever possible, and carry a detailed map to help you navigate between the many lakes and vistas scattered through Humphreys Basin.

This is a high-elevation hike, and it is best to spend the night before you start walking at either North Lake Campground or Sabrina Campground to let your body acclimate. Thunderstorms come up very quickly, and Piute Pass and the basin are very exposed. Be prepared at all times for changing weather; it may even snow!

**THE HIKE.** From the parking area, walk the road back to the campground and locate the Piute Pass Trailhead, at the far end of the walk-in campsites. Two trails start here: Take the one on the right and begin a

*Desolation Lake in Humphreys Basin*

gradual climb. At 1.3 miles, the trail proves that it was designed for horses rather than people by fording the North Fork and shortly beyond recrossing the creek (wet crossings in early season). Near the 2-mile point, arrive at the headwall of Piute Crags and Mount Emerson. With a series of steep switchbacks, the trail works its way up to Loch Leven (10,740 feet) at 3.1 miles. Campsites and picnic spots are located all around this rock-bound lake.

The trail continues its ascent through delightful meadows covered with wildflowers. Stumbling feet will remind you to watch the trail rather than

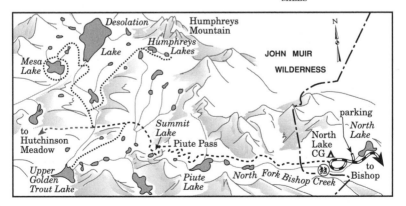

the scenery. Windblown Piute Lake (10,950 feet) and more campsites are passed at 4.2 miles. At 5.4 miles the trail crosses a small snowfield. Stop here for a final view over Piute Lake and Loch Leven and then head up to the crest of 11,423-foot Piute Pass for a spectacular view of Humphreys Basin, Muriel Peak, Goethe Cirque, and Pilots Knob.

At this point you have a myriad of possible destinations, some reached by well-traveled routes and others found by cross-country trekking. Good campsites may be found by an easy 2-mile cross-country walk from the pass to Marmot Lakes, Humphreys Lakes, and Muriel Lakes. Reach Upper and Lower Golden Trout Lakes by descending 1.5 miles west from Piute Pass to an unsigned but heavily used intersection. Go left for 1 mile to the lakes (10,800 feet). Camping is prohibited within 500 feet of the lower lake.

For a less-overused destination, go right at the Golden Trout Lake inter-section and head north toward the Desolation Lakes. The boot-beaten trail swings around the east side of Lower Desolation Lake (11,157 feet) and then divides. For the most seclusion, go left (west) to Mesa and Wedge Lakes. To the right is Desolation Lake (11,381 feet), the largest of the Humphreys Basin lakes, where you will find numerous campsites at 8.6 miles from the trailhead.

# 34 | EVOLUTION VALLEY

**One-way hike: 53 miles**
**Hiking time:** 5–7 days
**High point:** 11,980 feet
**Elevation gain:** 8,958 feet
**Difficulty:** Potentially difficult
**Hikable:** August through September

**Driving directions:** This description begins at North Lake (see Hike 33 for directions) and ends at South Lake (see Hike 35 for directions). Hik-ing direction is contingent on permit availability.
**Maps:** USFS John Muir Wilderness (North and Central Sections); USGS Mt. Darwin, Mount Tom, Mt. Hilgrad, Mt. Henry, Mt. Goddard, North Palisade, Mt. Thompson
**Permits:** White Mountain Ranger Station (Case 3)

Three exquisite High Sierran passes, fields of alpine flowers that are more like gardens than meadows, crystalline lakes, glacier-scoured canyons, dancing creeks, lofty peaks that cleave the sky well over the 13,000-foot mark, and ideal mountain weather make the semiloop hike of the Evolu-tion Valley from North Lake to South Lake one of the best extended treks found anywhere.

*Muir Pass Hut*

By map, North Lake and South Lake are close together. However, no complete trail link exists between the two lakes, so a two-car shuttle is the best system for traveling between trailheads. If you do not have two cars at your disposal, try the Backpackers Shuttle Service in Bishop

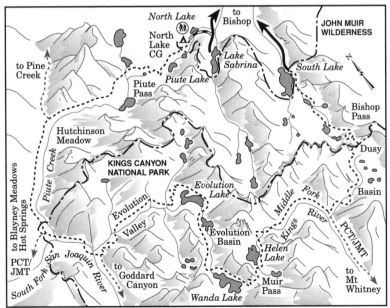

(contact the White Mountain Ranger District Office for details) or look to the friendly assistance of other hikers for transport.

This long hike follows well-maintained trails for the entire distance. However, many of the river and creek crossings do not have bridges, so be prepared to wade at some crossings. Even in early August some of the crossings may still be deep and fast. A pair of water shoes is a good idea for saving feet from cuts and bruises.

Snow lingers at the upper elevations, and if you hike in July, you should carry an ice ax. By August, falling through thin areas on snowbanks is the main hazard. When possible it is best to walk around snow patches.

Thunderstorms are an ever-present hazard in August and September. Your best defense is to try to cross high passes before midday, as storms are most common in the afternoons. Do not approach a pass if clouds are building.

The North Lake and South Lake Trailheads are both very popular, and you should apply for wilderness permits in early March. For experienced cross-county hikers, there is a third option when daily quotas are filled on the Piute Pass or Bishop Trails. From North Lake you may take the trail to Lower and Upper Lamarck Lakes. Just before Upper Lamarck Lake, a well-used but unmaintained trail branches left and climbs to the ridge above the lake. This trail ultimately crosses Lamarck Col. You then make a steep and difficult descent to Darwin Lakes and Darwin Canyon under Mount Mendel and follow a trail to the meadow near the Evolution Lake outlet. This trail is not shown on new maps, but old books and old maps show it clearly.

*Bridge below Dusy Basin*

As the North Lake and South Lake Trailheads are above 9,000 feet, it is advisable to acclimate by spending the night before your trip in a campground as close to 9,000 feet as possible.

**THE HIKE.** Begin your journey at the North Lake hikers' parking area (9,320 feet) and follow Hike 34 for 5.5 miles, to Piute Pass (11,423 feet). The trail then heads down, descending gradually past Summit Lake and through Humphreys Basin. The descent continues along Piute Creek through parklike meadows.

At 10.9 miles the trail levels and then crosses the French Canyon Creek delta. Even in August the crossing is a challenge, with at least six knee-deep fords in about 200 yards. Do not put your shoes back on until you have crossed all of them. At 11 miles reach the French Canyon Trail junction and campsites, in an area known as Hutchinson Meadow (9,440 feet).

Below the meadow, the descent is gradual through lodgepole forest for the next mile to East Pinnacles Creek (a moderately easy crossing). The rate of descent increases and the valley walls close in as the trail descends across the steep walls of The Pinnacles, while Piute Creek roars and froths below. At 13.4 miles ford West Pinnacles Creek, and at 14.6 miles ford Turret Creek. Piute Canyon Trail ends near the bottom of the canyon where it intersects the combined John Muir Trail/Pacific Crest Trail (JMT/PCT) at 15.8 miles (8,800 feet). At this point many hikers take a side trip down-valley to soak in Blayney Meadows Hot Springs, located near the John Muir Ranch, adding 6.4 miles to the trip.

From the intersection with the JMT/PCT, go left and cross Piute Creek on a steel bridge, then enter Kings Canyon National Park. Passing several campsites, the trail heads southeast, up the narrow South Fork San Joaquin River valley toward Evolution Valley. At 18.2 miles, the trail crosses the river on a solid bridge and passes several good campsites. Reach the Goddard Canyon Trail intersection at 19.1 miles and then recross the river on another strong bridge (8,470 feet).

Beyond the bridge the trail climbs a steep, sun-baked hillside where the spectacular waterfalls on Evolution Creek keep you interested even when feet seem to drag. A deep and wide ford of Evolution Creek, especially challenging on the fast-running south side, marks your entrance to Evolution Valley at 20.4 miles (9,210 feet). The trail then climbs gradually as you wander through alternating trees and meadows heading up-valley from Evolution Meadow for 2.2 miles to McClure Meadow (where a ranger station is located), fording several tributary streams as you go. Cross a couple more small tributary creeks on logs and rocks before reaching Colby Meadow at 24.4 miles (9,840 feet).

A mile beyond Colby Meadow the trail nears the end of Evolution Valley and heads steeply up, gaining 1,000 feet in a 1.5-mile climb to the high country of Evolution Basin. At the last switchback, pass an unsigned trail to Darwin Canyon. The trail reaches Evolution Lake (10,850 feet) at 26.9 miles. Head around the west side of the lake along the flanks of Mount

Darwin for 1.4 miles to a ford of Evolution Creek, at the inlet. The climb is gradual as the trail passes several tarns before reaching Sapphire Lake, and then it steepens a bit to switchback up and recross Evolution Creek near Wanda Lake (11,452 feet). Campsites are numerous.

From Wanda Lake the trail swings southwest to Lake McDermand. Snow patches are frequent; advice from the ranger or northbound hikers can be helpful in choosing your route. Above Lake McDermand, the trail climbs steadily to reach 11,955-foot Muir Pass, on the crest of the Goddard Divide at 32.9 miles. Scenery at the pass is spectacular, with views north over Evolution Basin and south to the Black Giant. Take time for a visit to the Muir Pass Hut, a well-known landmark. Careful hikers have kept it clean and in good shape for sixty years. Do your part and at least close the door when you leave.

From Muir Pass the trail descends quickly past Helen Lake, which is usually snow-covered until late summer. You may prefer to hike cross-country along the higher, exposed rock ribs running up the valley and avoid the snow.

Beyond Helen Lake the trail passes several campsites as it descends to Le Conte Canyon and Middle Fork Kings River. The best campsites are found at Big and Little Pete Meadow, and more sites are located near the Le Conte Ranger Station (8,700 feet). Leave the JMT/PCT at the 40-mile point of your hike and go left to begin the ascent of Bishop Pass. The trail climbs relentlessly, gaining 2,000 feet in the next 4.5 miles to lower Dusy Basin. The grade eases as you climb from the lower to the middle basin and then steepens as you head up to reach the crest of 11,980-foot Bishop Pass at 47 miles. The final 6 miles are an easy descent through a beautiful, lake-dotted valley, which brings you to the South Lake Trailhead at 53 miles.

# 35 | DUSY BASIN

**Round trip: 16 miles**
**Hiking time:** 2 days
**High point:** 11,980 feet
**Elevation gain:** 2,180 feet in; 600 feet out
**Difficulty:** Potentially moderate
**Hikable:** Mid-July through September

**Driving directions:** From the center of Bishop, drive west on Highway 168, following the signs to South Lake. After climbing steeply for 15.4 miles, the road divides. Go left on South Lake Road for another 7.2 miles to road's end, at the Bishop Pass Trailhead at South Lake. Park in the overnight area (9,800 feet). When the overnight area is full, cars must

be left over a mile back down the road, below Rainbow Pack Station.
**Maps:** USFS John Muir Wilderness (Central Section); USGS Mt. Thompson and North Palisade
**Permits:** White Mountain Ranger Station (Case 3)

Bring lots of film for this hike over Bishop Pass to renowned Dusy Basin. The scenery along the trail is outstanding and the basin is unbelievable. Do not expect solitude on the trail or in the basin. Day-of-hike permits are difficult to get; plan ahead and reserve your wilderness permit early.

**THE HIKE.** From the parking area, the trail descends 10 feet to join the horse packer's trail then heads around the east shore of South Lake for 0.5 mile before climbing a ravine filled with shooting stars and willows. Pace yourself, breathe steadily, walk with measured steps, and enjoy the scenery as you get used to the elevation.

Pass the Treasure Lakes Trail junction at 0.8 mile. Stay left and continue the well-graded ascent by small flower-covered meadows under the welcome shade of trees. The Mary Louise Lake spur trail branches right at 1.4 miles and at 1.9 miles, pass a trail to Bull and Chocolate Lakes. Continue up through a garden of wildflowers for another 0.2 mile to reach Long Lake (10,710 feet) at 2.1 miles. With its backdrop of knife-edged mountains and the appealing foreground of green meadows, granite boulders, and a sprinkling of trees, you may have to force yourself to continue.

Head around Long Lake, passing the spur trail to Ruwau Lake at 2.8 miles. The trail climbs to Spearhead Lake then to the Timberline Tarns to reach island-studded Saddlerock Lake at 4 miles (11,180 feet). At this point you leave the meadows and trees behind and head up into the rocky world of the High Sierra.

After passing an unsigned spur trail to Bishop Lake at 4.5 miles, your trail begins its final push to the pass. At 5.7 miles, cross a

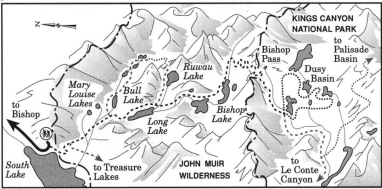

*Dusy Basin with Columbine Peak in background*

notch in the ridge crest and then head over a broad, open plateau for 0.3 mile to the 11,972-foot high point of Bishop Pass.

At the pass, the trail enters Kings Canyon National Park and then descends with an occasional switchback into Dusy Basin. The sandy trail contours southwest, dropping from one rocky bench to the next. Leave the trail at the small inlet creek at 11,360 feet and walk over alternating slabs of granite, interspersed with delicate meadows to the northernmost of the middle basin lakes. At this point your options are as vast as the basin. You may camp at this lake or head east and climb over a low ridge to more secluded campsites and lakes in the upper basin (11,393 feet).

Once you have set up camp, it is time to explore. The easiest trip is to head back to the trail and descend 0.5 mile below the basin's outlet to a bridge over a spectacular waterfall. Strong hikers with considerable cross-country experience can follow a rough route from the lower lakes over Knapsack Pass to Palisades Basin or to Rainbow Lakes.

# 36 | SOUTH LAKE TO WHITNEY PORTAL

**One-way trip: 92.8 miles**
**Hiking time:** 10–12 days
**High point:** 14,495 feet
**Elevation gain:** 20,353 feet
**Difficulty:** Difficult
**Hikable:** August through September

**Driving directions:** From the center of Bishop, drive west on Highway 168 following the signs to South Lake. After climbing steeply for 15.4 miles the road divides. Go left on South Lake Road for another 7.2 miles to road's end, at the Bishop Pass Trailhead at South Lake. Park in the

overnight area (9,800 feet). When full, cars must be left a mile back down the road, below Rainbow Pack Station.
**Maps:** USFS John Muir Wilderness (Central and South Sections); USGS Mt. Thompson, North Palisade, Split Mtn., Mt. Pinchot, Mt. Clarence King, Mt. Brewer, Mt. Williamson, Mt. Kaweah, Mt. Whitney, and Mt. Langley
**Permits:** White Mountain Ranger Station (Case 3)

Walk along the very crest of the Sierra on one of the finest hikes in the United States. Along the route you will scale six major passes, climb to dizzying heights and breathless views, and end your traverse by ascending to the highest point in the Lower 48 states. Your feet will follow a trail that crosses flower-covered meadows, skirts shores of crystalline lakes, passes bubbling cascades and thundering torrents, and scales cliffs of sparkling granidiorite, while your mind feasts on endless vistas and the enchanting aspects of the High Sierra.

The main portion of the hike, from South Lake to Whitney Portal, follows the combined John Muir Trail/Pacific Crest Trail (JMT/PCT). The trail is well maintained; however, you must be prepared to face numerous challenges along the route that require resourcefulness as well as

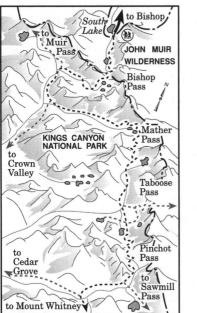

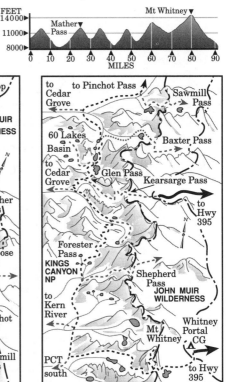

*South side of Forester Pass*

considerable hiking experience. The major challenges include unbridged river crossings, snow and ice that may cover the trail at the passes for most of the summer, heavy packs, high elevations, and sudden storms. You must also be prepared for routefinding, as trail signs are often not replaced for several years after they are stolen or damaged.

The best way to deal with the unbridged river crossings and the snowfields is to plan your hike for August or September. Check with the Forest Service and National Park Service concerning river and snow conditions before you start.

Transportation between trailheads is also a challenge for hiking groups that do not have two cars. From Whitney Portal, at the end of the trail, to Lone Pine, 12 miles below on the valley floor, if you have no other transportation you must use your charm to gain a ride. Once in Lone Pine, Greyhound provides once-a-day service north to Bishop. In Bishop you may call the Backpackers Shuttle Service (phone (619) 872-2721) to arrange transportation back to the South Lake.

**THE HIKE.** The initial 6 miles are spent climbing to the summit of Bishop Pass (see Hike 35). Although at 11,972 feet this is the lowest major pass crossed on the hike, it may feel like the hardest. Take it slow; the high elevation will drain your strength until you acclimate, and your pack, with its 10-day supply of food, will only get lighter. One of the best ways to face this initial climb is to plan a short first day and camp either near Long Lake, about halfway up to the pass, or just over the crest, in Dusy Basin.

From Bishop Pass the trail descends past lakes, meadows, and waterfalls to reach the Middle Fork Kings River and an intersection with the John Muir Trail/Pacific Crest Trail (JMT/PCT) at 12 miles from South Lake. Go left (south) and descend gradually through Grouse Meadows.

At 15 miles (8,000 feet) the trail begins to climb again. The elevation gain is gradual as you head up through Deer Meadow and then increases as you climb past Palisade Lakes to reach 12,100-foot Mather Pass at 25.2 miles.

From Mather Pass the trail descends nearly 2,000 feet through lake-studded Upper Basin to cross the South Fork Kings River (5.2 miles below the pass) before heading to the 12,000-foot crest of Pinchot Pass at 33.7 miles.

From Pinchot Pass, the trail descends gradually for 7 miles through meadows and forest to cross Woods Creek at 8,492 feet on a delightful suspension bridge. After Woods Creek you can expect a lot of company as you hike the most scenic portion of the famous Rae Lakes Loop (see Hike 57). The campsite on the south side of Woods Creek is well used and has a food-storage box. From Woods Creek, the trail climbs to Dollar Lake and beautiful Rae Lakes at the base of Fin Dome and the Painted Lady. There is a one-night limit at the campsites in this area, and there are food-storage boxes at most of them. At mile 49 cross 11,978-foot Glen Pass.

From Glen Pass, the trail descends briskly to the Kearsarge Plateau, passing spur trails to Charlotte Lake and Kearsarge Lakes (these beautiful and popular lakes also have a one-night camping limit). Continuing, the trail relentlessly descends a sparsely forested hillside to reach Vidette Meadow at 54.2 miles (9,510 feet).

At Vidette Meadow, the Rae Lakes Loop and many of your fellow hikers will head west, down Bubbs Creek. However, there is little solitude as numerous Whitney-bound hikers from Onion Valley join you for a breathtaking climb over 13,180-foot Forester Pass. On this difficult section of trail you will gain 3,670 feet of elevation in just 7.3 miles. Snow may linger on the north side of the pass for the entire summer. From the summit, descend 6 miles down the cliff walls on stony switchbacks then cross a high, open plain to reach Tyndall Creek and a popular, overused campsite (10,880 feet) at 67.5 miles.

The Tyndall Creek crossing can be dangerous and is best done in the early morning. Beyond the creek, the trail rolls over the forested Bighorn Plateau to Wallace Creek then climbs over Stony Meadow to the Crabtree Ranger Station and an intersection. Here the John Muir Trail and Pacific Crest Trail part company at 73.5 miles from South Lake. Go left on the John Muir Trail and follow it past several excellent campsites before beginning the climb to the 13,480-foot Trail Crest, reached at 78.9 miles.

At Trail Crest there is an intersection. Unless weather conditions prohibit continuing the ascent, go left and climb for another 1.8 miles to the summit of Mount Whitney (14,495 feet). Do not linger at the summit too long; it is still an 11-mile descent down the famous ninety-seven switchbacks to Whitney Portal. There are two campsites along the descent, at 5 and 7 miles below the summit. Walk-in campsites are available at Whitney Portal.

# 37 BIG PINE LAKES BASIN

**Loop trip to Summit Lake: 16 miles**
**Hiking time:** 2 days
**High point:** 10,920 feet
**Elevation gain:** 3,160 feet
**Difficulty:** Potentially difficult
**Hikable:** Mid-July through September

**Driving directions:** Drive Highway 395 to the town of Big Pine and then go west on Crocker Street, which soon becomes Glacier Lodge Road. Reach Upper Sage Flat Campground at 9.9 miles. The backpackers' trailhead is located 0.2 mile farther on (7,750 feet). Day hikers can continue another 0.6 mile and park at the end of the road.
**Maps:** USFS John Muir Wilderness (Central Section); USGS Coyote Flat, Mt. Thompson, and Split Mountain
**Permits:** White Mountain and Mount Whitney Ranger Stations (Case 3)

Big Pine Lakes Basin lies at the base of a wall of glaciated peaks whose summits pierce the sky at over 14,000 feet. The basin has nine lakes, each in its own granite bowl, exquisitely sculptured by ancient glaciers. Hike the basic loop to Summit Lake as described here, then plan to spend several more days exploring.

**THE HIKE.** From the backpackers' parking area, the trail heads up-valley, traversing a sage-covered hillside for 1.2 miles. As you round the hill and enter the North Fork Big Pine Creek valley, pass a trail on the left that descends to First Falls Walk-in Campground and the day hikers'

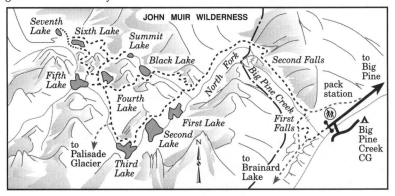

parking lot. At 1.7 miles the Baker Lake Trail branches off on the right.

The trail switchbacks up a narrow gorge at the edge of Second Falls then enters a verdant valley covered with forest and meadows. Near the 3-mile point, pass a beautiful old cabin that was once the property of actor Lon Chaney and is now the wilderness ranger's camp. The rate of climb increases as you continue, and an unbelievable wall of summits comes into view.

At 4.3 miles the trail divides and the loop portion of the hike begins. Go left and explore the dazzling spectacle of Big Pine Lakes one through seven, in numerical order. With the towering mass of Temple Crag reflecting in its waters, First Lake (9,900 feet), passed at 4.5 miles, is an

*Temple Crag rises above First Lake*

awesome sight. Just 0.2 mile beyond lies equally beautiful Second Lake. Third Lake, at 5.2 miles, is smaller and has several secluded campsites.

Beyond Third Lake the trail climbs steadily to an intersection at 5.7 miles. To the left, a rough trail scrambles over granite ledges and grassy meadows to the base of Palisade Glacier, an interesting side trip. For now, stay right for another 0.3 mile to the Fourth Lake intersection. The right-hand trail is your route back to the Big Pine Creek Trailhead, so go left and head toward Fourth and Fifth Lakes. Skirt the west shore of Fourth Lake, and at 6.2 miles pass the trail to Sixth and Seventh Lakes, on the left. Continue straight, crossing a small creek to reach Glacier Camp, a popular camp area for horse packers.

Continue uphill. After 100 yards, the horse trail to Sixth and Seventh Lakes branches off to the left. Stay to the right and continue climbing until you reach Summit Lake (10,920 feet), 8 miles from the start. This delicate lake has a granite fringe of some of the most impressive summits in the Sierra: the Inconsolable Range, North Palisade (14,242 feet), Mount Sill (14,162 feet), Mount Agassiz (13,891 feet), and Mount Winchell (13,768 feet). Camping is limited to a few sites along the west shore.

To return to your car, descend to the intersection below Fourth Lake and go left to Black Lake. Switchback down a very dry hillside to return to the North Fork Big Pine Trail to complete the loop portion of the hike.

# 38

# BRAINARD LAKE

**Round trip: 12 miles**
**Hiking time:** 7 hours
**High point:** 10,650 feet
**Elevation gain:** 2,900 feet
**Difficulty:** Potentially difficult
**Hikable:** Mid-July through September

**Driving directions:** Drive Highway 395 to Big Pine, then go west on Crocker Street, which soon becomes Glacier Lodge Road. At 9.9 miles reach Upper Sage Flat Campground. The backpacker's parking area (7,750 feet) is located 0.2 mile beyond. Day hikers may continue up the road another 0.7 mile to the small parking area at road's end (7,800 feet).
**Maps:** USFS John Muir Wilderness (Central Section); USGS Coyote Mountain and Split Peak
**Permits:** White Mountain and Mount Whitney Ranger Stations (Case 3)

Brainard Lake lies in a deep bowl of granite, surrounded by glacier-clad summits towering over 13,000 feet. Massive cliffs create a vertical shoreline for the icy blue waters. This scenic lake is located high up the South Fork Big Pine Creek valley. The trail to Brainard Lake is rough, steep, and hard to follow in some sections. Campsites are small and limited in number.

**THE HIKE.** If starting from the backpacker's parking lot, walk up the road to its end, at the upper trailhead. Head around the gate and then follow the South Fork Big Pine Creek Trail on an old road past several cabins. After a short 0.1 mile you will arrive at the confluence of the North and South Forks of Big Pine Creek. The trail goes right and climbs uphill to a sturdy bridge.

At 0.2 mile the trail divides; stay left on the South Fork Trail and follow it across a sage-covered hillside. The climb is gradual but steady with the river rumbling below and the glaciated Palisade Crest and Norman Clyde Peak above. The trail crosses the old roadbed and continues up-valley. Watch for prickly pear cactus as you walk. After 1.7 miles of easy going, cross the South Fork Big Pine Creek. (If the bridge is water-covered or missing, don't even think of crossing.)

The trail then heads up a talus-covered slope to the base of the valley headwall and begins a series of steep switchbacks that wind around boulders and scramble across ledges to reach the 9,800-foot ridge crest, where a spectacular view of mountains and glaciers bursts forth at 3.4 miles.

Descend across small meadows, losing 180 feet of elevation, before arriving at the Willow Lake intersection at 4.2 miles. Here you go left and cross a

*Trail above Willow Lake*

small creek with a long jump, then start uphill, paralleling a deep gorge.

The trail passes a small pond then dips to cross a marshy meadow. On the far side of the meadow the trail climbs past a second pond and then swings around a granite ledge to reach the shores of Brainard Lake (10,650 feet) at 5.7 miles.

Backpackers will locate tent sites to the left and right of the trail. Day hikers can scamper along the rocks to

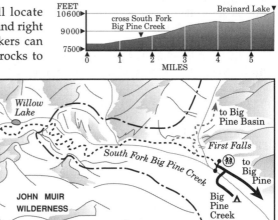

find the perfect combination of sun and wind. Cross-country hikers can work their way up the talus to Finger Lake on the bench above and then wander on to several small tarns with close-up views of the glaciers along the Palisade Crest.

# 39 | SAWMILL LAKE

**Round trip: 16 miles**
**Hiking time:** 2 days
**High point:** 10,040 feet
**Elevation gain:** 5,400 feet
**Difficulty:** Difficult
**Hikable:** Mid-June through September

**Driving directions:** From Independence, drive north on Highway 395 for 8 miles to Black Rock Spring Road. Go left (west) for 0.8 mile to a T intersection and then go right on Old Highway 395 for 1.3 miles. At Division Creek Road, turn left and head uphill for 2 miles to the trailhead (4,640 feet).
**Maps:** USFS John Muir Wilderness (Central Section); USGS Aberdeen Peak
**Permits:** White Mountain and Mount Whitney Ranger Stations (Case 3)

This trail begins in the near-desert conditions of the Owens Valley and climbs to a deep blue lake in the High Sierra. Along the way you will pass through a variety of ecosystems and sample some history as you walk beneath the ruins of a mill that supplied lumber to miners in the 1860s. Besides being a challenging weekend backpack, this trail offers an entry or exit from the combined John Muir Trail/Pacific Crest Trail (JMT/PCT) between Pinchot Pass and Glen Pass.

A word of warning: The Sawmill Trail is hot, dry, and exposed to the sun for the first 2,510 feet of this very strenuous 5,400-foot climb. Get an early morning or late afternoon start, and carry at least two quarts of water per person. Also note that this is a bighorn sheep preservation area; dogs and cross-country hiking are not allowed.

**THE HIKE.** The trail begins by meandering up a sage-covered hillside. At 0.5 mile you will arrive at the base of a steep hillside and begin the business of climbing. The grade is relentless as feet churn up dust in the soft soil of the trail. You climb past a couple of volcanic cones and then enter the bighorn sheep preservation area. Chances of seeing one of these animals are slim, but keep your eyes open nevertheless.

The trail climbs to a sharp ridge (6,831 feet) crested with weathered columns of granite and then makes a long, descending traverse, losing 150

*Trail to Sawmill Lake*

feet of elevation in the next 0.5 mile. Ahead at the center of this imposing valley is a ridge called The Hogsback. As you get closer you will see the old sawmill.

The descent ends when the trail reaches a creek, the first water encountered on this hike. Climb along the creek, passing several small,

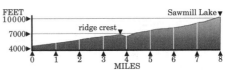

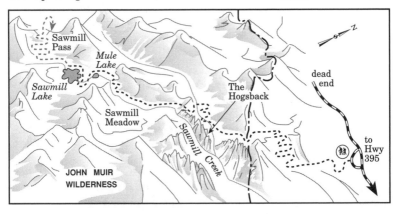

illegal campsites located too close to the water. You will cross the creek three times before you reach the 8,125-foot crest of The Hogsback. The climb continues to the 8,400-foot point, then the trail levels and traverses south to grassy Sawmill Meadow and a couple of nice (if you can ignore the mosquitoes) campsites.

Beyond Sawmill Meadow the trail climbs again, switchbacking up a talus-strewn headwall to little Mule Lake and more campsites, then up a lava-covered hillside to reach Sawmill Lake (10,040 feet) at 8 miles. Numerous scenic campsites are scattered around the lake among the foxtail pine.

If time allows, plan an extra day for exploring. From the lake it is only 2 miles to the top of 11,347-foot Sawmill Pass. On the west side of this open pass lies a beautiful high alpine basin where Mount Cedric Wright towers over lake-dotted meadows. If you descend all the way down the basin you will encounter the combined JMT/PCT (10,346 feet) 5 miles beyond Sawmill Lake.

# 40 | KEARSARGE LAKES TRAIL

**Round trip: 13 miles**
**Hiking time:** 8 hours
**High point:** 11,823 feet
**Elevation gain:** 2,623 feet in; 923 feet out
**Difficulty:** Potentially difficult
**Hikable:** Mid-June through September

**Driving directions:** Drive Highway 395 north from Lone Pine 16.7 miles to the town of Independence. Go left (west) on Market Street for 13.6 steep and twisting miles to the large Onion Valley Trailhead parking area and walk-in campground (9,200 feet).
**Maps:** USFS John Muir Wilderness (South Section); USGS Kearsarge Peak and Mt. Clarence King
**Permits:** White Mountain and Mount Whitney Ranger Stations (Case 3)

Nature has achieved near perfection in the Kearsarge Lakes area with its arrangement of crystal blue lakes, sculptured trees, and towering peaks. This is a popular area, so if you want to make the hike into an overnight adventure, get your reservation in early.

**THE HIKE.** Walk past the rest rooms to reach the start of the trail, which begins with long, moderately graded switchbacks—suitable for hikers starting out with heavy packs at high elevations. The climb is steady, and before long you will be rewarded with views east to the White Mountains.

The first lake, Little Pothole (10,020 feet), is reached after just 1.5 miles of steady climbing. This small lake has wonderful views and a couple of campsites near the trail. Continue up another series of switchbacks to reach beautiful Gilbert Lake at 2.2 miles. Campsites are located along the north side and at the upper end of the lake on a spur trail to the left. At 2.6 miles, pass a trail to Matlock Lake (a 0.7-mile side trip) and shortly afterward pass several campsites on the shores of Flower Lake. The climb continues with more switchbacks overlooking aptly named Heart Lake in a secluded basin.

At 3.7 miles you will arrive at the edge of a desolate plateau with a view of Kearsarge Pass. The pass is near; however, the trail extends the distance with a couple of long, well-graded switchbacks with views of

*East side of Kearsarge Pass*

Big Pothole Lake (very poor campsites). The trail crests the knife-edge Kearsarge Pass (11,823 feet) at 5.5 miles. Grab a seat on a rock and sit down to enjoy the magnificent panorama spread out below your feet. Kearsarge Lakes and Kearsarge Pinnacles dominate the scene below. To the left is University Peak, and to the right Mount Gould dominates the skyline.

With your goal in sight, descend into Kings Canyon

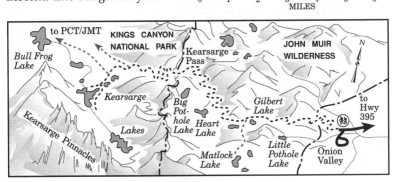

National Park. After 0.5 mile, leave the main trail and go left on the spur trail to Kearsarge Lakes. Campsites are spread out around the lakes. Due to the popularity of the area, there is a one-night camping limit.

## 41 | MEYSAN LAKE

**Round trip: 10 miles**
**Hiking time:** 8 hours
**High point:** 11,660 feet
**Elevation gain:** 3,960 feet
**Difficulty:** Potentially difficult
**Hikable:** Mid-June through September

**Driving directions:** From the Mount Whitney Ranger Station in Lone Pine, drive north on Highway 395 for 0.3 mile. Turn left (west) on Whitney Portal Road and follow it for 11.6 miles to the Meysan Lake Trailhead parking area, which is a dirt turnout on the south side of the road (7,900 feet).
**Maps:** USFS John Muir Wilderness (South Section); USGS Mt. Langley
**Permits:** Mount Whitney Ranger Station (Case 3)

The Mount Whitney Trail is the focus of most hikers at Whitney Portal, so anyone looking for a bit of solitude along with spectacular scenery can easily escape the crowds by making the arduous trek to Meysan Lake. Hikers who wisely spend a day acclimating before attempting Mount Whitney will find this hike a challenging test of strength while bodies adjust to the oxygen-deficient air.

**THE HIKE.** From the parking area, drop down into the Whitney Portal Campground, then go left on the paved campground loop road. Cross Lone Pine Creek on a car bridge, then go left at the first intersection and walk 200 feet, until you reach a trail that heads off to the right, climbing steeply. After gasping for breath a few times, hikers will be relieved to find that the trail levels into a traverse, which ends at a paved road. Walk past several summer cabins, and stay right when the road divides. The trail soon reappears on the right.

Climb steeply up a dry slope, switchbacking to the base of an impressive wall of granite, then head up-valley. There is a short section of extremely narrow trail on a precipitous slope where you must watch your step and not the extraordinary view; ahead is a massive headwall that must be climbed, to the south is Lone Pine Peak, and to the northeast are the Alabama Hills and the Owens Valley.

The ascent is steady as the trail moves up-valley with each well-graded switchback. At 3.5 miles descend, briefly, to a small, forested bench (10,250

*Route above Camp Lake*

feet). At the bench the wide, well-graded thoroughfare ends. From this point the trail is steep, rough, narrow, and sometimes overgrown with brush as it shoots uphill, gaining elevation rapidly. The route is faint in places as you climb over a rocky rib then up a sandy slope. At 4.7 miles the headlong uphill rush abates and you enter a grassy meadow

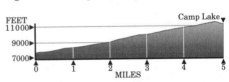

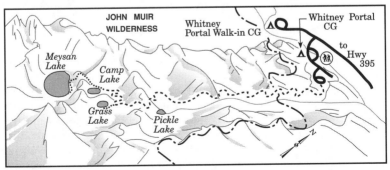

dotted with rounded granitic ribs where the trail divides. Campsites lie straight ahead. Meysan Lake is to the right.

The trail climbs, descends, and then climbs again to reach a meadow and Camp Lake (11,200 feet) at 5 miles. If backpacking, you may want to take advantage of the campsites in this area and save Meysan Lake with its rocky shores for a day hike.

No officially constructed trail exists between Camp Lake and Meysan Lake. Instead, you must follow one of several boot-beaten paths marked with ducks. Stay to the right as you round the large meadow surrounding Camp Lake until you reach a green gully and a seasonal creek bed. Follow the creek up to a first small bench and then on to a second. At this point, go left and head up the hillside on a well-beaten path. The track angles right to a rocky 11,660-foot draw above Meysan Lake. From this vantage point you have the best view of the lake and its imposing headwall, comprised of Mount Mallory and La Conte. From the saddle, descend the loose, rocky slope to the lakeshore, where a profusion of shooting stars grow in tiny pocket meadows.

# 42 | MOUNT WHITNEY

**Round trip: 21.4 miles**
**Hiking time:** 12–18 hours
**High point:** 14,495 feet
**Elevation gain:** 6,131 feet
**Difficulty:** Difficult
**Hikable:** Mid-July through September

**Driving directions:** From the Mount Whitney Ranger Station in Lone Pine, drive north on Highway 395 for 0.3 mile. Turn left (west) on Whitney Portal Road and head up for 12.6 miles to the Whitney Portal. Park in the hikers' area next to the walk-in campground (8,365 feet).
**Maps:** USFS John Muir Wilderness (South Section); USGS Mt. Langley and Mt. Whitney
**Permits:** Mount Whitney Ranger Station (Case 3)

People come from all over the world to hike to the top of the highest peak in the continental United States. The scenery from the trail and 14,495-foot summit of Mount Whitney bring people back to do this hike time and again.

Before your feet ever touch the trail, you must work your way through the preparation process. The first step in the process is to obtain an overnight or a day hiking permit. The process can be frustrating (put your sense of humor into high gear, then take a look at Case 6). Once you have your permit, the next step is to physically prepare yourself for the challenge. For most hikers, the length of the hike as well as the starting and ending elevations require a minimum of one night spent at the trailhead to acclimate and one or more nights spent on the trail.

All Mount Whitney hikers should carry a wide assortment of clothes to deal with adverse conditions such as thunder and lightning, heavy rains, arctic winds, snow, and ice. Always wear sunglasses and reapply sunscreen every hour or so. Carry lots of water: Day hikers should drink two to three quarts a day to avoid becoming dehydrated and sick. A large quantity of food is also a must. Day hikers must walk the entire 21.4 miles in a day, which requires being in excellent physical condition and having a willingness to start early, by 4:00 A.M. at the very latest.

Sudden electrical storms are common during the summer months and can be deadly on the exposed ridge and summit of the mountain. When thunderclouds appear, turn back immediately. If you are on the summit, wait out the entire storm in the cabin, even if it lasts for several hours. (The cabin is not always open and has been known to fill up during a bad storm). Altitude sickness, dehydration, and acute fatigue are major factors on the trail. If you feel ill, do not be afraid to turn back. You will be charged for the expense of the rescue if you cannot make it down on your own. To learn more about altitude sickness, look up *high-altitude pulmonary edema* and familiarize yourself with the symptoms before starting.

**THE HIKE.** The trail begins with a long switchback and then heads up the Lone Pine Creek Valley. Vertical walls of granite seem to surround you as you climb. Ahead, Thor Peak dominates the skyline. The climb is steady but never steep, and views expand as you go. To the east the Owens Valley and the amazing Alabama Hills soon become visible.

The trail crosses two small creeks. Near the second creek

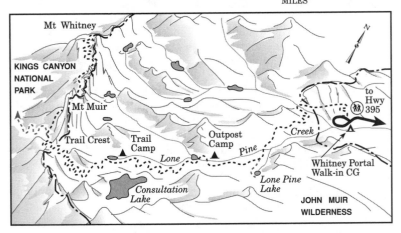

*Mount Whitney Trail at base of the famous ninety-seven switchbacks*

crossing, at 0.7 mile, pass the first of several unsigned climbers' trails branching off to the right. Beyond the creeks, the trail switchbacks up the headwall of the valley. At 2.7 miles cross Lone Pine Creek and 0.1 mile beyond pass a spur trail to Lone Pine Lake (9,850 feet). (Hikers without permits must turn around at the lake.) The trail continues to climb, heading up a boulder-filled valley then ascending granite walls on superbly engineered switchbacks. A short descent at 3.8 miles marks your entrance into a beautiful oasis of green known as Bighorn Park. At the upper end is Outpost Camp (10,365 feet), one of the two popular and convenient campsites along the trail. The camp has a solar toilet.

Beyond the camp, the trail climbs again (no big surprise), switchbacking up a granite-covered slope for 0.5 mile to Mirror Lake (10,640 feet). More switchbacks follow, heading up a granite stairway, leaving the trees and shade behind. At 5.3 miles feast your rock-weary eyes on a tiny swath of green known as Trailside Meadow (11,395 feet).

The switchbacks continue, the views expand, and the oxygen-rich air is left behind. The next mile goes slowly as the trail heads over the crest of a ridge to views of Consultation Lake and the summits of Mount Irvine and Mount McAdie. Follow the trail through one of nature's most glorious rock gardens to 12,000-foot Trail Camp, reached at 6.2 miles. The camp is located by a small lake and has a solar toilet and a ravenous population of marmots.

Beyond Trail Camp the fun begins. Head through a boulder field then start up the infamous ninety-seven switchbacks. Early morning hikers need to watch for ice on the trail in this section. At 8.5 miles you will complete the ninety-seventh switchback and arrive at Trail Crest (13,777 feet), where the trail enters Kings Canyon National Park and descends, briefly, to meet the John Muir Trail at 8.7 miles. Stay right at this intersection and follow the trail up the ridge crest. Watch your feet and not the amazing panorama around you.

In the next 1.9 miles you will pass some of the most expansive views found in the Sierra. At the end of the 1.9 miles the trail arrives at a hillside covered with blocks of rock. The trail disappears; however, the route is obvious. Head up the hillside and before long you will reach the crest of the broad plateau that is the summit of Mount Whitney. Head over to the hut, built by the Smithsonian Institute in 1909, and sign the register. Then wander over to the highest and most scenic toilet in America. Finally, relax and enjoy the natural high that comes from hiking to 14,495 feet.

Remember to keep an eye on the weather and be prepared to head down in a hurry. Clouds can build up suddenly and rapidly.

# 43 | NEW ARMY PASS LOOP

**Loop trip:** 19.7 miles
**Hiking time:** 2–4 days
**High point:** 12,340 feet
**Elevation gain:** 2,920 feet
**Difficulty:** Potentially difficult
**Hikable:** August through September

**Driving directions:** From the Mount Whitney Ranger Station in Lone Pine, drive north on Highway 395 for 0.3 mile and then go left on Whitney Portal Road. At 3.2 miles turn right on Horseshoe Meadow Road. After 19.3 miles the road divides; stay right for 0.3 mile to the Cottonwood Lakes Basin Trailhead and walk-in campground (10,060 feet).
**Maps:** USFS John Muir Wilderness (South Section); USGS Cirque Peak, Johnson Peak, and Mt. Kaweah
**Permits:** Mount Whitney Ranger Station (Case 3)

This loop has all the trappings that you expect from a trip in the High Sierra: beautiful lakes, verdant meadows, and incredible views.

**THE HIKE.** Begin your loop by following the Cottonwood Lakes–New Army Pass Trail over a low ridge, then descending gradually to cross Cottonwood Creek at 1.5 miles. At 3 miles pass the Golden Trout camp. The trail then climbs at a gradual pace to an intersection at 3.7 miles. Stay left here and follow a trail signed to South Fork Lakes and New Army Pass.

Recross Cottonwood Creek then climb steadily to reach the South Fork Lakes Trail intersection at 5 miles. Stay right and follow the trail over a low

*Small cascade near Lower Soldier Lake*

ridge to Cottonwood Lake 1 and views of the basin at 5.2 miles. This is a beautiful area, dotted with lakes and scenic campsites.

Following signs for New Army Pass, walk along the south shore of Cottonwood Lakes 1 and 2 then climb over a boulder-covered ridge to the South Fork drainage. The trail takes you past a small lake with an excellent campsite at the upper end and then up through meadows to Long Lake (11,440 feet). (Campsites are situated at the upper end of the lake.)

Above Long Lake the trail ascends a boulder-strewn basin to New Army Pass. Using long, moderately graded switchbacks, climb with a slow and steady pace to reach the crest of 12,340-foot New Army Pass at 8 miles. A snowbank lingers just below until mid-August. Use extreme caution when crossing.

From the pass, descend into Kings Canyon National Park for 2.3 miles to an intersection with the Siberian Pass Trail (10,800 feet). To the

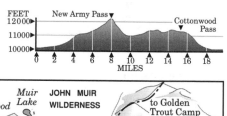

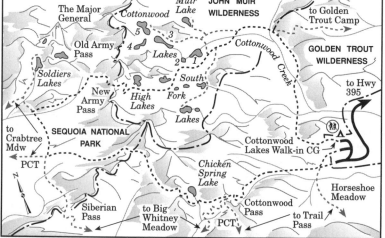

right is Lower Military Lake and good campsites, an easy 0.6-mile side trip.

The loop route heads south (left) on the Siberian Pass Trail, and the next 1.1 miles are spent crossing a forested ridge. At 11.4 miles, leave the Siberian Pass Trail and go left on the Pacific Crest Trail (PCT). The trail climbs with occasional views west to Siberian Outpost through the pines and re-enters the wilderness at 12.3 miles. At this point the trail becomes annoyingly sandy as it swings around a horseshoe basin where some maps show a lake, though the only water is a seasonal spring. At 15 miles, crest a rocky rib with views of Big Whitney Meadow to the west and Chicken Spring Lake to the east, and then descend to the lake (11,260 feet) to find a multitude of hikers and fellow campers.

From Chicken Spring Lake, continue south on the PCT for 0.2 mile to Cottonwood Pass (11,160 feet). Leave the PCT here and go left, descending first through forest then along the edge of Horseshoe Meadow to reach the Horseshoe Meadow Trailhead at 19.2 miles. Walk the road for the final 0.5 mile back to your car at the Cottonwood Lakes Basin Trailhead.

## 44 | ROCKY BASIN LAKES

**Round trip: 26 miles**
**Hiking time:** 2–4 days
**High point:** 11,160 feet
**Elevation gain:** 2,200 feet in; 1,160 feet out
**Difficulty:** Potentially moderate
**Hikable:** July through September

**Driving directions:** From Mount Whitney Ranger Station in Lone Pine, drive north on Highway 395 for 0.3 mile then go left on Whitney Portal Road. After 3.2 miles, turn left on Horseshoe Meadow Road and follow it for 19.6 miles to its end, at the Horseshoe Meadow Trailhead and a walk-in campground (9,960 feet).
**Maps:** USFS Golden Trout Wilderness; USGS Cirque Peak and Johnson Peak
**Permits:** Mount Whitney Ranger Station (Case 3)

Tucked away in a rocky basin (hence the name) is a chain of secluded lakes. The 13-mile trail access includes two major climbs and usually is hiked in two days with an overnight stop at Chicken Spring Lake or Big Whitney Meadow.

**THE HIKE.** Begin your hike on the Cottonwood Pass Trail, passing at 0.2 mile a spur to Trail Pass on the left followed by a horse trail to the Cottonwood Lakes Basin Trailhead on the right. Continue straight along the north side of Horseshoe Meadow for the remainder of the first mile.

At the upper end of the meadows the trail begins a gradual climb, which

*Chicken Spring Lake*

ends at 11,160-foot Cottonwood Pass, 4 miles from the trailhead. From the summit you can preview the rest of the trip down to Big Whitney Meadow and then up over a forested ridge to Rocky Basin. A four-way intersection with the Pacific Crest Trail (PCT) is located at Cottonwood Pass. Just 0.6 mile north is Chicken Spring Lake, which has excellent though usually crowded camping. To reach Rocky Basin Lakes you must go west and descend the sloping meadow below the pass, then head down gradual switchbacks along Stokes Stringer to another meadow. Cross this open and often damp area, then walk over a wooded knoll to reach Big Whitney Meadow (9,720 feet). The meadow is a combination of marsh, meadow, sand, and cow-churned mire, and the trail cuts straight through all of it. At the center of the meadow is an island of trees and an intersection with the first of two trails to Siberian Pass. The trail then crosses Golden Trout Creek, the last certain water before you reach the basin.

At 8 miles the trail leaves Big Whitney Meadow and passes the second trail to Siberian Pass. A good campsite

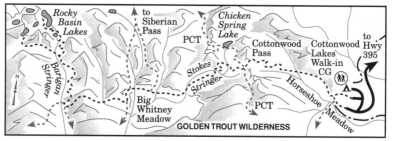

with a spring is located just 500 feet to the north in a fringe of trees at the edge of the meadow. (This is good water until the cows arrive, usually in mid-August.)

At 8.2 miles the trail divides. Stay to the right and immediately head up a forested hillside, gaining 640 feet in the next 1.7 miles. The trail crosses the crest of a low saddle, then drops 200 feet to an intersection at 10.1 miles in the Barigan Stringer drainage. Campsites are located to the left and straight ahead along the banks of the seasonal creek. Go right for the final gradual climb to the lakes. At 11.5 miles the trail divides. The horse trail goes left and crosses the creek; foot traffic stays to the right. A small, bug-infested pond at 12.2 miles marks the entrance to Rocky Lakes Basin, and soon after the trail reaches the first lake (10,745 feet). Follow the path along the south shore to reach the second and third lakes, at 13 miles. Johnson Lake, located just over the hill from the third lake, is a popular cross-country trip from the basin.

## 45 | COBALT AND CRYSTAL LAKES

**Round trip to Crystal Lakes: 9.8 miles**
**Hiking time:** 6 hours
**High point:** 10,788 feet
**Elevation gain:** 2,988 feet
**Difficulty:** Potentially difficult
**Hikable:** Mid-July through September

**Driving directions:** Drive east from Visalia on Highway 198. At the town of Three Rivers, check your odometer, then continue on for another 3.6 miles before turning right on Mineral King Road. The next 24 miles are slow going up a narrow, twisting, partly dirt-surfaced road to the Mineral King Ranger Station, where backpackers must pick up their permits before continuing the final 0.9 mile to the Sawtooth Parking Area (7,800 feet).
**Maps:** USFS John Muir Wilderness (South Section); USGS Mineral King
**Permits:** Mineral King Ranger Station (Case 4)

Just a few miles from the extremely popular and overused Monarch Lakes lie four scenic and often overlooked lakes in a rock-filled basin on a shoulder of the Great Western Divide. Due to a steep and rough access trail, these lakes are somewhat isolated, making them ideal destinations for day hikes and backpack trips.

**THE HIKE.** The trail begins on the north side of the road at the upper end of the parking area and heads nearly straight up the sage-covered hillside. This initial hot, steep climb does not last long. As you approach the

*Lower Crystal Lake*

trees, the trail heads into a long switchback. The first intersection is reached at 0.5 mile. The left fork heads up to Timber Gap (Hike 46). Stay right and continue the long, traversing switchback.

At 0.9 mile the trail changes character again, heading nearly straight uphill along the edge of Monarch Canyon. After a difficult 0.1 mile you will enter Groundhog Meadow (8,540 feet). Pass the abandoned trail to Glacier Pass on the left then cross Monarch Creek with a running long jump. The trail then heads up a forested hillside with well-graded switchbacks.

At 3.2 miles (9,850 feet), arrive at the Cobalt and Crystal Lakes junction. Go right, leaving the wide thoroughfare with its crowds of horses and hikers

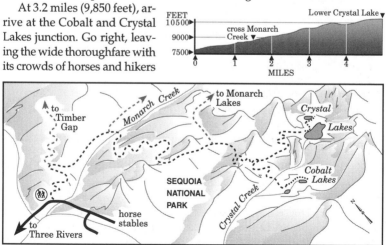

and head south on a rough, narrow track. Traverse the open hillside into Chihuahua Bowl, where the trail begins to climb again, heading past an old mine to a narrow, tree-fringed gap (10,340 feet).

From the gap, you will descend steeply for 0.1 mile to the Cobalt Lakes junction. To reach the Cobalts, go right and continue down to the floor of a 10,000-foot basin. The trail heads across meadows to granite slabs, where it disappears. Continue straight to reach lower Cobalt Lake, sandwiched between cliffs and a narrow band of rock, at 4.4 miles. Campsites here have views west to the San Joaquin Valley. To gain Upper Cobalt Lake, follow a boot path along the left side of the band of rocks above the lower lake. Mosquitoes plague these two lakes until the first frost.

If you have chosen the Crystal Lakes as your destination, continue on from the Cobalt Lakes junction, traversing the open basin to Crystal Creek. The trail climbs steeply over talus and bands of weathered rock to Southern California Edison–enhanced Lower Crystal Lake at 4.9 miles (10,788 feet). Campsites are located on a narrow ledge at the base of the dam (don't sleepwalk) and at the upper lake, reached by a rough trail that branches off 200 feet below the dam.

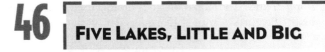

# 46 | FIVE LAKES, LITTLE AND BIG

**Loop trip: 28.4 miles**
**Hiking time:** 3–4 days
**High point:** 11,600 feet
**Elevation gain:** 9,310 feet
**Difficulty:** Potentially difficult
**Hikable:** Mid-July through September

**Driving directions:** Drive east from Visalia on Highway 198. At the town of Three Rivers, check your odometer, then continue on for another 3.6 miles before turning right on Mineral King Road. The next 24 miles are slow going up a narrow, twisting, partly dirt-surfaced road to the Mineral King Ranger Station, where backpackers must pick up their permits before continuing the final 0.9 mile to the Sawtooth Parking Area (7,800 feet).
**Maps:** USFS John Muir Wilderness (South Section); USGS Mineral King and Chagoopa Falls
**Permits:** Mineral King Ranger Station (Case 4)

Three passes with unbelievable views and fourteen outstanding lakes make this the kind of hike you do not want to rush through. (*Note:* This loop is best hiked in a clockwise direction to avoid an exhausting ascent of the sandy west side of Sawtooth Pass.)

**THE HIKE.** The trail climbs the steep sage-covered hillside for 0.5 mile to a junction. Take the left fork to Timber Gap; you will return by the trail on the right. A steady climb leads to forested Timber Gap (9,400 feet) at 2.2 miles. This is the first legal (though waterless) campsite on the loop. From the gap descend to Timber Gap Creek and then parallel it through forest and flower-covered meadows. At 4.4 miles the trail leaves the creek and then heads over a ridge and drops into Cliff Creek Canyon. Cross Cliff Creek on rocks or logs and then go right, to a camp area and intersection, at 5.5 miles (7,040 feet).

Next is a grueling 4,560-foot ascent of Black Rock Pass. Climb from forest, through flower-dotted meadows, and into rock gardens to reach the Pinto Lake food locker (8,690 feet) at 8.4 miles, where the trail divides. Campsites are to the right. The trail to the pass heads left, crossing the basin to begin the final ascent to Black Rock Pass. Very little shade is found along this steep trail, which reaches 11,600-foot Black Rock Pass at the 12-mile point of your loop. On a clear day, views from the pass extend east over Little Five Lakes all the way to Mount Whitney.

From the pass it is a relatively easy descent to Little Five Lakes and campsites. At 13.8 miles, the trail crosses the outlet of the second lake (10,480 feet) and divides. The loop route goes straight (east) to reach a junction with the Big Five Lakes Trail at 15.7 miles. The uppermost of the Big Five Lakes is located just 1.3 miles to the right. The loop trail continues straight, descending 1 mile to the lowest of the Big Five Lakes. All the lakes have excellent campsites.

From the lowest Big Five Lake, the trail heads to Lost Canyon Creek and a junction at 17.7 miles (9,600 feet). Stay right and cross the creek twice as you head up-valley. At the head of the valley, the trail makes

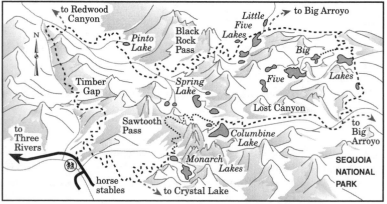

a short climb to Columbine Lake (11,040 feet) at 22.4 miles. For the most spectacular views of this very scenic loop, ascend the hills near the outlet; Cyclamen and Spring Lakes sparkle below. If you camp in this delicate area, stay off the surviving grass.

From Columbine Lake to Sawtooth Pass, the trail is a sketchy route that frequently disappears on the rocky hillside. Consult your map and look for a low notch in the ridge above; Sawtooth Pass is to the right of the notch and slightly higher. The summit of Sawtooth Pass (11,600 feet) is reached at 23.9 miles.

From Sawtooth Pass, head down slippery rock and loose scree on an unmaintainable trail. At the base of the long, open slope is an unsigned intersection; go left and traverse the open hillside to Monarch Lake (10,380 feet), a popular destination for day hikers and backpackers

*Resting on food locker at Columbine Lake*

coming from the Mineral King area. From this point there is a wide, overused trail for the final 4.7 miles back to the Sawtooth Trailhead.

# 47 | FRANKLIN LAKES

**Round trip: 10.8 miles**
**Hiking time:** 6 hours
**High point:** 10,337 feet
**Elevation gain:** 2,527 feet
**Difficulty:** Potentially moderate
**Hikable:** Mid-July through September

**Driving directions:** From Visalia, drive northeast on Highway 198. At 3.6 miles beyond Three Forks, turn right on narrow and winding Mineral King Road. At 24 miles pass the Mineral King Ranger Station, where backpackers must stop and pick up permits, and then continue on another

1.3 miles to the road's end, at Eagle Crest Trailhead (7,800 feet).
**Maps:** USFS John Muir Wilderness (South Section); USGS Mineral King
**Permits:** Mineral King Ranger Station (Case 4)

Enclosed in a snow-dappled cirque below Mount Franklin and Tulare Peak, Lower Franklin Lake is as beautiful as nature and man could make it. Nature did an excellent job sculpting the scene, leaving sand-covered ledges on the granite slopes for scenic campsites. Man, in the form of Southern California Edison, created the large, deep lake. Upper Franklin Lake was left as nature intended, wild and beautiful.

**THE HIKE.** From the parking area, walk back down the road 0.1 mile, crossing the creek to an intersection. Go right and follow a dirt road upvalley to the Mineral King Pack Station. Walk past the corral to the start of the trail.

Just over the hill from the pack station, at an unmarked intersection, stay left. At 0.7 mile cross Crystal Creek, which, like all creek crossings on this trail, will be a very damp experience in early season. Beyond the creek, the trail begins to climb, steeply at the start and then moderately through a series of well-graded switchbacks. Franklin Creek offers a pleasant place to take a break and catch your breath at 1.5 miles.

After a couple more switchbacks the trail enters Farewell Canyon, where the rich meadows support a beautiful display of wildflowers throughout the summer. At 3.5 miles the trail divides (9,200 feet). To the right, the Farewell Gap Trail continues its climb for another 2.7 miles over open meadows. The Franklin Lakes Trail goes left for a long, climbing traverse back into the Franklin Creek drainage.

In the middle of a damp meadow, the trail recrosses Franklin Creek and then heads past the Lady Franklin Mine site. Before long the dam

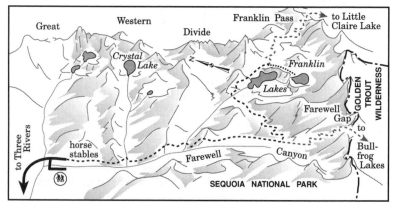

*Lower Franklin Lake*

comes into view, and at 5.4 miles the trail reaches a rocky promontory overlooking Lower Franklin Lake (10,337 feet). This is a great picnic spot for day hikers. Backpackers should continue on climbing about halfway up the next hill and then descend to a scenic campsite and food locker overlooking the lake.

If you would like to escape the crowds, continue on to a saddle above Lower Franklin Lake to reach an unsigned, boot-beaten path on the right. Follow this brush-covered path to the peaceful seclusion of the upper lake.

# 48 | EAGLE CREST

**Round trip to Upper White Chief Basin: 8 miles**
**Hiking time:** 4 hours
**High point:** 9,980 feet
**Elevation gain:** 2,180 feet
**Difficulty:** Potentially moderate
**Hikable:** Mid-July through September

**Driving directions:** From Visalia, drive northeast on Highway 198. At 3.6 miles beyond Three Forks, turn right on narrow and winding Mineral King Road. At 24 miles pass the Mineral King Ranger Station, where

backpackers must stop and pick up permits, and continue on another 1.3 miles to the road's end, at the Eagle Crest Trailhead (7,800 feet).
**Maps:** USFS John Muir Wilderness (South Section); USGS Mineral King
**Permits:** Mineral King Ranger Station (Case 4)

The Eagle Crest Trail offers you a perplexing choice of three beautiful and very different valleys: White Chief Canyon, Eagle Creek, and Mosquito Creek.

In White Chief Canyon, the rocks on the hillsides will dazzle you with their varying shades of white, red, and gray. The hillsides, which appear to have oozed down from somewhere above, end abruptly at the edge of the rich green meadows that coat the valley floor. Eagle Lake Trail leads to an enchanting, man-enhanced (dammed) lake and is the most popular of the three destinations. Mosquito Creek Valley, the most challenging hike of the three, lives up to its name with plenty of the plaguey critters at each of the five pretty lakes and the countless fascinating ponds.

**THE HIKE.** Begin at the upper end of the parking lot and walk past a private cabin. The trail plows its way through fields of corn lilies as it climbs above the Kaweah River. At 1 mile the White Chief Basin Trail forks off to the left.

**Upper White Chief Basin.** From the intersection you will climb steadily for 1 mile and then enter a narrow valley (9,169 feet). Follow the trail across the meadow to White Chief Creek, where the trail divides. Go right and cross the creek and then head up the hill, passing several old mine shafts and a couple of sinkholes. The trail crosses the bare rock, dividing then rejoining as it climbs to the top of the rock band. Recross the creek and then walk through meadows toward a rocky basin ringed with cliffs. At 4 miles the trail divides; the right fork goes to a camping area and the left fork to a small pothole. Anglers

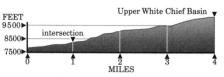

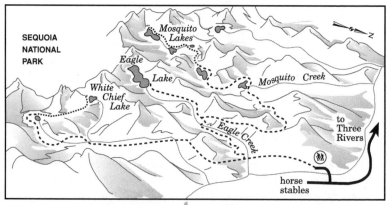

with cross-country experience can head northwest up a rising shelf to reach White Chief Lake in about a mile.

**Eagle Lake.** Although the trail to the lake is short and well marked, this is not an easy hike. The trail gains 2,240 feet of elevation in the 3.4 miles from the trailhead to the lake. From the White Chief Basin Trail intersection, go right and spend the next mile switchbacking uphill. The trail divides a second time at 2 miles (9,500 feet). Go left, climbing steadily for the final 1.4 miles to Eagle Lake (10,000 feet). Campsites may be found on the right (west) side of the lake.

**Mosquito Lakes.** From the Eagle Lake intersection at 2 miles, stay right and follow the trail over a low ridge and then descend, losing 300 feet of elevation, before arriving at First Mosquito Lake (9,100 feet) at 3.6 miles. Cross the outlet creek and follow the best-looking of several paths around the west side of the lake, up the forested valley, and then over a steep, rocky headwall to Second Mosquito Lake (9,590 feet).

Cross the outlet creek and follow a chain of ducks and your map up the forested hillside to the next bench. Once you reach this point, the remainder of the hike is easy. If you find the trail, follow it. If not, just head up-valley, passing east of Third Mosquito Lake and west of Fourth Mosquito Lake. The fourth lake has the best campsites, and Fifth Mosquito Lake (10,440 feet), reached at 5.1 miles from the trailhead, has the best scenery.

*White Chief Lake*

# 49 | GIANT FOREST LOOP

**Loop trip: 9.5 miles**
**Hiking time:** 6 hours
**High point:** 7,300 feet
**Elevation gain:** 960 feet
**Difficulty:** Potentially easy
**Hikable:** May through mid-October

**Driving directions:** Drive the Generals Highway to the General Sherman Tree parking lot (6,840 feet), located 2.6 miles northeast of the Giant Forest Museum or south 2 miles of Lodgepole Village.
**Maps:** Sequoia National Park—Giant Forest; USGS Giant Forest and Lodgepole
**Permits:** *No camping is allowed on this loop*

With meadows, Indian grinding holes, tree houses, and some of the largest trees on earth to look at, an entire day is needed to walk the 9.5-mile-long Giant Forest Loop. You may even wish to plan a little extra time for side trips, intentional or otherwise.

The best way to negotiate the maze of trails in this area is to buy the Giant Forest map issued by the Sequoia Natural History Association and sold at all park visitor centers.

**THE HIKE.** Begin with a short stroll over to the General Sherman Tree to get a feel for the size and history of the largest living thing on earth, and

*The Senate Group*

then walk east on the Congress Trail. At 0.4 mile, go left and cross over to the western leg of the Congress Trail then go left to the McKinley Tree. Continue left at all intersections to the General Lee Tree, the House Group, and the Senate Group (a short side trip is required to see the whole grove). Stay on the Congress Trail until you reach a signed trail to the President Tree, then go right for 100 feet to the Chief Sequoyah Tree. Go right again on to the Trail of the Sequoias and follow it for the next 2.8 miles through lodgepole forest to Tharps Log.

Located at the edge of Log Meadow, Tharps Log was used as summer quarters for Hale Tharp from 1861 to 1890 while he grazed his cattle in the meadow. From the log cabin, leave the Trail of the Sequoias and head west on a paved trail that parallels the meadow for 0.5 mile to a T junction, then go right for 0.3 mile to the Chimney Tree.

From the very charred Chimney Tree, go left, following signs to Huckleberry Meadows. Take the second left at 0.2 mile, and continue another 0.3 mile to the Squatters Cabin. Take a right here and walk the Huckleberry Meadow Trail for the next mile. At the Alta Trail junction, go right for the next 0.6 mile, watching for bedrock mortars where native people ground acorns into flour.

Shortly beyond the bedrock mortars, the trail divides. To the right a 0.3-mile side trip leads to the Washington Tree, a giant nearly 30 feet in diameter and almost 250 feet high. The loop route follows the left fork, staying right at two junctions to reach Bears Bathtub. This area along the edge of Circle Meadow has some amazing trees. After passing Bears

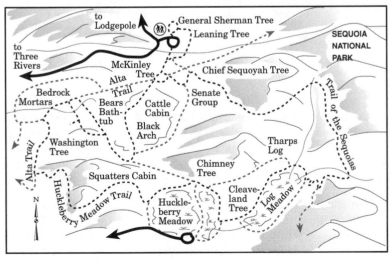

Bathtub, go left at the next intersection and head toward Crescent Meadow for the next 0.3 mile. At the next junction, go left, and in 100 yards go left again and follow signs to Cattle Cabin. Cut through Circle Meadow, and in the next 0.8 mile walk past the Black Arch, the Pillars of Hercules, Cattle Cabin, the towering Founders Group, and the Room Tree to reach an intersection at the McKinley Tree. From this point it is a straight shot along the Congress Trail for 0.7 mile back to the General Sherman Tree.

## 50 | ALTA MEADOW AND ALTA PEAK

**Round trip to Alta Meadow: 11.4 miles**
**Hiking time:** 6 hours
**High point:** 9,300 feet
**Elevation gain:** 2,060 feet
**Difficulty:** Potentially moderate
**Hikable:** Mid-June through September

**Round trip to Alta Peak: 13.8 miles**
**Hiking time:** 8 hours
**High point:** 11,204 feet
**Elevation gain:** 3,936 feet
**Difficulty:** Potentially difficult
**Hikable:** July through September

**Driving directions:** Drive the Generals Highway 1.6 miles southeast from Lodgepole Village. Take the Wolverton turnoff and head uphill, passing a spur road to the corral. Continue for 1.5 miles to the winter sports area at the road's end, and take the first left to find the trailhead in the upper parking area (7,240 feet).
**Maps:** Sequoia National Park—Lodgepole/Wolverton; USGS Lodgepole
**Permits:** Lodgepole Visitor Center (Case 4)

Two destinations lure you deep into the backcountry, one a green meadow fringed by the magnificent summits of the Great Western Divide and the other a peak with views so expansive you may want to sit down and applaud Mother Nature. Either destination can be reached by a long day hike. However, if you can spare an entire weekend, treat yourself to an overnight hike to the meadow and from there climb to the summit of Alta Peak for an inspirational sunset.

**THE HIKE.** Head uphill 0.1 mile on the Lakes Trail to the ridge crest and a junction with a trail from Lodgepole Campground. Go right and in a few feet pass the Long Meadow Trail, on the right. Continue straight, following the wide and dusty forested ridge crest. As you climb, the forest gives way

*Alta Meadow and the Great Western Divide range*

to flower meadow. At 1.8 miles the trail crosses a creek and shortly after arrives at the Lakes Trail junction (8,000 feet). Continue straight, heading up through a red fir forest to reach Panther Gap (8,450 feet) at 2.7 miles. Here you meet the official Alta Trail, which begins in the Giant Forest. Go left, climbing along the crest of the gap to views of the Kaweah River, 5,000 feet below, and west (depending on the clarity of the atmosphere) to the green orchards of the San Joaquin Valley and the coast mountains.

The views improve as the trail crosses a steep, open hillside to include the peaks of the Mineral King area and the Great Western Divide. At

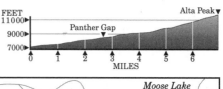

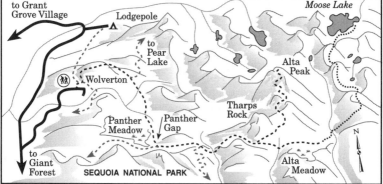

3.7 miles the Seven-mile Trail branches off on the right, and 0.3 mile beyond you will walk through little Mehrtern Meadow, a small but popular camp area.

The next 0.8 mile is spent in a nearly level traverse to the base of Alta Peak where, at 4.8 miles, the trail divides. To the right, Alta Meadow is an easy 1-mile walk from the junction. Campsites may be found at either end of the meadows; however, water is scarce by mid-September. A hikers' route continues on from the meadow for another 4 miles, to Moose Lake.

If Alta Peak is your destination, go left and begin the steep ascent to the summit. Plan at least 2 hours for this hot, dry climb. At the top, all your efforts seem minor compared to the rewarding view. The High Sierra surrounds you; the mighty peaks of the Great Western Divide, Mount Whitney, and the Kaweah Peaks are visible. To the north, Mount Silliman stands alone, while below your feet are the deep blue waters of Emerald and Pear Lakes. The summit of Alta Peak is a rocky mound with a register box at its precipitous crest. To reach the register you must scramble up the rocks. Be very careful; a misstep could be fatal.

# 51 | PEAR LAKE

**Round trip: 13.4 miles**
**Hiking time:** 8 hours
**High point:** 9,510 feet
**Elevation gain:** 2,290 feet
**Difficulty:** Potentially moderate
**Hikable:** June through mid-October

**Driving directions:** Drive the Generals Highway 1.6 miles southeast from Lodgepole Village. Take the Wolverton turnoff and head uphill, passing a spur road to the corral. Continue for 1.5 miles to the winter sports area at the road's end, and take the first left to find the trailhead in the upper parking area (7,240 feet).
**Maps:** Sequoia National Park—Lodgepole/Wolverton; USGS Lodgepole
**Permits:** Lodgepole Visitor Center (Case 4)

The Lakes Trail to Heather, Emerald, and Pear Lakes is the most popular hike in the Lodgepole/Wolverton area of Sequoia National Park. With an early start, day hikers will have time to visit all three lakes; however, to fully experience this beautiful area requires an overnight stay. (Plan ahead; day-of-hike permits are in high demand for the limited number of designated campsites along this busy trail.)

**THE HIKE.** A food locker and large sign mark the start of the Lakes Trail. Head uphill for 0.1 mile to an intersection with a trail from Lodgepole Campground, then go right along the ridge crest. Just 100 feet after the first

*Pear Lake*

intersection, the Long Meadow Trail branches off on the right. Continue straight and ascend the forested ridge.

At 1.8 miles the trail divides. To the right lies Panther Gap (Hike 50). Go left on the Lakes Trail, which heads up the forested hillside for 0.2 mile before splitting. Both trails go to Heather and Pear Lakes and both are about the same length. To make optimum use of shade and views, take the left fork past The Watchtower on the way up and return via The Hump Trail.

The trail climbs gradually for the next mile to The Watchtower, a large wing of granite that juts out of the hillside. Beyond The Watchtower the

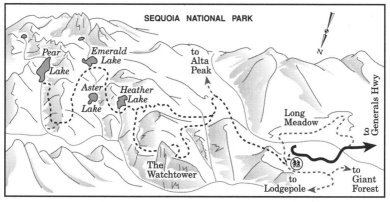

trail has been etched into the nearly vertical granite hillside, and there are breath-grabbing views every step of the way.

At 3.8 miles The Watchtower Trail rejoins The Hump Trail. The combined trail continues on for a nearly level 0.3 mile to reach Heather Lake (9,180 feet) at 4.1 miles. This quaint lake has been trampled by enthusiastic visitors for many years and is open for day use only.

The trail continues over gently rolling terrain for 1.1 miles to Emerald Lake (9,170 feet). Ten numbered campsites and a solar toilet are located near the lake.

It will take a great deal of willpower to pull yourself away from beautiful Emerald Lake and continue the gradual climb. Before long you will have a view of the Tokopan Valley and The Watchtower. At 5.9 miles a trail to the backcountry ranger station branches off to the left. Stay right and complete the final ascent to reach Pear Lake (9,510 feet) and the end of the trail at 6.2 miles.

Pear Lake is surrounded by towering peaks and granite spires that bristle into the sky. The most notable is Alta Peak, which towers over the south end of the lake. There are twelve numbered campsites at the lake and the most scenic solar toilet for miles around.

## 52 | TWIN LAKES

**Round trip: 13.6 miles**
**Hiking time:** 8 hours
**High point:** 9,500 feet
**Elevation gain:** 2,975 feet
**Difficulty:** Potentially difficult
**Hikable:** June through mid-October

**Driving directions:** Follow the Generals Highway to Lodgepole Village and Visitor Center and then drive east, into the campground. Park in the large open area between the Nature Center and the Amphitheater (6,760 feet).
**Maps:** Sequoia National Park—Lodgepole/Wolverton; USGS Mt. Silliman
**Permits:** Lodgepole Visitor Center (Case 4)

Fraternal rather than identical is the best way to describe the twin lakes situated in a small basin below the Silliman Crest. The smaller twin is surrounded by a marsh beautifully highlighted with masses of shooting stars, in season, and an abundance of grass. The larger twin is partially surrounded by forest and partially by heather and lupine meadows.

**THE HIKE.** Walk to the upper end of the parking area, then go left and

*Twin Peaks on Silliman Crest above Twin Lake*

cross the Middle Fork Kaweah River on a car bridge. Pass the Tokopan
Trail and continue on another 100 feet to a large signboard that designates
the beginning of the Twin Lakes Trail.

The trail contours along the edge of the campground and then heads
west up the forested hillside. The climb is brisk as the trail gains 500 feet in
the first 0.8 mile before it bends north on a large sloping bench above Silliman
Creek. The trail descends a bit and then begins a gradual climb through
lodgepole forest.

The climb intensifies as
you approach Silliman Creek
at 2.1 miles, where great dex-
terity is required to keep your
feet dry when crossing in

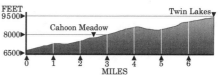

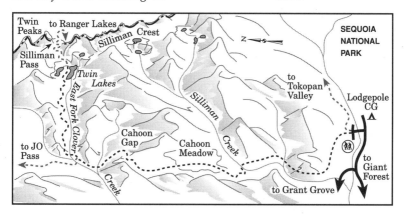

early season. Just 0.5 mile beyond the creek you will find the first camp-sites at the edge of Cahoon Meadow (7,740 feet). As the damp meadows are breeding grounds for a healthy population of ambitious mosquitoes, it is best to pass these campsites by and continue the steady climb to reach the forested crest of 8,645-foot Cahoon Gap at 4.2 miles.

From the gap the trail descends, losing 250 feet of elevation in the next 0.6 mile before arriving at East Fork Clover Creek. After crossing the creek on a log or with a mighty long jump, you will pass a popular forested camp area, complete with a food locker. The trail then traverses the nearly level valley for 0.3 mile to an intersection with the JO Pass Trail (see Hike 53). Stay right and begin a 2-mile climb. The forest thins and soon you are climbing through flower gardens interspersed with large slopes of granite. At 6.8 miles the trail arrives at Twin Lakes (9,500 feet), on a forested bench surrounded by the towering cliffs of the Silliman Crest. Campsites are nu-merous, and you will find food lockers and a backcountry toilet, as well. From the lakes it is an easy hike over 10,100-foot Silliman Pass to Ranger and Beville Lakes.

# 53 | JENNIE LAKE

**Round trip: 14 miles**
**Hiking time:** 7 hours
**High point:** 9,170 feet
**Elevation gain:** 1,774 feet
**Difficulty:** Potentially moderate
**Hikable:** Mid-June through mid-October

**Driving directions:** Drive south on the Generals Highway 8.3 miles from Grants Grove Visitor Center or 18.1 miles north of the Lodgepole Visitor Center. Turn east on Forest Service Road 14S11, signed to Big Meadow. Follow paved Road 14S11 for 3.8 miles to the Big Meadow Trailhead (elevation 7,680 feet).
**Map:** USFS John Muir Wilderness (South Section)
**Permits:** *No backpacking permits, fire permits only*

Just outside the Sequoia and Kings Canyon National Parks boundaries and free from all the associated rules and regulations, little Jennie Lake is a popular destination. Day hikers will find pleasant picnicking on lake shores; backpackers can use one of four well-trampled tent sites.

**THE HIKE.** The trail officially starts at the vault toilet. It climbs over the granite dome that runs through the center of the parking lot and then de-scends to cross Meadows Creek, opposite a small campground. The trail then passes the official trail register and begins to climb. At 1.8 miles, pass

*Jennie Lake*

a short spur trail, which descends to Road 14S16 (an alternate starting point when the road is passable).

The trail divides at 2.2 miles (8,165 feet). The left fork climbs another 1.4 miles to 8,700-foot Weaver Lake, a potential return route if you decide to loop on the way back. For now, head right on the Jennie Lake Trail, climbing steadily around the south flank of Shell Mountain. On a clear day you can see for miles to the west from the open hillsides.

The next intersection is reached at 4.7 miles (9,035 feet). Here, a rarely used trail heads downhill for 6 long miles to Stoney Creek Campground.

Stay left and continue climbing for another 0.2 mile to the forested crest of Poop Out Pass (9,170 feet).

The descent from the pass is rough; the trail zigzags steeply along the edge of a shattered granite dome. Once down, the trail heads east and shortly after begins climbing again. In 2003, the turnoff to Jennie Lake was unsigned but obvious. If you miss the turnoff, you will cross the lake outlet about 200 feet beyond the turnoff. Jennie Lake (9,012 feet) is reached at 7 miles. Campsites are located along the forested north and west shores.

A loop return can be made by following the trail on from Jennie Lake. It is 1.9 miles to an intersection at 9,416-foot JO Pass, where you will turn north toward Rowell Meadow and hike 3.2 miles to another intersection at 8,960 feet. Go left to reach Weaver Lake in 5.5 more miles. The entire loop is 21.2 miles.

# 54 | REDWOOD CANYON LOOP

**Loop trip: 9.5 miles**
**Hiking time:** 5 hours
**High point:** 6,980 feet
**Elevation gain:** 1,240 feet
**Difficulty:** Potentially easy
**Hikable:** Mid-May through October

**Driving directions:** From Grants Village, drive south along General Grants Highway for 5 miles. The turnoff is not marked, so look for the Quail Flat sign on the east side of the road. Your turnoff is just opposite this sign, on the right (west) side of the highway. Head downhill on a narrow dirt road for 1.8 miles to Redwood Saddle, then turn left into the large parking area (6,080 feet).
**Map:** USGS General Grants Grove
**Permits:** Grants Grove Visitor Center (Case 4)

Explore one of the world's largest groves of the world's largest trees on this walk to some of grandest sequoias in Sequoia National Park. Although the trees are the undoubted stars of this hike, you will find numerous other delights, such as a small waterfall, a well-shaded creek, meadows, vistas, delightful picnic sites, and even a place to camp.

This is an excellent early or late-season hike. However, no matter when you walk it, do not underestimate the time required to complete the loop. The trees command your attention and the pace slows frequently as eyes are lifted to the treetops.

**THE HIKE.** The loop hike begins on the right side of the parking lot and follows the Sugar Bowl Grove Trail south. Walk the forested ridge crest to

*Giant sequoias on Redwood Creek Trail*

reach, at 1 mile, Burnt Grove. This group of giant sequoias looks very healthy even though it has been subjected to terrible fires.

You will gain only 250 feet of elevation in the first 2.5 miles of ridge walking to Sugar Bowl Grove, where the trail meanders through the giants and then leaves the ridge crest and descends into Redwood Canyon through a forest of cedars, ponderosa pines, sugar pines, and oaks. Near the end of the 2.5-mile descent, the trail crosses an old burn where young sequoias are growing as thick as grass.

At 5 miles (5,720 feet), the Sugar Bowl Trail intersects the Redwood Creek Trail and ends in a grove of giant sequoias. Go right on the Redwood Creek

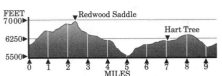

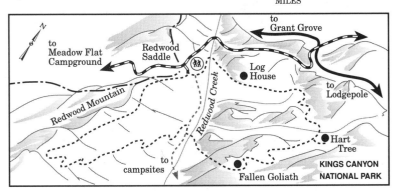

Trail for 0.1 mile to a second intersection and then take a left on the Hart Tree Trail. (Backpackers will continue straight at this intersection to campsites down the canyon.)

The Hart Tree Trail immediately crosses Redwood Creek (not an easy task in early season) and then climbs out of the canyon through a mixed conifer forest. At 5.6 miles the trail divides; to the left is the Fallen Goliath, a once-mighty tree that is now rather tired looking. Continue climbing, and at 7.2 miles you will arrive at the turnoff to the Hart Tree, which is located 100 yards to the right. This great tree ranks as the seventh tallest and sixteenth most massive in the world.

Beyond the Hart Tree, the trail crosses the East Fork of Redwood Creek just below a small waterfall and then heads northwest, climbing over a couple of low ridges. On the way you may walk through a burnt log and look over Redwood Canyon from a rocky overlook viewpoint. The trail then descends, passing an old log house near Burton's Post Camp (an old sequoia logging site remarkable for its high stumps with deep springboard notches). At 9 miles, the Hart Tree Trail intersects the Redwood Creek Trail and ends. Go right for the final 0.5-mile climb to the parking lot at Redwood Saddle.

# 55 | EAST KENNEDY LAKE

**Round trip: 23 miles**
**Hiking time:** 2–4 days
**High point:** 10,800 feet
**Elevation gain:** 6,100 feet
**Difficulty:** Difficult (very)
**Hikable:** Mid-July through September

**Driving directions:** After picking up your backcountry permit at Cedar Grove Village Junction, drive west, back down-valley, for 1.4 miles to the Lewis Creek Trailhead. Park on the south side of the road (4,720 feet).
**Maps:** USFS John Muir Wilderness (Central Section); USGS Cedar Grove and Slide Bluffs
**Permits:** Cedar Grove Ranger Station (Case 4)

The trail up the Lewis Creek drainage to East Kennedy Lake is long, steep, and blazing hot in the midday sun. This 6,100-foot climb is a daunting proposition; however, hikers who go the entire distance are rewarded with tremendous views. This area also boasts a great deal more solitude and wilderness feeling than the other, more accessible trails from Cedar Grove.

**THE HIKE.** This trail does not mess around. You have a great deal of

*View of East Kennedy Lake from overlook near Kennedy Pass*

climbing to do and the long ascent begins with your first step. By 1.9 miles you will have already gained 1,030 feet of elevation when you reach a junction with the Hotel Creek Trail from Cedar Grove Village.

Your trail dodges in and out of the forest, trading shade for sweltering heat on the open hillsides. The heat can be so intense that you may actually welcome the ford of Comb Creek at 3.3 miles (a difficult crossing in early season) and the ford of East Fork Lewis Creek at 4.2 miles (also difficult in early season).

The unmaintained trail to Wildman Meadow, which branches off to the left at 6 miles, marks your entrance to the Frypan Meadow area

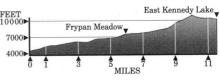

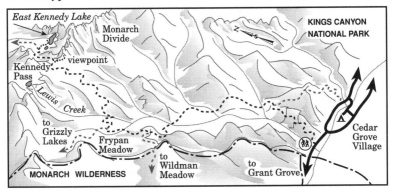

(7,480 feet). Here the climb eases, and at 6.1 miles you will pass the first campsites. Continue on, crossing a creek and a swampy meadow, to more campsites. At this point you will have gained nearly half the elevation needed to reach the pass, making it a reasonable, though not very scenic, place to spend a night.

Just above the camp area, pass the unmaintained trail to Grizzly Lakes and then settle into the long ascent to the pass. The climb begins in forest, where you ford two small, unnamed creeks followed by a ford of Lewis Creek. Before long you will reach an open, manzanita-covered slope and continue the climb with views of the Great Western Divide. You will trade off between open slopes and shady groves of trees for the rest of the way to the top.

Reach the 10,800-foot summit of Kennedy Pass at 10 miles. There is a treasure chest of views over the Middle Fork of the Kings River and ridge line after ridge line of rugged High Sierra peaks. Before leaving the pass, walk east 100 feet to an overlook of East Kennedy Lake, your destination.

From the pass follow the trail north, passing several tarns, where with a bit of searching you can find several nice campsites. Continue down to the second set of tarns 0.5 mile below the summit. Here the trail makes a turn to the right and heads into the Kennedy Creek drainage. After dropping for another 0.5 mile to reach 10,280 feet, look for a small tarn below you, to the right. Leave the trail and drop down a wide, grassy gully to the tarn, then traverse the left shore to a rocky hillside where you will make your final ascent to East Kennedy Lake (10,250 feet) at 11.5 miles.

Small campsites are located along the west shore. To the south is the impressive wall of the Monarch Divide, and the view to the north is almost as good as from the pass. If you are lucky enough to have this place to yourself, the solitude is almost deafening.

# 56 | GRANITE LAKE AND GRANITE PASS

**Round trip to Granite Lake: 21 miles**
**Hiking time:** 2–4 days
**High point:** 10,100 feet
**Elevation gain:** 5,392 feet
**Difficulty:** Difficult
**Hikable:** Mid-July through September

**Driving directions:** From Grant Village, drive 32 miles northeast to Cedar Village, where you may pick up your permit at the ranger station before continuing up-valley another 6 miles. At Roads End are a huge parking area, rest rooms, running water, and an information station (5,035 feet).

**Maps:** USFS John Muir Wilderness (Central Section); USGS The Sphinx and Marion Peak
**Permits:** Cedar Grove Ranger Station and Roads End Information Station (Case 4)

Nestled between sweeping meadows and the base of skyscraping mountains, Granite Lake attracts many visitors for reasons that need no further explanation. However, the often-overlooked crown jewel of this area is the glorious ascent to Granite Pass, an easy morning stroll from the lake. (*Note:* The ascent from the valley floor to the lake and pass is long and can be extremely hot. Even hikers who are in good physical condition should plan an early start to avoid the midday heat, and carry at least two quarts of water per person.)

**THE HIKE.** The trail begins at the far north end of the parking area and soon begins to climb. You start off with a long series of switchbacks that take you up the first 1,400 feet of your climb. The trail then swings into Copper Creek Canyon and continues to climb with the occasional welcome shade of a sugar pine, Jeffrey pine, or white fir.

Reach Lower Tent Meadow (7,600 feet) at 3.5 miles. This is the first comfortable campsite with a reliable water source and several almost-level tent sites. Upper Tent Meadow (8,160 feet), located another 1.5 miles farther up, has more campsites and a food locker.

At 7 miles, the trail switchbacks up a 10,347-foot saddle between the Copper Creek and the Granite Creek drainages. At this point you must convince your aching legs to change modes and descend, losing 348 feet of hard-gained elevation, to reach the floor of aptly named Granite Basin. The next 2 miles are an agreeable climb through forest and meadows to the Granite Lake

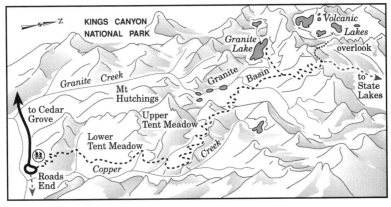

*Granite Basin from Granite Pass*

Trail intersection at 9.5 miles. Go west for 1 mile to Granite Lake (10,080 feet), where you will find a campsite with a view. If you continue west, you will find more campsites at the upper lake.

After you have settled in and explored the immediate neighborhood, it is time to check out the view. Head back 1 mile to the main trail and then go left for a 1.5-mile ascent to 10,673-foot Granite Pass. After taking in the deluxe view from the pass, head west (uphill), skirting a large flaking dome of granite. Just beyond a low saddle you will find a panoramic view of the Volcanic Lakes.

## 57 | RAE LAKES LOOP

**Loop trip: 46 miles**
**Hiking time:** 5 days
**High point:** 11,978 feet
**Elevation gain:** 6,943 feet
**Difficulty:** Potentially difficult
**Hikable:** August through September

**Driving directions:** From Grants Grove, drive Highway 180 east for 32 miles to Cedar Grove, where you will pick up your reserved permit. Continue for another 6 miles to Roads End. Park in the backpackers' area (5,035 feet).

**Maps:** USFS Kings Canyon National Park—Rae Lakes Loop; USGS The Sphinx and Mt. Clarence King
**Permits:** Cedar Grove Ranger Station and Roads End Information Station (Case 4)

Besides being a perfect loop with good trails and ideally located campsites, the Rae Lakes Loop embodies the spirit of Kings Canyon National Park: the granite-walled canyons, the cascading creeks and rivers, the green meadows brilliant with wildflowers, the sparkling clarity of the high mountain lakes, and the euphoric views from the lofty crest of a High Sierran pass.

This is a popular loop, and you will have lots of company on your long trek. To keep hikers from congregating at scenic points, a one-night camping limit has been established at Kearsarge Lakes, Charlotte Lake, and Rae Lakes. In Paradise Valley, you must use a numbered campsite and abide by a two-night limit. Bullfrog Lake is closed to camping. Food lockers have been installed at all major camping areas along the loop and are significantly helping to reduce the bear problem. If you camp away from the food lockers to avoid the crowds, you must store your food in bear-resistant canisters.

Clockwise is the most popular direction for hiking the Rae Lakes Loop. The standard 5-day itinerary places camps in Paradise Valley, Woods Creek Crossing,

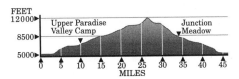

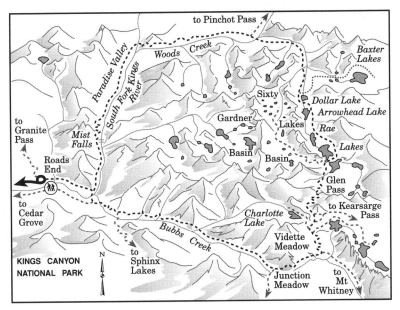

Rae Lakes, and Junction Meadow. If you have extra time, plan side trips to Sixty Lakes Basin, Charlotte Lake, Kearsarge Lakes, and Lake Reflection. If the clockwise direction is full, reverse the itinerary and head up Bubbs Creek. When hiking counterclockwise, make a special effort to start your hike early to avoid the oppressive afternoon heat in the Bubbs Creek valley.

**THE HIKE.** Walk past the Information Station and head up-valley on a wide, dusty, and poorly signed trail. After 2 miles of nearly level hiking the trail divides. This is the start of the loop portion of the hike. If hiking in a clockwise direction, go left and head up Paradise Valley. You will return by the trail on the right.

The Paradise Valley Trail parallels the South Fork Kings River, climbing gradually for the next 2 miles to Mist Falls (5,663 feet). At this point, you leave most of the day hikers behind and the trail begins switchbacking up the steep hillside. The trail climbs to the cliffs and then traverses along the sandy base of the granite wall. The ascent is steady until the trail enters Paradise Valley at 6.9 miles. Just 0.1 mile beyond, you will reach Lower Paradise Valley Camp (6,586 feet).

From the camp, the trail heads up the nearly level valley, climbing and descending over forested ribs. At 9 miles pass Middle Camp, and at 10 miles reach Upper Paradise Valley Camp (6,879 feet).

Above the upper camp, the trail crosses the South Fork Kings River on a large log and then heads east, up Woods Creek Valley. The trail steepens and before long climbs out of the forest onto the brushy avalanche slopes of the upper valley. It is a long, hot ascent beneath giant granite walls and domes that tower above on both sides of the valley. Try to complete this portion of the hike in the cool of the morning.

Pass a stock fence and then make a short descent into Castle Domes Meadow at 14.5 miles. A camp area with a food locker is located at the upper end of the meadow (8,200 feet). Beyond the meadow, the climb is gradual for the final 1.5 miles to the combined John Muir Trail/Pacific Crest Trail (JMT/PCT) intersection. Stay right and head south on the JMT/PCT, which immediately crosses Woods Creek on a swaying, swinging suspension bridge. On the south side of the creek is the popular Woods Creek Crossing Camp (8,492 feet), at the 16-mile point of your loop.

From Woods Creek the trail climbs constantly, paralleling the South Fork Woods Creek up the open valley. You will gain 1,748 feet of elevation in the next 5 miles, to Dollar Lake (10,240 feet) and your first view of Fin Dome. There are campsites near the lake but no food lockers.

Follow the trail around the west shore of Dollar Lake and then make a short climb to a large bench just above. Here you will find the lowest Rae Lake and the first of three official Rae Lakes campsites (10,300 feet). The most popular campsites as well as the best views of the famous Fin Dome and the Painted Lady are found at the upper two camp areas, located on the middle lake (10,560 feet).

Beyond Rae Lakes, the trail climbs at a steady pace. Vegetation is left

*Mist Falls*

behind as you head up through a moonscape spotted with deep blue tarns. The trail switchbacks up to a dark ridge that marks the crest of 11,978-foot Glen Pass at 26.5 miles. The remainder of the loop is all downhill.

The trail descends past a small lake with a couple of campsites at the south end and then crosses over a saddle to contour above a smaller lake, with limited camping, before swinging west and then south for a high traverse of Charlotte Lake. At 2.5 miles below Glen Pass, the horse trail to Kearsarge Pass branches off to the left, and shortly beyond you will reach the Charlotte Lake intersection (10,800 feet). Charlotte Lake, a backcountry ranger station, and a camp area with food lockers are reached by a 1.5-mile side trail.

Follow the JMT/PCT past the second Kearsarge Pass intersection, and after another 0.5 mile pass a third trail to Kearsarge Pass that passes by Bullfrog Lake, Kearsarge Lakes, and a backcountry camp area. At this point you are 29 miles into the loop. Continue down a seemingly endless descent with views of East and West Vidette Peaks and Vidette Meadow. At 31 miles you will arrive at the Vidette Meadow camp area (9,520 feet).

At Vidette Meadow the Rae Lakes Route leaves the JMT/PCT and heads west (right) down the spectacular Bubbs Creek Valley. After a 3-mile descent, the trail levels off in Junction Meadow (8,100 feet). The most popular campsites are located beyond the stock gate at the lower end of the meadow. The next camp is located 2.3 miles down the valley at the Charlotte Creek crossing, and the last camp on the loop (or the first camp on the counterclockwise loop) lies at the Sphinx Creek Trail junction, at the 42-mile point of the loop. The trail then descends out of the Bubbs Creek valley to complete the 46-mile loop at Roads End.

## 58 | WOOD CHUCK LAKE

**Round trip: 18 miles**
**Hiking time:** 2–3 days
**High point:** 9,812 feet
**Elevation gain:** 3,380 feet
**Difficulty:** Potentially difficult
**Hikable:** Mid-July through September

**Driving directions:** Drive Highway 168 northeast from Fresno to the center of Shaver Lake, then turn right on Dinkey Creek Road and head east. After 12.1 miles, turn right on McKinley Grove Road, following signs to Wishon Reservoir for the next 18 miles. At the reservoir, go across the spillway and then continue on 0.2 mile to the Woodchuck Trailhead (6,660 feet).
**Maps:** USFS John Muir Wilderness (Central Section); USGS Rough Spur and Courtright Reservoir
**Permits:** Prather Ranger Station and Dinkey Creek Ranger Station (Case 5)

Located in the midst of rolling ridges, small meadows, and a shady forest, Wood Chuck Lake is the largest of the picturesque lakes in scenic Woodchuck Basin. Although lacking in the broad vistas and moonlike landscapes of the High Sierra, the lake and basin area is ideal for hikers throughout the entire summer.

**THE HIKE.** The hike begins with a brisk climb up the rocky hillside. At 0.5 mile the trail intersects a dirt road. Cross the road and rejoin the trail a few feet to the right, then head north in a long, rolling traverse above the reservoir. At 2.5 miles the trail turns east, enters the wilderness, and then descends for 0.5 mile to Woodchuck Creek (7,300 feet) and a couple of campsites. The trail crosses the creek and then follows it up the forested hillside to Woodchuck Basin, passing several campsites.

At 6.5 miles the trail divides. The right fork follows Woodchuck Creek to Chuck Pass, creating all sorts of loop possibilities. However, for now, go left on the Crown Pass Trail. The climb is steady, through alternating bands of forest, rocky ribs, and grassy meadows. At 7.2 miles (8,840 feet), leave the Crown Pass Trail and go left, toward Wood Chuck Lake. The trail descends

*Wood Chuck Lake*

to cross a creek and passes several small campsites before it begins a steady climb through thinning forest to reach Wood Chuck Lake (9,812 feet) at 9 miles. The lake is pleasantly nestled among granite boulders and rolling granite domes with just enough trees to provide shade on a hot day. Campsites are located on the west shore.

For your return trip, you have three routes to choose from. You may return the way you came; you may continue around the east shore of Wood Chuck Lake and follow

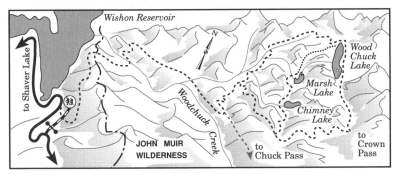

the trail until it rejoins the Crown Pass Trail 3 miles above the point where you originally left it; or you may try a cross-country route.

The cross-country route begins from the camp area at the northwest end of Wood Chuck Lake. Look down through the trees and spot a large meadow with two small ponds to the southwest. Descend to the meadow and then follow the outlet stream from the ponds down to Marsh Lake (9,330 feet). Walk to the west side of Marsh Lake to find a well-used trail and follow it over a small rise to Chimney Lake. Continue on this trail until you intersect the Crown Pass Trail, 2 miles below Wood Chuck Lake. Go right and descend 1.5 miles to close the loop at the Wood Chuck Lake intersection.

## 59 | DISAPPOINTMENT LAKE

**Round trip: 27 miles**
**Hiking time:** 3–4 days
**High point:** 10,420 feet
**Elevation gain:** 3,020 feet
**Difficulty:** Potentially difficult
**Hikable:** Mid-July through September

**Driving directions:** From Fresno, drive northeast on Highway 168 to the town of Shaver Lake. At the center of town, go right on Dinkey Creek Road for 12.1 miles. At Dinkey Creek the road divides. Go right on McKinley Grove Road for 14.2 miles then turn left, following signs to Courtright Reservoir for another 7.7 miles. At the reservoir, head to the right and cross the dam to reach the road's end, at the Maxson–Dusy Trailhead, in 1.3 miles (35.3 miles from Shaver Lake). The trailhead has rest rooms but no running water (8,150 feet).
**Maps:** USFS John Muir Wilderness (Central Section); USGS Courtright Reservoir, Ward Mtn., and Mt. Henry
**Reservations:** Prather Ranger Station and Dinkey Creek Ranger Station (Case 5)

From its beginning among the granite domes of the exotic Courtright Reservoir to its objective, Disappointment Lake, set in the green meadows at the edge of the rocky world of the High Sierra, this is a remarkably scenic hike.

**THE HIKE.** The jeep road, hikers' trail, and horse trail start from three different locations around the parking area and come together at the base of the first hill. Follow the jeep road up the nearly level valley for 1 mile. At Maxson Meadow, the road and trail part company. The intersection is marked with a small sign reading "Trail."

Head to your right, crossing Maxson Meadow and then climbing the

*Eight-hour nighttime exposure of campsite at Disappointment Lake*

forested hillside to the crest of an 8,900-foot ridge and an intersection with the Hobler Lake Trail at 3.7 miles. Stay right and descend to Long Meadow and the first campsites with water on this hike.

At the lower end of Long Meadow, cross a creek (expect damp feet) and then continue down-valley on a horse-churned trail. At 7 miles,

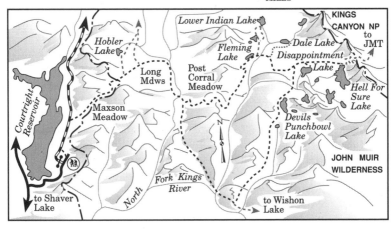

ford Post Corral Creek to find campsites, mosquitoes, and an intersection at the edge of Post Corral Meadow (8,220 feet). Go left on a trail signed to Red Mountain Basin and begin your climb to the High Sierra on a dusty horse trail.

At 9 miles, cross a granite ridge and then follow a narrow, forested bench into the Fleming Creek drainage. The climb resumes again near the 10-mile mark. At 11.3 miles the trail passes subalpine Fleming Lake (9,724 feet) and several enticing campsites.

Cross the Fleming Lake outlet and head through meadows for 0.2 mile, to the Rae Lakes intersection. To the left are sheltered base camps for extended stays in this area. From the Rae Lakes intersection, go right and cross Fleming Creek. The trail then heads steeply uphill, passing a spur trail to Dale Lake. Shortly after, cross a 10,240-foot saddle and enter Red Meadows Basin.

Follow the trail across a granite-dotted meadow fringed by the barren summits of the Le Conte Divide to the east and an unnamed line of summits stemming from 11,998-foot Mount Hutton to the south. At 13 miles, the trail crosses a small creek and arrives at an intersection. Stay left, following signs to Hell For Sure Pass. The trail is nearly invisible as it crosses granite slabs for 0.5 mile to a sandy, unmarked intersection on the bench above. Go right to Disappointment Lake, which has excellent campsites (10,360 feet).

Check your map for other lakes to explore in the basin and do not miss the view from Hell For Sure Pass. On your return trip, consider doing a loop by heading to Devils Punchbowl Lake and then descending 5 miles to the North Fork Kings River. Head north for 4 miles to close the loop at Post Corral Meadows.

# 60 | DINKEY LAKES

**Loop trip to Island Lake: 9 miles**
**Hiking time:** 5 hours
**High point:** 9,810 feet
**Elevation gain:** 1,250 feet
**Difficulty:** Potentially easy
**Hikable:** July through mid-October

**Driving directions:** From Fresno, drive Highway 168 northeast through Clovis to the town of Shaver Lake. Continue to the center of town, where you will take a right on Dinkey Creek Road. After 9.1 miles, turn left on rough, semipaved Rock Creek Road and continue for 6 miles. At a signed T intersection, go right for an even rougher 4.7 miles to the crest of a wooded ridge. Turn right again on an extremely rough, steep, and narrow spur road for 2 more miles. Where the road divides, stay left for a

final rocky descent to a surprisingly busy parking area (8,560 feet).
**Maps:** USFS Dinkey Lakes Wilderness; USGS Dogtooth Peak
**Permits:** Prather Ranger Station (Case 5)

In comparison with the hundreds of other lakes in the Sierra, the Dinkey Lakes are nothing out of the ordinary. The lakes are subalpine with trees on at least one side and spectacular walls of granite on the other. The meadows around the lakes are grassy, festooned with Labrador tea and a profusion of flowers such as colorful paintbrush, monkeyflower, primrose, penstemon, and shooting star.

What makes this area so unusual is the short and easy access to the lakes and views. It is a great area for a day hike, an ideal place to take beginners backpacking, and a wonderful trail for families.

**THE HIKE.** The trail begins with a short, steep drop to Dinkey Creek. Cross the creek and then follow it up-valley in the cool shade of the forest. At 0.5 mile you will recross the creek and enter the wilderness. The climb remains gradual but steady to the first of many intersections, at 1.3 miles, and the beginning of the loop portion of this hike.

For now, stay left on the well-graded trail to First Dinkey Lake. At 2.9 miles pass a marshy lake, and shortly after you will arrive at a junction. Stay right and walk along the shore of First Dinkey Lake, passing several signed and unsigned junctions on your way to Second Dinkey Lake.

Second Dinkey Lake and the Island Lake intersection are reached at 3.1 miles. Go right, along the shore of Second Dinkey, and then head steeply up over a band of rocks. Once on top of the rocks, the ascent is gradual for the remainder of the way to Island Lake (9,810 feet), reached at 3.6 miles.

Tucked into the base of the Three Sisters, Island Lake is the rockiest and wildest lake in the wilderness. Camping is excellent.

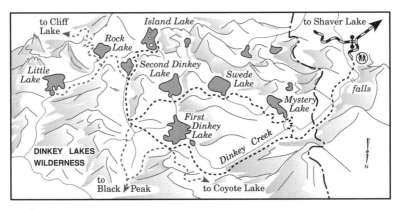

*Dogtooth Peak near Rock Lake*

On your return, descend from Second Dinkey Lake to find an intersection at 9,325 feet, just before the trail enters the meadows that surround the First Dinkey Lake. Go left on a well-trampled path through the forest for 0.5 mile to South Lake. After enjoying the serenity of this area, head west across the outlet creek and then over a forest ridge. The trail then descends steeply to Swede Lake, another place to linger, although the fishing is reported to be bad.

From Swede Lake, the trail drops over the hill to reach Mystery Lake 1.2 miles from South Lake. Walk along the northeast side of the lake to its outlet and then descend again to close the loop at the Dinkey Lake Trail, 1.9 miles from South Lake. Go left and head back to the trailhead.

# 61 | KAISER LOOP TRAIL

**Loop trip: 15 miles**
**Hiking time:** 9 hours
**High point:** 10,310 feet
**Elevation gain:** 3,110 feet
**Difficulty:** Potentially difficult
**Hikable:** Late June through mid-October

**Driving directions:** From Fresno, drive northeast on Highway 168 for 71 miles to its end, at Huntington Lake. Go left on Huntington Lake Road for 1 mile to Kinnikinnick Campground, then turn right on Upper Deer Creek

Road, following signs to the stables for 0.6 mile. Just before you reach the pack station, find the hikers' parking, on the left (7,200 feet).
**Maps:** USFS Kaiser Wilderness; USGS Kaiser Peak and Huntington Lake
**Permits:** Pine Ridge Ranger Station at Prather (Case 5)

The Kaiser Loop is a strenuous trail that combines a climb to an outstanding panoramic view of the High Sierra with a tour through the forest and meadows of the lower portions of the Kaiser Wilderness.

Backpackers may find it difficult to obtain permits as the Deer Creek Trailhead (where the loop begins) has a daily quota of six people. However, Billy Creek Trailhead is a good second choice and adds only 1.8 miles to the total loop.

**THE HIKE.** From the parking area, walk up the road to the trailhead, at the upper end of the pack station. Head uphill 100 yards to intersect the Kaiser Loop Trail. You will return to this point by the trail to your left. For now, go straight.

Near the 0.6-mile point, pass an unmarked intersection with the Potter Pass Trail. Continue straight, and shortly afterward the steep climb will give way to well-graded switchbacks. At 1.9 miles a rocky outcropping offers your first view of Huntington Lake. The trail levels off in a small basin at 3.5 miles but soon resumes climbing with a final steep push to the open crest of the ridge. Walk past a carpet of miniature alpine flowers to a saddle overlooking George Lake and then follow the ridge to an intersection at 5.3 miles, just a few feet below the summit of 10,310-foot Kaiser

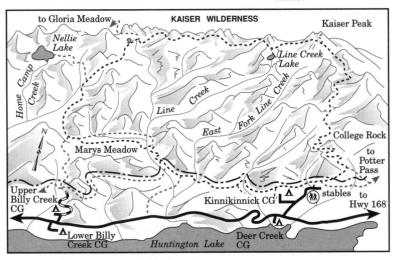

Peak. Go left to the high point for a view of the High Sierra and the great reservoirs: Shaver, Huntington, Mammoth Pool, and Thomas A. Edison.

From Kaiser Peak the loop trail heads west, descending for 0.5 mile to Line Creek Lake. When the weather is good, this is a great campsite. Continue west along the ridge and then switchback down to a small meadow and an unsigned intersection. Stay left, and continue your descent to a small creek and signed junction with the Gloria Meadow–Hidden Lake Trail at 8.8 miles (8,800 feet). Go straight, cross the creek, and then head down the forested valley, passing the Nellie Lake intersection at 9.6 miles.

At 11.3 miles (8,140 feet), leave the Kaiser Loop Trail temporarily and go left on Marys Meadow Trail. Descend the forested hillside for 0.3 mile to Marys Meadow, where the trail disappears. Walk around the left side of the meadow, crossing first a marshy creek and then a seasonal creek, to the northeast end, where you will find a trail on the left that heads into the forest and divides. Take the right fork and continue down-valley, paralleling a small creek.

At 12.2 miles (7,850 feet) the trail crosses Line Creek and then descends, often steeply, for 0.7 mile until it intersects the Kaiser Loop at 12.9 miles (7,540 feet). Go left for a final 2.1 miles of forest walking. Several signed and unsigned spur trails branch off to the right; ignore them. At Bear Creek the trail intersects an old road. Go right 10 feet and then go left, back onto the trail. The loop ends at 15 miles.

*View from summit of Kaiser Peak*

# 62 | GEORGE LAKE

**Round trip: 9.6 miles**
**Hiking time:** 5 hours
**High point:** 9,100 feet
**Elevation gain:** 1,460 feet in; 480 feet out
**Difficulty:** Potentially moderate
**Hikable:** Mid-June through October

**Driving directions:** From Fresno, drive northeast on Highway 168, passing through Clovis, Prather (where backcountry permits are picked up), and then Shaver Lake before reaching Huntington Lake at 71 miles. Where Highway 168 ends, go right and head up Kaiser Pass Road for 4.8 miles. The trailhead is a large turnout on the right (south) side of the road marked by a sign that reads "Riding and Hiking Trail 24E03." A small pit toilet is the only facility (8,120 feet).
**Maps:** USFS Kaiser Wilderness; USGS Kaiser Peak and Mt. Givens
**Permits:** Pine Ridge Ranger Station at Prather (Case 5)

Granite-speckled lakes and a grand vista make this low-mileage trek a great day hike or an easy backpack, perfect for families and beginners. Of course, this ideal hiking area is very busy on weekends, so backpackers should reserve their permits as early as possible.

**THE HIKE.** Cross Kaiser Pass Road to find the trail on the north side and begin your hike with a climb through mixed coniferous forest. Around 1 mile you will cross a creek and walk past the first of many meadows.

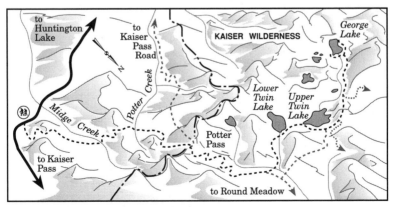

*Granite boulders near Upper Twin Lake*

Wildflowers attempt to grow here in early summer; later, the cows trim the meadows to a uniform size and color.

The trail crosses a saddle, where a couple of old roads and some large stumps indicate logging activity in the not-too-distant past. Continue on with a nearly level traverse into the Potter Creek drainage. Watch for views to the west, which extend all the way to the San Joaquin Mountains.

The ascent resumes, and at 2 miles you will arrive at 8,990-foot Potter Pass. Walk by the signed intersection with the Potter Creek Trail and then enter the Kaiser Wilderness. An unsigned trail to Idaho Lake branches off to the right near the wilderness sign. To the northeast, 13,157-foot Mount Ritter and the Minarets stand proud on the horizon.

From the pass, the trail heads steeply down a dusty hillside. Descend 480 feet through forest and meadows in the next 0.7 mile to an intersection. Go left here, heading to Twin Lakes.

The shallow Lower Twin Lake, with its headwall of tumbled granite, is reached at 3.3 miles. Continue on another 0.3 mile to Upper Twin Lake (8,601 feet). Campsites are numerous and excellent on the rocky shelves above the upper lake, larger than those found ahead at George Lake.

The George Lake Trail follows the east shore of Upper Twin Lake to an unmarked intersection at the upper end. Go left and climb steeply to a flower-covered ridge crest, where you will pass an unmarked trail to Walking Lake. Continue straight to reach the shores of George Lake (9,100 feet) at 4.8 miles. Pick a glacier-polished granite slab for a picnic lunch or search around the rocky shores for one of the two good campsites.

# 63 | BLAYNEY MEADOWS HOT SPRINGS

**Round trip: 18 miles**
**Hiking time:** 2–3 days
**High point:** 7,790 feet
**Elevation gain:** 780 feet
**Difficulty:** Potentially moderate
**Hikable:** Mid-August through mid-October

**Driving directions:** From Fresno, drive northeast on Highway 168 for 71 miles to Huntington Lake Reservoir. Where the highway ends, go right on Kaiser Pass Road. At 16.2 miles from Huntington Lake, pass the High Sierra Ranger Station, and at 17.2 miles the road divides. Stay right and head to Florence Lake for another 6.1 miles, to the hikers' parking area (7,360 feet).
**Maps:** USFS John Muir Wilderness (North Section); USGS Florence Lake and Ward Mountain
**Permits:** Pine Ridge Ranger Station and High Sierra Station (Case 5)

Because of a dangerous ford of the South Fork San Joaquin River, the extremely popular Blayney Meadows Hot Springs is a late-summer destination. However, if you skip the hot springs and simply enjoy a hike in the scenic South Fork River valley to excellent fishing, wide meadows, and shady riverside campsites, then this trail is ideal from the time the snow melts in June until it falls again in October.

The hot springs hike is long but not strenuous. In midsummer, this 18-mile trip can be shortened to 8 miles by taking advantage of the

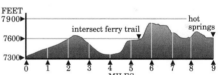

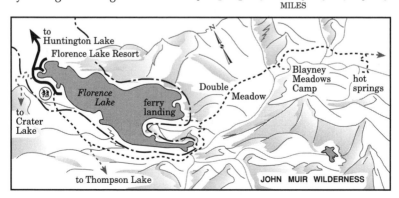

*Fishing the South Fork San Joaquin River at the head of Florence Lake*

hikers' ferry up Florence Lake.

**THE HIKE.** Hikers making use of the ferry service should take the road at the lower left side of the parking area. If hiking the entire distance, go right and descend through the picnic area, then walk the paved road past a gate and the Crater Lake Trail to reach the Florence Lake Trail at 0.2 mile. Go right and climb to a bench, where the trail traverses the west side of the lake with views of the dam, Ward Mountain, Mount Shinn, Mount Darwin, and Mount Mendel.

Climb a granite ridge where an unmarked trail branches right to Thompson Lake and Hot Springs Pass, then descend to the upper end of the lake, where the trail divides. Stay left for a bridged crossing of Boulder Creek, which is followed by a bridged crossing of the South Fork of the San Joaquin River. Pleasant campsites are located on either side of the river.

Once across the river, climb a sparsely forested hillside to intersect the trail from the ferry at 5.5 miles. Shortly beyond you will cross a 4x4 road (one of those strange wilderness anomalies). The trail and 4x4 road are intertwined for the remainder of the hike. The climb ends at 7,790 feet and the trail levels off, passes Double Meadow, and then descends.

At 7.6 miles, pass a signed trail on the right to Blayney Meadows camp area, a delightful site along the edge of the river. Continuing up the nearly level valley, pass Lower Blayney Meadow and then enter the private land holding of the Muir Trail Ranch (the Double D). Once through the stock gate, hikers are requested to stay on the trail and hike without stopping, picnicking, camping, or otherwise lingering for the next 1.2 miles.

At 8.3 miles the trail divides. Go left and in a few feet exit the private land by a second gate. Just 150 feet beyond is an intersection. Go right for

10 feet, then left, and descend to the campsites along the river.

Cautiously ford the river, walking with a stick for balance and shoes for traction on some of the most slippery and rounded boulders found anywhere. Once across, walk through a couple of campsites then head to the right, following a boot-beaten path. Use the fence line to guide you across a damp meadow. You will pass two small pools before reaching the deep hot springs pool. The path continues another 100 feet to end at a small, clear lake at the base of Ward Mountain.

# 64 | DEVILS BATHTUB

**Round trip: 10 miles**
**Hiking time:** 6 hours
**High point:** 9,167 feet
**Elevation gain:** 1,327 feet
**Difficulty:** Potentially moderate
**Hikable:** July through mid-October

**Driving directions:** Drive Highway 168 northeast from Fresno for 71 miles to Huntington Lake. Where the road ends at a T intersection, go right on the Kaiser Pass Road. The first 5.9 miles are easy driving, then the road narrows to a paved, single lane that twists and winds over Kaiser Pass and passes the High Sierra Station (where backpackers can pick up their wilderness permits) to reach an intersection at 17.2 miles from Huntington Lake. Go left, toward Lake Thomas A. Edison. At 6 miles the road divides at the base of the dam. Go left and after 0.5 mile go left again, following signs to the High Sierra Pack Station. Pass the Vermillion Valley Resort to reach the campground entrance in 1.8 miles. Go left again and then stay right at all the remaining intersections for the final 0.3 mile to the large trailhead. Pit toilets, picnic tables, and fire pits are available (7,840 feet).
**Maps:** USFS John Muir Wilderness (North Section); USGS Sharktooth Peak and Graveyard Peak
**Permits:** Pine Ridge Ranger Station and High Sierra Station (Case 5)

If the devil really did pick this lake for a bathtub, he obviously prefers scenery to such amenities as hot water and smooth porcelain. The bathtub picked out by the Devil has a necklace of granite boulders along a narrow band of trees, with the imposing wall of the Silver Divide and Graveyard Peak dominating the horizon.

**THE HIKE.** With two trails beginning from the same trailhead, there can be a bit of confusion. The Devils Bathtub Trail is located at the upper left side of the sign and follows the route of an old road. After a nearly level 0.3 mile,

*Devils Bathtub with Graveyard Peak in background*

the trail crosses an unmarked horse packers' trail. Go right for 20 feet and then go left, back on the trail.

Due to heavy use by feet, horses, and cattle, the trail bed has been beaten to a fine powder. Battle your way through the dust, climbing gradually up the forested hillside. At 1.1 miles, the trail levels off on a broad bench and then fords Cold Creek (7,980 feet). Find a convenient log to cross the creek, and then follow the trail as it wanders through the forest before passing the lower end of a large meadow. Stock herders have built a small dam here, providing a constant flow of water.

Climb to a platform at 2 miles, where you leave the old road for good and continue straight ahead on trail. Shortly after, the trail levels

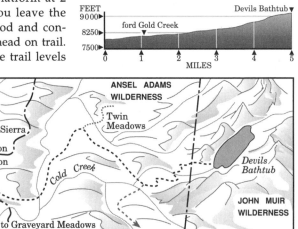

off on a bench covered with lodgepole pines. At 3.2 miles (8,340 feet), reach an intersection with a trail to Graveyard Meadows. Go left and continue across the forested bench.

At 4 miles the trail begins to climb again. The soft soil makes this last mile slow going as you head steeply upward. At 4.8 miles begin paralleling the Devils Bathtub outlet creek. Campsites are located here and around the lakeshore, which is reached at 5 miles (9,167 feet).

# 65 | SILVER DIVIDE LOOP

**Loop trip: 27.2 miles**
**Hiking time:** 3–4 days
**High point:** 10,970 feet
**Elevation gain:** 4,527 feet
**Difficulty:** Potentially difficult
**Hikable:** August through September

**Driving directions:** Drive Highway 168 northeast from Fresno for 71 miles to Huntington Lake. Where the road ends at a T intersection, go right on the Kaiser Pass Road. The first 5.9 miles are easy driving, then the road narrows to a paved single lane that twists and winds over Kaiser Pass. It passes the High Sierra Station (where backpackers can pick up their wilderness permits) to reach an intersection at 17.2 miles from Huntington Lake. Go left, toward Lake Thomas A. Edison. At 6 miles the road divides at the base of the dam. Go left, and after 0.5 mile go left again, following signs to the High Sierra Pack Station. Pass the Vermillion Valley Resort to reach the campground entrance in 1.8 miles. Go left again and then stay right at all the remaining intersections for the final 0.3 mile to the large trailhead. Pit toilets, picnic tables, and fire pits are available (7,840 feet).
**Maps:** USFS John Muir Wilderness (North Section); USGS Sharktooth Peak and Graveyard Peak
**Permits:** Pine Ridge Ranger Station and High Sierra Station (Case 5)

Six beautiful lakes, two passes (both near 11,000 feet in elevation), and flower-covered meadows make this loop one of the best hikes in the area. Part of this loop follows the route of the combined John Muir Trail/Pacific Crest Trail (JMT/PCT), which is well maintained and easy to follow even in early season. However, the Goodale Pass Trail, the return leg of the loop, is designed for stock rather than human use and requires several difficult fords of Cold Creek, making late season the best time for the complete loop.

**THE HIKE.** This description assumes you are planning to walk the entire loop. However, if you choose to ride the hikers' ferry from Vermillion

Valley Resort to the upper end of Lake Thomas A. Edison, you can cut 5 miles off your trip total. The ferry departs daily at 9:00 A.M. and 4:00 P.M. from July 1 to the middle of September.

The official start of the loop is from the upper end of the parking lot (7,840 feet). Take the lower of the two trails and follow the signs for Graveyard Lakes and Quail Meadows. This dusty trail descends gradually along the north shore of the Lake Thomas A. Edison. At 0.3 mile, an unsigned trail from the pack station joins in from the left, and shortly after the trail divides. Stay left and cross Cold Creek on a horse bridge. The intersection at 0.8 mile marks the start of the loop. Stay right; you will return to this point by the trail on the left.

Before long the trail leaves the dense lodgepole forest and begins a roller-coaster traverse of the granite slabs that comprise the shore of Lake Thomas A. Edison. Views from the slabs are a delightful reward for hiking instead of taking the boat. Pass several tempting campsites overlooking the lake before you reach the upper end and the trail from the ferry landing at 5 miles.

The trail crosses a seasonal creek (a difficult ford during early summer runoff) and then climbs steadily for the next mile along boisterous Mono Creek to Quail Meadows (7,820 feet). The meadows are mostly forested, and campsites are numerous. At the upper end of the meadows, the Lake Edison Trail meets the JMT/PCT and ends. Continue straight ahead on the JMT/PCT, following signs to Silver Pass. The trail climbs steadily up the rapidly narrowing valley to reach the Mono Creek Trail intersection at 7.5 miles (8,380 feet). Continue straight on the JMT/PCT.

The climb steepens as the trail switchbacks up a granite headwall and then levels

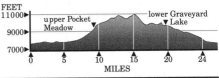

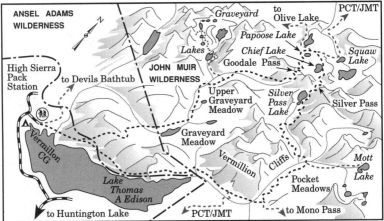

out to traverse Pocket Meadow, passing several inviting campsites and thousands of mosquitoes along the way. At 9 miles reach the upper end of the meadows, where the 1.8-mile spur trail to Mott Lake branches right.

The loop route continues straight, crossing the North Fork Creek and then climbing the steep cliff on the west side of the valley. At 9,530 feet you will arrive at the top of the cliffs and pass the first of several meadows along Silver Creek. The climb remains steady through this beautiful valley, gradually leaving the forest and heading into the open wonderland that is the High Sierra. Silver Pass Lake (10,380 feet), lying to the left of the trail in the shadow of the jagged crest of the Silver Divide, is passed at 12 miles. Several excellent campsites are located here.

From Silver Pass Lake, the trail crosses open meadows and then climbs to a false pass. Go right and continue up to the real 10,880-foot Silver Pass and view of Mount Ritter and the Minarets to the north.

From the pass, the trail descends over a semipermanent patch of snow and then passes rocky Warrior and Chief Lakes to reach an intersection at 14 miles (10,475 feet). At this point the loop route leaves the JMT/PCT and heads left, descending 0.3 mile to Papoose Lake. Small, rocky, and very scenic campsites may be found around all these lakes.

At Papoose Lake the trail crosses the outlet and then climbs to an intersection. The loop route goes straight, heading steeply up to Goodale Pass. After climbing the first pitch, the trail levels in an open gully. An unsigned spur trail branches right here, descending to Lake of the Lone Indian. Ahead on an open bench is a false summit where the trail bends left and then splinters, as stock and hikers take different routes around lingering snowfields.

Crest the 10,970-foot summit of Goodale Pass at 15.8 miles. At this point the trail crosses back to the south side of Silver Divide and begins a rocky, switchbacking descent into the Cold Creek valley. The trail stair steps past

*Upper Graveyard Lakes Basin*

several small meadows to reach Upper Graveyard Meadow and the Graveyard Lakes Trail intersection, at 18.7 miles (9,355 feet).

Although off the main loop, Graveyard Lakes are an essential part of this trip. So go right for 1 mile and trudge up the rough trail to lower Graveyard Lake (9,900 feet). Campsites are numerous around the shore of this large subalpine lake. View seekers will want to follow the trail on for another 0.3 mile to visit the two smaller lakes in the basin above. Cross-country hikers can continue on climbing northeast to a larger lake with an incredible view of the peaks of the Mono Divide to the southeast.

The loop route returns to the Goodale Pass Trail at 20.7 miles and then continues down the valley, descending gradually to Graveyard Meadows. Due to overuse, the trail does not enter the meadows; that privilege is left for the cows. Instead, the trail makes two difficult fords of Cold Creek. Numerous forested campsites may be found in this section.

At 23.5 miles, just before the second Cold Creek ford, an unsigned but well-defined trail branches off to the right to join the Devils Bathtub Trail. Stay left and follow the Cold Creek valley trail on down through a couple of pocket-size meadows to reach the Lake Edison Trail at 26.5 miles. Go right for the final 0.8-mile, slightly uphill, and trudge back to the parking lot to complete your hike, at 27.2 miles.

# 66 | POST PEAK LOOP

**Semiloop trip: 25.1 miles**
**Hiking time:** 3–4 days
**High point:** 10,800 feet
**Elevation gain:** 4,040 feet
**Difficulty:** Potentially difficult
**Hikable:** Mid-July through September

**Driving directions:** From the town of North Fork, drive north on Minarets Highway for 54 miles, following signs to Mammoth Pool and Clover Meadow. Where the pavement ends, go right on Forest Road 5S30 for 1.8 miles to Clover Meadow Station (7,001 feet). Continue on Forest Road 5S20 for 0.5 mile then go left for 2.4 miles, following signs to Isberg Trailhead (7,040 feet). If hiking the full loop, park at Clover Meadow Station and walk the road to the trailhead. Car shuttlers should park their second vehicle at Fernandez Trailhead.
**Maps:** USFS Ansel Adams Wilderness; USGS Timber Knob and Mt. Lyell
**Permits:** Bass Lake Ranger District in North Fork (Case 5)

With the soft green forest and the rugged High Sierra; from lakes, creeks, and meadows to sweeping visits; from main trails to spur trails to boot-beaten paths—this is an ideal area for an extended backpack trip. Although the recommended hike is a semiloop, a complete loop around Post Peak is possible. The full loop is 31.2 miles long and involves several miles of walking on forest roads. Most hikers prefer to do a car shuttle between trailheads and spend their extra time exploring the high country.

**THE HIKE.** The trail begins with a 1.5-mile climb to the Ansel Adams Wilderness boundary at The Niche (8,000 feet). Soon after entering the wilderness you will pass two junctions. Stay left at the first and right at the second, following the Cora Lakes signs.

At 3.2 miles the trail skirts forested Cora Lake (8,400 feet). (Camping is not allowed from the stream flow dam northward around the shoreline for 0.25 mile.) At 3.7 miles pass a trail to Chetwood Cabin on the right and 100 feet beyond pass a second, unmarked trail, also on the right.

Following signs to Sadler Lake, continue the generally gradual ascent. Campsites are nonexistent along the seasonal creeks. At 6.2 miles, a 1-mile side trail takes off left to pretty Joe Crane Lake. At 7.8 miles reach the turnoff to Sadler and McClure Lakes. The very popular Sadler Lake (9,345 feet) is located 100 feet west of the junction. Camping is prohibited from the junction of the Isberg and McClure Trails northward around the shoreline for 0.25 mile to preserve the scenic lake. Dazzling McClure Lake is located 0.7 mile beyond.

Continuing, reach the high alpine country at Lower Isberg Lake (9,920 foot) and campsites at 9 miles. From Isberg Lakes, the trail climbs 2.4 miles to the crest of 10,560-foot Isberg Pass and outstanding views. From the pass, you must descend to

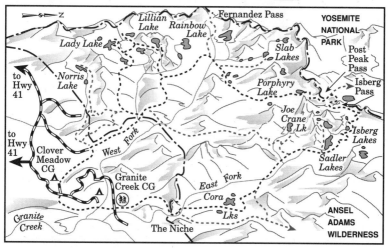

*Rocks near Porphyry Lake*

the Post Peak Pass Trail and then climb back up to reach 10,800-foot Post Creek Pass at 13.2 miles. (If the trail is blocked by snow, stay right and ascend the rocky hillside to the ridge crest above the pass.)

From the pass, descend to Porphyry Lake, which has only limited camping among the fascinating boulders. Good campsites can be found 2 miles below, at the Post Creek crossing. If the creek is dry, you must continue on another mile, to two small tarns. Water and campsites can be found at Fernandez Creek (8,640 feet) at 18.5 miles. Continuing down, pass junctions to Fernandez Pass, Rainbow Lake (no camping allowed within 0.25 mile of the lakeshore), and then Lillian Lake. At the Lillian Lake junction you can choose between two routes. If time allows, go right to Lillian, Stanford, Chittenden, Lady, and Vandeburg Lakes. If you are in a hurry, take the left fork and continue your forested descent. At the Walton Trail junction go left and, after 0.3 mile, ford Fernandez Creek. The trail traverses the forested hillside to the Fernandez Trailhead. If hiking the full loop, follow the horse trail through the forest to Clover Meadow Campground.

# 67 | CHAIN LAKES

**Round trip: 13.8 miles**
**Hiking time:** 8 hours
**High point:** 9,300 feet
**Elevation gain:** 2,100 feet
**Difficulty:** Potentially moderate
**Hikable:** July through mid-October

**Driving directions:** Drive Highway 41 north from Fresno or south from Yosemite to the northeast side of Oakhurst. Turn east on Bass Lake Road No. 222 and follow it for 6 miles, then go left on Beasure Road No. 7. Stay on this road for the next 20.7 miles, following signs to Beasure Meadows and then to Clover Meadow and Granite Creek. The pavement ends at mile 20.3; continue on for another 0.4 mile to Globe Rock

and take a left turn on Road 5S04. At 2.4 miles you will reach the
Chiquito Lake Trailhead (7,200 feet).
**Maps:** USFS Ansel Adams Wilderness; USGS Sing Peak
**Permits:** Minarets Ranger Station in North Fork (Case 5)

The remote southwest corner of Yosemite National Park is the location of
the three superb subalpine lakes that compose the Chain Lakes group. Although quite isolated, these lakes are not the place to look for solitude; they
are much too pretty.

**THE HIKE.** The initial 0.2 mile of this trail follows a jeep road. Where the
road ends, the trail climbs steeply over a rocky outcropping and then levels off in a forested valley. At 2 miles you will arrive at the swampy shores
of Chiquito Lake (7,960 feet). Campsites are located at the south end of the
lake; mosquitoes can be found everywhere.

Head around the west side of the lake, passing the first of several unsigned trails on the left to the Quartz Mountain Trailhead, then make a short
climb to 8,039-foot Chiquito Pass at 2.5 miles. Ignoring the spur trails on the
left, cross the pass and enter Yosemite National Park. Walk through an old
cattle fence and then take an immediate right on the Chain Lakes Trail.

The trail remains nearly level as it traverses through forest and across
small meadows. At 3 miles you will cross the outlet creek from Spotted
Lake and then begin a gradual climb along an old moraine. The trail traverses
a meadow at the top of the moraine and then descends, gradually, to cross
the Chain Lakes outlet creek at 6 miles (8,575 feet).

On the north side of the
creek the trail divides. Go left
and climb steadily for the next
0.5 mile to reach the lower
Chain Lake (8,845 feet) at 6.5

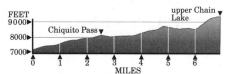

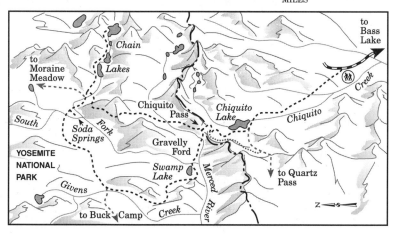

*Middle Chain Lake below Gale Peak*

miles. Located in a delightful granite saucer, this lake has several protected campsites. To reach the upper lakes, follow the trail along the north side of the lower lake and then climb the rocky hillside to the island-studded middle lake (9,050 feet). The trail continues, climbing past several marshy tarns and crossing the outlet creek before entering the granite bowl at the base of Gale Peak that holds the rugged upper lake (9,300 feet).

# 68 | BUENA VISTA LAKES LOOP

**Loop trip: 28.1 miles**
**Hiking time:** 4 days
**High point:** 9,315 feet
**Elevation gain:** 2,400 feet
**Difficulty:** Potentially difficult
**Hikable:** July through mid-October

**Driving directions:** Drive Highway 41 north from Oakhurst for 33 miles, then go right on Glacier Point Road for 9.4 miles to the Ostrander Lake Trailhead (7,000 feet).
**Maps:** Wilderness Press Yosemite; USGS Half Dome and Mariposa Grove
**Permits:** Wawona and Yosemite Valley Wilderness Offices (Case 6)

This rambling forest walk explores six of the lesser-known lakes along the southern border of Yosemite National Park. While there are a few magnificent vistas, and two of the lakes are subalpine gems, it is the flowers that cover the meadows and forest floor that make this an outstanding hike.

Water is the chief problem on this loop. In early season, the streams flood and are miserable to ford. By mid-September, these same creeks dry up and the lakes are the only reliable sources of water.

**THE HIKE.** Follow the nearly level Ostrander Lake Trail through fire-damaged forest and meadows for 1.5 miles to an intersection. Go right, toward Bridalveil Campground, for 0.2 mile. After fording Bridalveil Creek (not difficult), reach a second intersection and go left, toward Buck Camp and Wawona, for the next 0.8 mile. After fording another small creek at 2.5 miles, arrive at a third intersection. Stay right and head through meadows of waist-high lupine, columbine, mountain bluebells, sneezewort, and corn lilies (to name a few).

At 3.5 miles, ford (easily) two small creeks and pass a small campsite. Soon after you will climb to the crest of a dry ridge (7,640 feet) and then descend back to verdant forest. The Deer Camp Trail branches off to the right at 4.9 miles. Continue straight, descending to good campsites at Turner Meadow (no water in late summer).

The descent eases at 6.2 miles after a lateral trail to Wawona is passed. At 7 miles you will reach the Chilnualna Lakes Trail intersection (7,300 feet), which is the start of the loop portion of this hike. Go straight and ford rocky Chilnualna Creek (a hazardous crossing in early season), then head up a forested ridge to a second Wawona junction, at 7.7 miles (7,590 feet). Go left and climb through forest wildflower gardens. After 2 miles, pass little Grouse Lake and several campsites, to the right. At 10.7 miles the trail passes another campsite, at marshy Crescent Lake (8,380 feet).

Prepare to battle mosquitoes as you walk the next mile to campsites at Johnson Lake. From there it is just 0.5 mile to the Buck Camp Trail intersection. Stay left for a 0.7-mile climb to Royal Arch Lake (8,700 feet) and more campsites. The name comes from the distinctive wall arch on

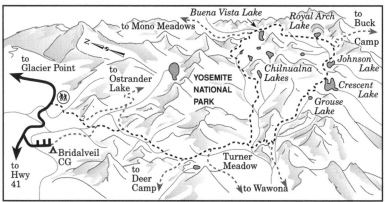

*Royal Arch Lake*

the granite hillside above the lake.

From Royal Arch Lake, climb over granite slabs and then through park-like forest to 9,315-foot Buena Vista crest. The trail then descends to scenic Buena Vista Lake (9,090 feet) at 15.5 miles. Campsites can be found along the north shore and on the granite shelves above the south side of the lake.

Beyond Buena Vista Lake, descend 0.5 mile to the Buena Vista Trail junction and then go left, down the Chilnualna Creek valley. The trail is steep and rocky as it descends past Upper Chilnualna Lake and several campsites at 16.7 miles. A mile beyond you will pass the shallow lower lake. From this point the descent is gradual, through brightly colored meadows, to the intersection with the Bridalveil Campground Trail, where the loop portion of the hike ends at 21.1 miles. Go right and retrace your steps for the final 7 miles back to the Ostrander Trailhead.

# 69 | OSTRANDER LAKE

**Round trip: 12.4 miles**
**Hiking time:** 7 hours
**High point:** 8,600 feet
**Elevation gain:** 1,560 feet
**Difficulty:** Potentially moderate
**Hikable:** Mid-July through September

**Driving directions:** Drive Highway 41 north from Oakhurst for 33 miles, then turn right on Glacier Point Road and continue for 9.4 miles. Park at the small, dirt-surfaced Ostrander Lake Trailhead (7,040 feet).
**Maps:** Wilderness Press Yosemite; USGS Half Dome and Mariposa Grove

**Permits:** Wawona and Yosemite Valley Wilderness Offices (Case 6)

The powerful beauty and peaceful setting attract year-round visitors to Ostrander Lake. This granite-rimmed, tree-fringed lake is an ideal weekend family outing or long day trip for the hardy hiker.

**THE HIKE.** The trail begins with a level ramble through fire-scarred forest and grassy meadows. After 0.7 mile of easy going, the trail gradually begins to climb. At 1.5 miles the trail divides; stay left. You will come to a second junction at 2.3 miles. Once again, stay to the left.

Shortly after the second junction, the trail begins ascending Horizon Ridge on an old roadbed. Head southeast, following the old road first through forest and then up the dry, rocky ridge to an 8,641-foot high point with a stunning view of Half Dome, Liberty Cap, and Star King.

At 6.2 miles the trail reaches Ostrander Lake (8,580 feet). To the right is the large stone ski hut, which is usually locked during the summer. Campsites are located along the north, east, and west sides of the lake.

*Ostrander Lake*

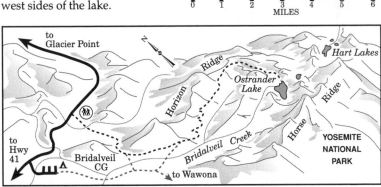

# 70 | YOSEMITE POINT

**Round trip: 8.4 miles**
**Hiking time:** 6 hours
**High point:** 6,935 feet
**Elevation gain:** 3,040 feet
**Difficulty:** Potentially difficult
**Hikable:** Mid-June through October

**Driving directions:** Parking is a problem in the valley. If you arrive early in the day you can drive to the trailhead at Yosemite Falls and park across the street at the lodge. By 8:00 A.M., leave your car in any available parking area and ride the shuttle to the falls (3,990 feet).
**Maps:** Wilderness Press Yosemite; USGS Half Dome and Yosemite Falls
**Permits:** Yosemite Valley Wilderness Office (Case 6)

One of the most popular activities for Yosemite National Park visitors is to stand in the valley with necks arched back and look up at the Lower Yosemite Falls. Bending their necks a little more, they can see Upper Yosemite Falls free-falling down massive granite walls in delicate plumes. With a final stretch of the neck muscles, they can see all the way to the top of the falls, where the glowing granite meets the blue sky.

The strenuous hike to Yosemite Point offers you a chance to reverse this activity and look down from the top of the granite walls to the green valley below. Start early in the day to avoid the heat, and carry plenty of water.

**THE HIKE.** Begin your walk with a short side trip to the base of Yosemite Falls, then head back to the parking area and go west on a trail that parallels the highway for 0.3 mile to Sunnyside Walk-in Campground. Go right and head up the first of hundreds of switchbacks. Much of the trail is paved with slick stone cobbles that, in turn, are covered with an even slicker dusting of sand. Watch your step.

Pass the first viewpoint, Columbia Rock (5,031 feet), at 1.2 miles. Soon afterward the trail levels and then, appallingly, descends for 0.2 mile. Pass below a near-vertical cliff and then resume the climb at 1.7 miles, near the base of Upper Yosemite Falls. In early season, a cooling mist from the falls can blow across the trail as the water tumbles freely for 1,430 feet to crash on the rocks near your feet.

The climb continues—and so do the switchbacks—until you reach an intersection at 3.4 miles. Go right, toward Yosemite Point. In 100 feet pass some excellent campsites to the left of the trail. Continue on another 150 feet to a second intersection. One hundred yards to the right is an unprotected viewpoint over the Upper Falls and the valley.

Continuing on, your trail heads east over a small rise and then drops to

## Yosemite Point Trail

cross Yosemite Creek. Ascend again to reach a junction with the North Dome Trail at 4.2 miles, then continue straight for a final 100 yards to Yosemite Point (6,936 feet). Walk to the railing and gasp at the view. Half Dome and North Dome dominate the eastern horizon. To the south are Glacier Point and Sentinel Rock. The top of Lost Arrow and the granite walls of the Three Brothers are visible to the west. For the ultimate thrill, look down and watch the cars and people scurrying around in the valley below your toes.

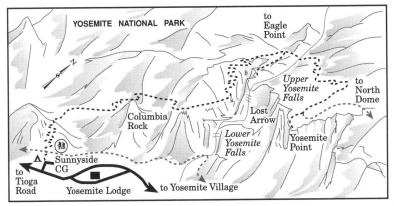

# 71 | HALF DOME

**Round trip: 16.4 miles**
**Hiking time:** 9 hours
**High point:** 8,842 feet
**Elevation gain:** 4,870 feet
**Difficulty:** Potentially difficult
**Hikable:** July through September

**Driving directions:** Drive into Yosemite Valley and park at the large lot at Curry Village (3,970 feet).
**Maps:** Wilderness Press Yosemite; USGS Yosemite Falls and Half Dome
**Permits:** Yosemite Valley Wilderness Office (Case 6)

Some people hike to the summit for the view. Others go to the top just to say they did it. No matter what your reason, it is important to understand that the climb to the top is not for everyone. The final ascent of the dome requires strong arms to pull yourself up a set of near-vertical cables. The exposure is extreme. If you are not comfortable with extreme exposure, do not go.

**THE HIKE.** If you are getting an early start, you must walk up-valley 0.8 mile to Happy Isles. By 7:30 A.M. you can catch a free ride on the shuttle bus. From the Happy Isles bus stop, walk up-valley on the road and cross the Merced River bridge before heading left along the river terrace for 0.1 mile. Before long you will find yourself on a paved trail that heads steeply up the forested hillside.

At 1 mile, recross the Merced River just below Vernal Falls to reach an important junction on the opposite side. Both trails lead to the top of Nevada Fall. On the right, the John Muir Trail (JMT) climbs the steep hillside with well-graded switchbacks. To the left, the Mist Trail climbs with incredible steepness, making giant steps up the rock. The Mist Trail is wonderfully scenic—ascending through the spray of Vernal Falls and past the base of Nevada Fall—and is a whole mile shorter than the JMT, but it requires a great deal of concentration with each foot placement.

At 2.5 miles from Happy Isles, the Mist Trail rejoins the JMT at the top of Nevada Fall (6,000 feet). Go left and continue the climb on well-graded switchbacks to the entrance of Little Yosemite Valley, where the trails levels off and parallels the Merced River. At 4.4 miles the trail splits (6,285 feet). To the right in 0.3 mile is a large camp area. Half Dome is to the left. The trails rejoin 10 feet north of the solar toilet.

At 6.2 miles (7,000 feet) the combined trails divide. Go left on the Half Dome Trail and continue the ascent for another 1.5 miles. At 7.9 miles (7,860 feet) you leave the forest and begin the assault of Half Dome. The climb begins with a series of steep granite steps that lead to the top of a small granite dome at the eastern base of Half Dome. Cross the top of this dome and descend to a saddle (8,400 feet), where cables will guide you to the summit.

At the base of the cable is a pile of used work gloves. If you did not bring your own, grab a pair to spare your hands from cable burns, then grasp the cables and begin hauling yourself up 442 feet to the summit. Before you go too far, stop and ask yourself if you really want to go on, because this is the last convenient turnaround point.

Once on the broad 8,842-foot summit, make a full tour for the complete 360-degree view. Stay away from the edges; it is a long drop to the valley. No camping is allowed on the summit.

*Cable route to summit of Half Dome*

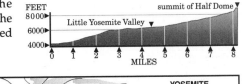

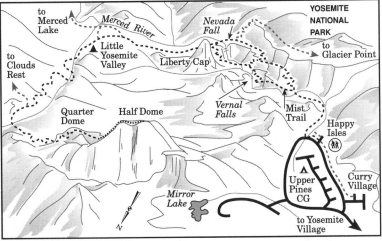

# 72 | MERCED LAKE

**Round trip: 27.4 miles**
**Hiking time:** 3–4 days
**High point:** 7,216 feet
**Elevation gain:** 3,181 feet
**Difficulty:** Potentially difficult
**Hikable:** Mid-June through September

**Driving directions:** Drive to Yosemite Valley and pick up your wilderness permit at the Wilderness Center. Leave your vehicle at the backpackers' parking lot near Curry Village, then either walk or catch a free shuttle bus for the 0.8 mile to Happy Isles (4,035 feet).
**Maps:** Wilderness Press Yosemite and Merced Peak; USGS Half Dome, Merced Peak
**Permits:** Yosemite Valley Backcountry Office (Case 6)

Granite surrounds you. You walk on granite and climb granite stairways. Huge walls of granite tower to lofty heights above you, the river below you cascades over a bed of granite, and everywhere you look there are slabs of granite, granite domes, and even massive blocks of granite.

The trail to Merced Lake is not an easy one, as it climbs steeply for extended periods. Your efforts are rewarded with marvelous scenery. If possible, plan to do most of this hike either early in the morning or late in the afternoon to avoid the midday sun.

**THE HIKE.** From the bus stop, follow the road across the Merced River bridge and then go right. Walk along the Merced River until you reach the paved trail. Head up the forested hillside on the steep and very busy John Muir Trail (JMT). The JMT is wide and partially paved, and often seems too small for the number of people on it. At 0.9 mile, cross the Vernal Fall bridge to an intersection with the Mist Trail. Here you must choose between the steady grade of the very scenic JMT or the steep and often slippery ascent on the extraordinarily scenic and often very crowded Mist Trail.

The two trails rejoin at the top of Nevada Fall (5,980 feet), at 3.5 miles. Continue on the JMT for 0.9 mile to an intersection at the entrance to Little Yosemite Valley. Stay right to reach the extremely popular Little Yosemite Campground at 4.7 miles (6,300 feet).

At the campground the trail divides again; stay right. The next nearly level 2 miles is a no-camping zone. At 6.7 miles the valley narrows. The trail passes a forested camp area, then enters a zone of granite. Climb briefly to enter Lost Valley, another no-camping area, and walk for the next mile under a canopy of sugar pines, sequoias, lodgepole pines, and incense cedars.

At the upper end of Lost Valley, the trail passes a small camping area

*Granite wall in Little Yosemite Valley*

and then heads steeply up a granite wall, climbing past Bunnel Cascade before leveling out again (6,500 feet). At 8.9 miles, pass another camp area on the left, then cross to the south side of the valley. The next stage is a steep climb over the granite flank of Bunnell Point (an official discrepancy in spelling from the cascade courtesy of the USGS). At the crest, walk across sloping granite before descending to recross the river (7,000 feet).

The trail continues up the nearly level valley, passing several appealing campsites. At 10.8 miles, pass the trail to Sunrise High Sierra Camp and Sunrise Creek (an excellent alternate return route). Continue straight,

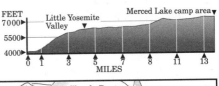

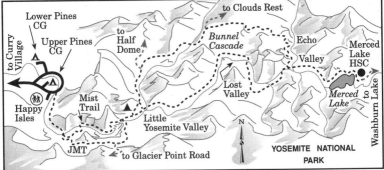

crossing Echo Creek on three major bridges, then walk on up-valley for another mile before beginning your final climb at 11.9 miles.

The valley narrows and the walls tower above you on both sides. The trail reaches the west end of granite-bound Merced Lake at 12.8 miles. No camping is allowed along the lakeshore, so walk on 0.3 mile around the lake to reach the official campsite at 13.1 miles, located next to the Merced Lake High Sierra Camp (7,216 feet). Food-storage boxes, toilets, and running water (when the High Sierra Camp is open) are provided.

# 73 | RANCHERIA FALLS

**Round trip: 13 miles**
**Hiking time:** 6 hours
**High point:** 4,800 feet
**Elevation gain:** 1,800 feet
**Difficulty:** Potentially difficult
**Hikable:** May through October

**Driving directions:** Drive Tioga Pass Road (Highway 120) to the Evergreen Road turnoff (located on the north side of the road 1.1 miles west of the Big Oak Flat Entrance to Yosemite National Park). After 7.2 miles, the road passes under an archway and enters Camp Mather. Continue straight to an intersection and go right, passing the park entrance gate (check for open hours). Drive on to make your official entrance into the park at 8.7 miles from Tioga Pass. The road climbs and then descends to the reservoir. Day hikers park near the dam; overnight hikers park at the campground, open to hikers with backcountry permits only (3,830 feet).
**Maps:** Wilderness Press Hetch Hetchy; USGS Hetch Hetchy Reservoir
**Permits:** Big Oak Flat Visitor Center and Hetch Hetchy Entrance Station (Case 6)

Located partway up the sparkling Hetch Hetchy Reservoir is a long, rambunctious waterfall on Rancheria Creek. This is one of nature's finest waterslides, where you can enjoy spirited water play in the sloping granite chutes and crystal clear pools or relaxing siestas along the granite banks.

**THE HIKE.** From your parking lot, head toward the lake. Walk across O'Shaughnessy Dam and then on through the tunnel at the far end. Follow the old road up the reservoir for 0.7 mile to a junction with the Laurel Lake–Lake Vernon Trail. Go right on the lake trail and continue up the reservoir, traversing from one eye-catching viewpoint of Hetch Hetchy Reservoir to another.

After 1.5 miles, pass under Tueeulala Falls. This is a seasonal fall, spectacular in late spring, usually dry by August. One mile beyond, the trail crosses a

*Playing in a pool below Rancheria Falls*

series of solidly constructed footbridges at the base of Wapama Falls. This fall dries to a bare trickle by August; however, the pools at the base generally linger throughout the summer, luring overheated hikers off the trail for cooling dips.

Beyond Wapama Falls, the trail climbs up and over rock ledges while dipping in and out of gullies. The trail heads through alternating bands of blazing sun on the open rock and deep shade in sheltered oak and manzanita groves. Be mindful of the poison oak and the occasional rattlesnake that lives in the vegetation and suns on the rocks.

At 6.4 miles Rancheria Falls come into view. As the trail enters the broad Rancheria Valley, an unmarked path veers off to the right, heading to the Rancheria backcountry

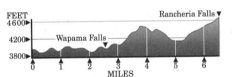

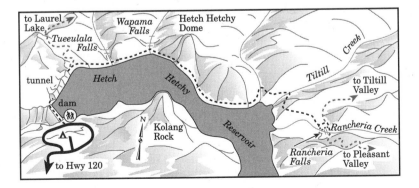

camp and the pools at the base of Rancheria Falls. The official, signed entrance to the backcountry camp is located in a stand of trees another 0.2 mile up the main trail. Once you reach the falls, peel off your dusty shoes and enjoy.

# 74 | GRAND CANYON OF THE TUOLUMNE

**Loop trip: 48.8 miles**
**Hiking time:** 4–6 days
**High point:** 9,840 feet
**Elevation gain:** 6,935 feet
**Difficulty:** Potentially difficult
**Hikable:** July through mid-October

**Driving directions:** From Yosemite Valley, drive east on Tioga Pass Road (Highway 120) to the White Wolf Campground exit. Go left and descend 1.1 miles to the White Wolf Trailhead (7,840 feet).
**Maps:** Wilderness Press Tuolumne Meadows and Hetch Hetchy Reservoir; USGS Falls Ridge, Hetch Hetchy Reservoir, Tamarack Flat, Ten Lakes, Tenaya Lake, and Yosemite Falls
**Permits:** Big Oak Flat and Tuolumne Meadows Wilderness Centers (Case 6)

Hikers who follow the Tuolumne River down the spectacular granite-bound canyon can expect superb scenery. The river provides a constantly changing spectacle as it flows from the placidly reflective pools of Tuolumne Meadows to foaming cascades, thundering waterfalls, and churning catch-basins on its turbulent journey down the Grand Canyon. On either side of the river are magnificent walls of granite that rise a breathless 4,000 feet above the canyon floor.

The most pleasing way to do this hike is as a loop that includes a trek to Ten Lakes. However, using the park's excellent transportation system (summer only), the Grand Canyon may also be hiked as a one-way trip from Tuolumne Meadows to White Wolf.

**THE HIKE.** Head east through forest, skirting the campground, to reach an intersection at 0.4 mile. Go right, toward Ten Lakes, on a trail that climbs through alternating whispering pines and small meadows ablaze with wildflowers. At 5.5 miles your trail intersects the Ten Lakes Trail. Go left and ascend to the crest of a 9,690-foot ridge and magnificent views at 8.3 miles. The trail then descends 600 feet to Ten Lakes Basin, reached at 9.7 miles. From the basin the trail heads into the South Fork Cathedral Creek valley, then climbs around the southeast flanks of Tuolumne Peak to the hike's 9,840-foot high point, on an open ridge. Descend to the May Lake

*Tuolumne River from Glen Aulin*

Trail junction and continue on to reach the Polly Dome Lakes–Tenaya Lake junction at 21 miles (8,700 feet). Good campsites may be found near Polly Dome Lakes.

Continue the gradual descent to reach McGee Lake at 24.1 miles and the very popular Glen Aulin at 25.3 miles (7,840 feet), location of a High Sierra Camp and a thirty-site backpackers' camp with running water.

The loop route crosses the Tuolumne River on a bridge, then turns left and climbs a rocky rise to a view of the upper Grand Canyon. Descend into the canyon, passing California Falls and Le Conte Falls before reaching

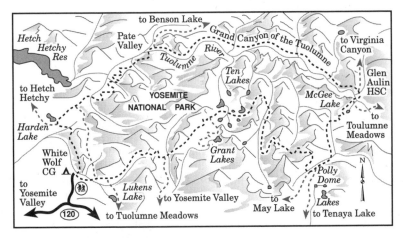

the famous Waterwheel Falls at 28.6 miles. Watch for rattlesnakes on or near the trail as you descend, and check your campsite before setting your pack down.

At 39.4 miles the trail reaches Pate Valley, a junction, and a popular camp area (4,400 feet). Below Pate Valley the trail crosses the Tuolumne River on a footbridge and then continues down the nearly level canyon for another 1.3 miles before starting the long, steep grind out of the valley. There are two main camp areas on the way up: one at 5,690 feet and the second at 6,780 feet. At the 45.6-mile point of the loop is a junction (6,970 feet). Go right for the final 3.2 miles on trail and dirt road, passing swampy Lukens Lake and the sewage treatment area to reach White Wolf at 48.8 miles.

# 75 | TEN LAKES

**Round trip: 12.6 miles**
**Hiking time:** 7 hours
**High point:** 9,690 feet
**Elevation gain:** 2,190 feet in; 750 feet out
**Difficulty:** Potentially moderate
**Hikable:** July through mid-October

**Driving directions:** Drive the Tioga Pass Road (Highway 120) east 5.3 miles from the White Wolf Campground exit to Yosemite Creek/Ten Lakes Trailhead and park on the south side of the road. The trail begins on the north side of the road (7,520 feet).
**Map:** Wilderness Press Tuolumne Meadows
**Permits:** Big Oak Flat and Tuolumne Meadows Wilderness Centers (Case 6)

Hike to a lake-studded basin, isolated from the rest of the park by granite walls towering overhead and by precipitous granite cliffs below that plunge 3,000 feet into the Grand Canyon of the Tuolumne River. The isolation and beauty of this basin attract large numbers of visitors, so plan to reserve your permit well ahead of time.

**THE HIKE.** The trail heads away from the road for 75 feet to reach its first junction. To the left a trail descends 11.5 miles to Yosemite Valley. Go right, following the signs to Grant Lakes and Ten Lakes, and begin a steady climb.

Before long you will leave the forest and continue the ascent on barren granite slabs. At 2 miles, pass the trail from White Wolf Campground on the left and continue the climb. A brief descent at 4 miles leads to Half Moon Meadow, a lush green patch of earth that is an ideal resting spot (if the bugs do not run you out) before the final climb.

After skirting the meadow, the trail heads steeply upward using several

*Ridge crest above Ten Lakes*

switchbacks to complete the 700-foot grind. At 4.8 miles, just below the crest of the ridge, pass the Grant Lakes Trail on the right. This 1-mile side trip is an ideal day hike from the lakes basin; it also is a good destination for hikers who prefer to avoid the crowds.

At 5 miles, the Ten Lakes Trail reaches the crest of the ridge and 9,690-foot high point of the hike. Walk across the lupine-covered saddle to view a seemingly endless succession of ridges filling the northern horizon. Just as the trail begins its descent, a boot path branches off to the left leading to a rock outcropping with a breath-stopping view over Ten Lakes Basin and into the Grand Canyon of the Tuol-umne.

The next mile is spent in a 750-foot descent to one of the largest of the Ten Lakes (8,940

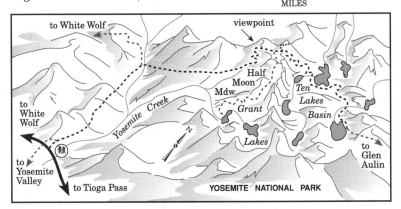

feet). If you do not like the campsites at this first lake, move on and descend a terrace to the next lake. You have seven large lakes and several small ones to choose from.

# 76 | CLOUDS REST

**Round trip: 14 miles**
**Hiking time:** 8 hours
**High point:** 9,926 feet
**Elevation gain:** 2,300 feet
**Difficulty:** Potentially difficult
**Hikable:** July through September

**Driving directions:** Drive Tioga Pass Road (Highway 120) west 8.9 miles from the Tuolumne Meadows Store, or east 16.6 miles from the White Wolf turnoff, to the Sunrise Trailhead, located at the west end of Tenaya Lake (8,150 feet).
**Maps:** Wilderness Press Tuolumne Meadows; USGS Tenaya Lake
**Permits:** Big Oak Flat and Tuolumne Meadows Wilderness Centers (Case 6)

Most veteran Yosemite Park hikers consider the view from Clouds Rest to be the best in the park. What more needs to be said?

This is a long trip, and many hikers prefer a backpack trip over a one-day marathon hike with a chance of thunderstorms rather than views at the end. No water is available on the dry ridge that leads to Clouds Rest. The closest water and comfortable campsites are located 3 miles below the summit, along a tributary of Tenaya Creek.

**THE HIKE.** From the parking area, head into the forest on the trail signed to Sunrise High Sierra Camp (HSC). Follow this trail out into a meadow for 300 feet to a junction. Go left. After just 500 more feet the trail crosses Tenaya Creek and then heads right to another intersection. Go straight, still following signs to Sunrise HSC.

The trail crosses a second stream and then begins a rocky ascent of a forested hillside. After 1.5 miles the ascent becomes even more aggressive, and at 2.8 miles the trail attains the crest of a broad, sandy ridge and a junction (9,200 feet). The trail to the Sunrise HSC goes to the left. Continue straight and descend from the ridge, losing 280 feet of hard-earned elevation.

Once down, the trail heads northwest over a broad bench, winding in and out of forest interspersed with verdant meadows. Pass a small tarn at 4 miles, and 0.5 mile beyond cross a small, unnamed tributary of Tenaya Creek. This is the last camp area with water before Clouds Rest. One site is located below the trail, and several sites may be found above.

*View of Yosemite Valley from Clouds Rest*

At 5 miles the trail to Sunrise Creek heads off to the right (9,120 feet). Continue straight and begin a steady climb through thinning forest cover. Your goal, a bald, rocky ridge, can be seen to the west. At 6.7 miles the trail arrives at the crest of the ridge (9,766 feet). At the last large tree, the trail splits. Stock goes left while sure-footed hikers stay right, ascending slabs of granite that look like stacks of pancakes to reach the summit of Clouds Rest at 7 miles (9,926 feet).

To the north and east are Tenaya Lake, the Cathedral Range, and a sea of granite domes and jagged ridges. To the west lie Little Yosemite Valley and Merced Lake. However, the most impressive view is to the southwest, over Half Dome to Yosemite Valley. Your eye can trace the path of the glaciers from Tuolumne Meadows to the valley. While viewing, keep a weather eye open for thunderstorms, and leave as soon as you spot even a slightly suspicious cloud.

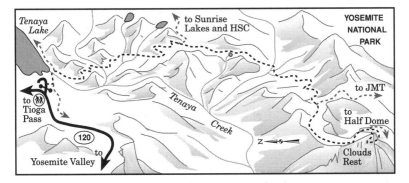

# 77 | CATHEDRAL LAKES TRAIL

**Round trip to Cathedral Lakes: 7 miles**
**Hiking time:** 4 hours
**High point:** 9,580 feet
**Elevation gain:** 1,010 feet
**Difficulty:** Potentially easy
**Hikable:** July through September

**Semiloop trip to Sunrise High Sierra Camp: 12.8 miles**
**Hiking time:** 7 hours
**High point:** 9,850 feet
**Elevation gain:** 1,760 feet
**Difficulty:** Potentially moderate
**Hikable:** July through September

**Driving directions:** Drive Tioga Pass Road (Highway 120) west 1.6 miles from the Tuolumne Meadows Store, or east from the White Wolf turnoff, for 23.9 miles. Park along the edge of the road at the Cathedral Lakes Trailhead (8,570 feet). During the summer months you may leave your car at the Wilderness Center in Tuolumne Meadows and ride the free shuttle bus to the trailhead.
**Maps:** Wilderness Press Tuolumne Meadows; USGS Tenaya Lake
**Permits:** Toulumne Meadows Wilderness Center (Case 6)

From the stately spires of Cathedral Peak cleaving the deep blue sky to the serene lakes in broad granite saucers, the lavish scenery on the Cathedral Lakes Trail is guaranteed to please even the most jaded hiker.

The Cathedral Lakes Trail offers hikers a choice of scenic destinations. The Cathedral Lakes are an ideal destination for a day hike or a low-mileage backpack. Hikers looking for a longer trip may continue on to campsites at the Sunrise High Sierra Camp (HSC) and then complete their trip by making a semiloop to Tenaya Lake. The summer shuttle bus will solve any transportation difficulties involved in starting and ending at different trailheads.

**THE HIKE.** From the parking area, follow the trail into the forest for 500 feet to a four-way junction. Go straight, on the John Muir Trail (JMT), and begin your climb toward Cathedral Lakes. The trail is steep and rough, ravaged by stock use. This first climb is short, and soon you are heading across the broad bench between Fairview Dome and Cathedral Peak. A second climb takes you to the forested crest of a 9,540-foot saddle.

From the saddle, the trail descends gradually to an intersection at 3 miles. To the right, a 0.5-mile spur trail descends to lower Cathedral Lake

*Glacier-polished granite at lower Cathedral Lake*

(9,250 feet), where broad slabs of granite invite you to relax and contemplate the meadows and needlelike Cathedral Peak. Campsites are located in a grove of trees at the lake's northeast corner.

To reach the Sunrise HSC, stay on the main trail, which climbs to upper Cathedral Lake and more campsites at 3.5 miles. A short climb above the lake leads to Cathedral Pass (9,700 feet). The trail continues its well-graded ascent above the pass, traversing the flanks of Tresidder Peak to a saddle on the side of the Columbia Finger. The view is impressive; to the south and east, looking like waves on the ocean, are endless rows of granite ridges.

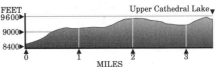

From the saddle, descend through coniferous forest to

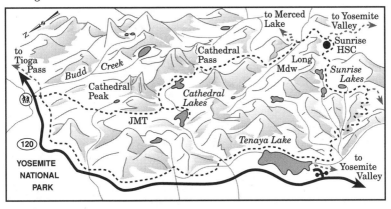

an intersection at the northern end of Long Meadow at 7.4 miles. Go straight for a final 0.4-mile stroll over the open meadow to Sunrise HSC (9,300 feet). Several trails branch off to the right. The first is the horse access to the camp; the second is for hikers. Just beyond is a major intersection, where you leave the JMT. Go right, uphill, for 100 feet and then go right again to the backpacker camp, toilet, and running water (midsummer only).

To complete the semiloop, continue up the Clouds Rest/Tenaya Lakes Trail. Climb to a saddle, then descend past the three Sunrise Lakes to intersect the Clouds Rest Trail. Go right and descend to Tenaya Lake, 5 miles from Sunrise HSC.

# 78 | VOGELSANG LOOP

**Loop trip: 20.9 miles**
**Hiking time:** 2–4 days
**High point:** 10,600 feet
**Elevation gain:** 2,300 feet
**Difficulty:** Potentially moderate
**Hikable:** July through mid-October

**Driving directions:** From the Tuolumne Meadows Store, drive east on Tioga Pass Road (Highway 120). After 1.4 miles turn right and follow the signs to the Wilderness Permit Office. You may park next to the office or continue on 0.4 mile to a second parking area (8,640 feet).
**Maps:** Wilderness Press Tuolumne Meadows; USGS Tioga Pass and Vogelsang Peak
**Permits:** Tuolumne Meadows Wilderness Center (Case 6)

Tucked away in a rocky basin at the foot of the Cathedral Range, Vogelsang Lake is an ideal place to set up a base camp for several days of high country exploring.

**THE HIKE.** From the second parking area, descend to the combined John Muir Trail/Pacific Crest Trail (JMT/PCT) at the edge of Dana Fork Creek. At 0.2 mile cross the Dana Fork on a footbridge, then stay right at the Gaylor Lakes Trail junction. Follow the JMT/PCT across upper Tuolumne Meadows and cross the Lyell Fork of the Tuolumne River on a second footbridge.

Shortly after crossing the Lyell Fork, a trail from Tuolumne Meadows Campground joins in from the right. Stay left, following the JMT/PCT for another 0.4 mile to the Rafferty Creek junction, where the loop portion of this hike begins. Leave the JMT/PCT here and go right, following signs to Vogelsang High Sierra Camp. For the next couple of miles the trail climbs steadily through the forest to reach the meadows and dramatic views of

Fletcher Peak at 4 miles. Rafferty Creek, which slices through the heart of the meadow, may run dry in late summer.

At 6.1 miles, crest the 10,000-foot summit of Tuolumne Pass and arrive at an intersection. Go left and continue to climb for another 0.8 mile to Vogelsang High Sierra Camp (10,160 feet). Walk straight past the backpackers' camp area and the tent cabins. You may fill up your bottles before continuing the final 0.7 mile on the Vogelsang Pass Trail to wildly beautiful Vogelsang Lake (10,341 feet) and peaceful wilderness campsites.

To continue the loop, retrace your steps from Vogelsang Lake to the High Sierra Camp, then go right (northeast) to Upper Fletcher

*Trail near Tuolumne Pass*

Lake and a very busy camp area. The trail ascends a low saddle and then drops down to reach Evelyn Lake at 9.8 miles. The lake, located on a barren plateau, is an excellent location for a camp.

Continuing on, the trail takes you over two more low ridges and begins the long descent

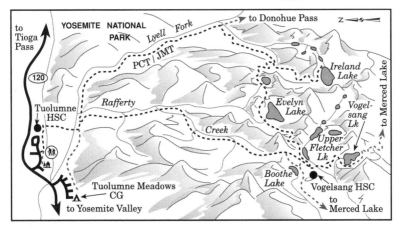

into Lyell Canyon by zigzagging down granite ledges. At 11.8 miles you will pass the Ireland Lake Trail junction (10,420 feet). Ireland Lake, and associated lakelets, is located 2.5 miles to the south and is an excellent side trip and delightful place to camp.

Below the junction the trail heads into forest, paralleling Ireland Creek into Lyell Canyon, where you will intersect the JMT/PCT at 15.7 miles. There is an excellent campsite at the intersection.

From the intersection, go left and follow the JMT/PCT down the canyon through beautiful meadows along the Lyell Fork. The loop portion of the hike ends after you cross Rafferty Creek on a wide bridge at 19.8 miles. Follow the JMT/PCT back to the parking area to end your hike at 20.9 miles.

# 79 | YOUNG LAKES

**Loop trip: 12.9 miles**
**Hiking time:** 7 hours
**High point:** 10,230 feet
**Elevation gain:** 1,620 feet
**Difficulty:** Potentially moderate
**Hikable:** Mid-July through September

**Driving directions:** Drive to the Dog Lake/Lembert Dome Trailhead (8,610 feet), on the north side of Tioga Pass Road (Highway 120), located 0.3 mile east of the Tuolumne Meadows Store or 0.4 mile west of the Tuolumne Meadows Wilderness Office.
**Maps:** Wilderness Press Tuolumne Meadows; USGS Tioga Pass and Falls Ridge
**Permits:** Tuolumne Meadows Wilderness Center (Case 6)

Young Lakes lie in a broad basin surrounded by jagged ridges, sheer cliffs, and towering mountains. From Tuolumne Meadows there are two trails to the lakes, creating a delightful loop.

**THE HIKE.** Begin your loop with a walk north on the stables' access road. Where the road divides at 0.3 mile, go straight, pass a gate, and then head across Tuolumne Meadows, following signs to Glen Aulin. At 0.6 mile, pass Soda Springs. Head uphill and to the right on a wide trail. Walk over a low ridge, then descend to cross Delaney Creek (an easy boulder hop except in early season). At 1.7 miles the trail divides; go right, toward Young Lakes.

The Young Lakes Trail climbs to the crest of a 9,700-foot ridge, then levels off. After descending to cross a creek at 5 miles, the trail divides. Go left, toward Young Lakes (the trail on the right is used when you loop back to the parking area). The final 1.5 miles to Lower Young Lake (9,850 feet) is an easy stroll around the base of Ragged Ridge. Campsites are located along

*Lower Young Lake and Mount Conness*

the north shore of the lake. (No campfires are allowed at the lakes.)

To reach the two upper lakes, go around the north side of the lower lake and cross the outlet. Where the trail divides, stay left for about 0.2 mile to a second junction, where you will go right. From the middle lake, simply follow the creek up the slope to the upper lake (10,230 feet).

To complete the loop, retrace your steps from Lower Young Lake back 1.5 miles to the intersection and go left. The trail climbs over a

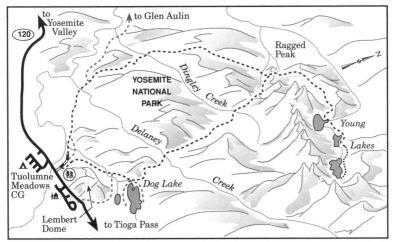

10,095-foot ridge and then descends open hillsides. Cross Dingley Creek, then leave the meadows, heading northwest through forest to a long meadow where the trail crosses Delaney Creek and arrives at an unmarked intersection. Stay left and continue descending to reach the Dog Lake intersection at the 11.4-mile point of the loop. Dog Lake (9,240 feet) is a pleasant 0.2-mile side trip.

A couple hundred feet below the Dog Lake Trail is an intersection with the Lembert Dome Trail. Stay right, and descend steeply along the west side of the dome. Pass three more intersections and, following signs to the parking area, stay left at the next two intersections and right at the third.

# 80 | GLEN AULIN AND McCABE LAKES

**Round trip to Glen Aulin: 11 miles**
**Hiking time:** 6 hours
**High point:** 8,610 feet
Elevation loss: 770 feet
**Difficulty:** Potentially easy
**Hikable:** July through mid-October

**Round trip to McCabe Lakes: 29 miles**
**Hiking time:** 3–4 days
**High point:** 9,900 feet
**Elevation gain:** 2,060 feet
**Difficulty:** Potentially moderate
**Hikable:** Mid-July through October

**Driving directions:** Drive Tioga Pass Road (Highway 120) to Tuolumne Meadows. At 0.3 mile east of the Tuolumne Meadows Store, or 0.4 mile west of the Tuolomne Meadows Wilderness Office, turn north on a small dirt road, signed to the stables. Where the road makes a sharp turn to the right at 0.3 mile, find a parking place along the edge (8,610 feet).
**Maps: Glen Aulin:** Wilderness Press Tuolumne Meadows; USGS Tioga Pass and Falls Ridge; **McCabe Lakes:** Wilderness Press Tuolumne Meadows; USGS Tioga Pass, Falls Ridge, and Dunderberg Peak
**Permits:** Tuolumne Meadows Wilderness Center (Case 6)

The easy hike to Glen Aulin is a Yosemite classic. Wide meadows, sweeping vistas of rounded granitic domes, and pulsating waterfalls on the Tuolumne River all combine to make this an exceptional area.

Even if this trail were not so spectacular, it would still be very well used. In addition to the High Sierra Camp, Glen Aulin lies on the Pacific Crest Trail (PCT) and the Tahoe–Yosemite Trail, and it is also a pivotal point for many hikes on the east side of the park. Because of the popularity of this area, make your backpacking reservations early.

If you would like to see more of this beautiful area and less of your fellow visitors, continue on from Glen Aulin to the relative peace of the subalpine McCabe Lakes.

**THE HIKE. Glen Aulin.** Following signs to Glen Aulin, walk around the gate and begin your hike on a road that heads across Tuolumne Meadows. This is a popular short-hike area, and the meadows are laced with well-signed trails. At 0.3 mile pass the famous Soda Springs. Just ahead is Parsons Memorial Lodge. At this point, the Glen Aulin Trail leaves the road and climbs over a low hill where you will pass a spur trail to the stables. The trail fords a couple channels of Delaney Creek (easy crossings except during the early season snowmelt) and at 1.5 miles passes the trail to Young Lakes (Hike 79). Stay left and continue the nearly level trek along the edge of meadows.

The trail stays in the forest, skirting the meadows. Below you will see the Tuolumne River as it meanders over the level plain. Cross several slabs of granite where the trail disappears on the hard rock. In these areas you must follow a scattered line of boulders. Pay attention to the trail when you are crossing the sheets of sloping granite; it is easy to meander off the route while watching the scenery rather than the trail.

Where the valley narrows, the hike gets exciting. The trail heads along a ledge of granite at the edge of the Tuolumne River. Steep and somewhat slippery ramps of cobblestones have been built to aid hikers and horses on and off the granite. As you walk, look west across the river for a view of Little Devils Postpile, an anomalous wall of columnar basalt set in a granite landscape. At 3.8 miles cross the Tuolumne River on bridges and begin the descent to Glen Aulin. Keep your eyes on your feet along this rough

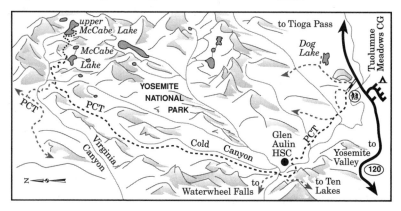

*Tuolumne Meadows*

section of trail and not on the expanding view over the upper Grand Canyon of the Tuolumne River. Descend past Tuolumne Falls and then the frothy White Cascade to reach an intersection with the May Lake/Ten Lakes Trail at 5.3 miles. Go right and descend for the final 0.2 mile to the large pool and waterfall that keynote Glen Aulin.

Recross the Tuolumne River on a large bridge to reach a four-way intersection (7,840 feet). To the right is the Glen Aulin High Sierra Camp and a thirty-site backcountry camp area with a solar toilet and running water. To the left is the Tuolumne River Trail. The 3.3 miles down the Grand Canyon of the Tuolumne to Waterwheel Falls makes an excellent side trip from Glen Aulin. On the way, the trail passes three waterfalls and several campsites before reaching its objective.

**McCabe Lakes.** From Glen Aulin, go straight at the four-way junction, following the PCT north up Cold Canyon. The trail climbs granite slabs to expanding views of Cathedral, Echo, Cockscomb, and Unicorn Peaks to the south. Ragged Peak, Mount Conness, and Sheep Peak fill the northeastern skyline.

The trail passes a couple of damp meadows—mosquito havens and potential campsites in July—and then ascends to an 8,800-foot defile between two granite domes at 3.3 miles from Glen Aulin. A short descent leads to a mile-long meadow, which ends opposite Elbow Hill. This meadow offers your best chance for water before the lakes.

The trail resumes its gradual climb as it heads back into the forest, and at 7 miles from Glen Aulin it arrives at the McCabe Lakes intersection (9,215 feet). Leave the PCT here and go right on a narrow trail that climbs gradually up the forested hillside. At 9 miles from Glen Aulin, the trail ends at lower McCabe Lake (9,900 feet). The lake is ringed by the granite slopes of Sheep Peak on two sides and by trees and boulders around the other two sides. Campsites are located on both sides of the outlet. No wood fires are allowed.

No maintained trail exists between the lower and upper McCabe Lakes; however, there is a well-traveled route that traverses along the north shore of lower McCabe Lake and then ascends through the forest. Pass a couple of tarns, then continue up to the crest of a saddle marked by cairns. Head east from the saddle to the outlet of the upper McCabe Lake.

# 81 | MONO PASS

**Round trip: 9 miles**
**Hiking time:** 5 hours
**High point:** 10,599 feet
**Elevation gain:** 902 feet
**Difficulty:** Potentially easy
**Hikable:** Mid-July through September

**Driving directions:** Drive Tioga Pass Road (Highway 120) west 1.4 miles from Tioga Pass summit, or east 6 miles from Tuolumne Meadows Store, to the Mono Pass Trailhead, located in the forest on the south side of the road (9,697 feet).
**Maps:** Wilderness Press Mono Craters; USGS Tioga Pass and Koip Peak
**Permits:** Tuolumne Meadows Wilderness Center (Case 6)

The trail to Mono Pass offers a remarkably easy entry into the starkly beautiful world of the High Sierra. Meadows, lakes, long-abandoned miners' cabins, and panoramic views attract crowds of visitors. Hikers seeking solitude are advised to go elsewhere.

**THE HIKE.** The trail begins by descending an old road through Dana Meadows. Once in the meadows, the trail leaves the road and heads left to cross the Dana Fork of the Tuolumne River (usually a simple matter of hopping boulders). The trail crosses a couple of old moraines, then settles into a gradual but steady climb.

At 2 miles pass an old miners cabin and 0.3 mile beyond pass a spur trail to Spillway Lake (10,060 feet). Stay left and continue up through the forest. Walk by the ruins of a second cabin shortly before the trail reaches the Parker Pass intersection, at 3.7 miles (10,540 feet). This intersection has

*Old Golden Crown Mine cabins at Mono Pass*

neither a sign nor a visible trail. However, by looking across the meadow you can spot the Parker Pass Trail on the far hillside.

To reach Mono Pass, stay left and continue climbing for another 0.3 mile. The trail divides again, a few feet below the crest of the pass. The right fork leads across the meadow to an old miners' encampment. The trail on the left continues up to 10,599-foot Mono Pass. For the best views, continue

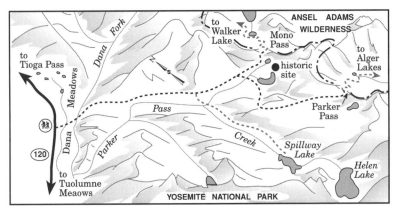

beyond the pass for another level 0.5 mile to glacier-polished rocks over-looking Upper Sardine Lake, Bloody Canyon, Mono Lake, and the Great Basin. No camping is allowed in the Parker Pass Creek drainage; however, there are excellent campsites at Upper Sardine Lake, in the Ansel Adams Wilderness.

If you have extra time, walk over to the miners' cabins. Silver was discovered in the Mono Pass area in 1879, and the cabins were part of the Golden Crown Mine. Long winters made mining difficult, and eventually the project was abandoned.

To escape the crowds, walk over to 11,100-foot Parker Pass, located just 2 miles from Mono Pass. Parker Pass is very different from Mono Pass. It is dry and open with unobstructed views. No camping is allowed at the pass; however, you can descend south 0.2 mile into the Ansel Adams Wilderness and find small, rocky campsites near several of the small tarns.

# 82 | 20 LAKES BASIN

**Loop trip: 8.4 miles**
**Hiking time:** 4 hours
**High point:** 10,400 feet
**Elevation gain:** 523 feet
**Difficulty:** Potentially easy
**Hikable:** Mid-July through September

**Driving directions:** Drive Tioga Pass Road (Highway 120) east 2.2 miles from Tioga Pass. Turn north on Saddlebag Lake Road and continue 2.4 miles to the backcountry parking area and Wilderness Permit Kiosk, located opposite the Saddlebag Lake Dam (elevation 10,087 feet). Alternate parking spaces are located 0.1 mile up the road at the small lakeside resort and along the edge of the road near the dam.
**Maps:** USFS Hoover Wilderness; USGS Tuolumne Meadows and Matterhorn Peak
**Permits:** Mono Lake Ranger Station and Saddlebag Lake Kiosk (Case 7)

Twenty beautiful high alpine lakes in one small basin is certainly a good enough reason for a visit, and the beautiful backdrop of glacier-clad mountains will make you want to return again and again. The relatively short access trails and minor elevation gain are added incentives to make repeated visits. If this sounds like a paradise with easy access and beautiful scenery, it is. Naturally, this perfection attracts large numbers of hikers. Then, to compound the overuse problem, a passenger ferry makes several trips a day carrying swarms of additional hikers to the upper end of Saddlebag Lake, cutting 3 miles off the loop's total distance.

*Lake Helen*

**THE HIKE.** Walk up the road from the backcountry parking area, passing the campground turnoff on the right and the small resort on the left. Traverse the day-use parking area and pass the toilets to find the start of the trail to 20 Lakes Basin.

The trail heads around the east side of Saddlebag Lake on an abandoned mining road. The views start immediately, with grand vistas into the Harvey Monroe Hall Natural Area. At 1.5 miles reach the upper end of Saddlebag Lake, where the trail divides. For the loop, stay right, heading to Lundy Pass and entering the Hoover Wilderness. After ascending

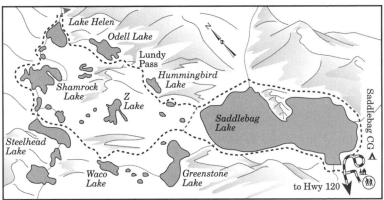

gradually through green meadows, Hummingbird Lake is passed and soon after the trail crosses over Lundy Pass (10,360 feet).

Descend around Odell Lake and then down to Lake Helen (10, 240 feet), where the trail divides at the outlet. Stay left here and head around the north end of Lake Helen, then follow the trail over a low rise to reach Shamrock Lake. From this scenic gem, the trail scrambles over a rocky rib. This is the trickiest part of the loop; the trail is easy to lose on the rock slabs. Watch carefully for a line of stones and an occasional duck marking the route.

From the top of the rib, the trail descends steeply to another intersection. To the right, the old mining road heads west to Steelhead Lake and on to the old Hess Mine. The loop route bears left, climbing a low knoll and then following the shoreline along the east side of the lake. At the upper end of Steelhead Lake, notice a spur trail branching off to the right, heading west to Towser, Potter, and Cascade Lakes.

The main trail crosses a 10,400-foot high point, then descends past Wasco Lake and onto the narrow rib of rock that divides Greenstone Lake from Saddlebag Lake. Once again the trail divides. The left fork heads down to the ferry dock; the right fork contours the west side of Saddlebag Lake to the dam. When the water is not running, you may cross the dam. If the water is running, descend to the bridge, then hike back up to the close the loop at the backcountry parking area.

# 83 | PETERS CREEK GROVE

**Round trip: 12 miles**
**Hiking time:** 7 hours
**High point:** 1,440 feet
**Elevation gain:** 1,040 feet in; 760 feet out
**Difficulty:** Potentially moderate
**Hikable:** All year

**Driving directions:** Drive Skyline Boulevard (Highway 35) south 7.1 miles from Highway 84, or 6.2 miles north from Highway 9, to Alpine Road. Follow Alpine Road for 3.1 miles, then take a left on Portola State Park Road and descend, steeply, for 3.5 miles to the Visitor Center. Day hikers park in the picnic area; backpackers park behind the Visitor Center (400 feet).
**Maps:** Portola Redwoods State Park Map; USGS Mindego Hill (trail not shown)
**Permits:** Portola Redwoods State Park (Case 8)

Like all of the old and magnificent redwood groves, the tall trees of Peters Creek show signs of the fires and floods they have survived. However, the

*Hillside of redwood sorrel in Peters Creek Grove*

most amazing survival story is their miraculous escape from the axes that leveled most of the forests in this area before the turn of the century.

The entire hike to this remarkable grove may be completed in one day, or it may be spread out over 2 days with an overnight stop at Slate Creek Trail Camp. No drinking water is available at the trail camp. All water must

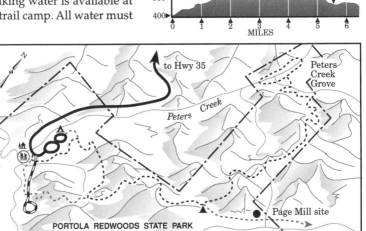

be packed in or taken from Slate Creek, a less-than-pristine source located 0.4 mile from the campsite.

**THE HIKE.** Walk the main road downhill from the Visitor Center. Cross Peters Creek and head up to an intersection. Follow the road to the right for 300 feet, then go left and head uphill on the Slate Creek/Old Tree Trail.

After an initial 0.1-mile climb, reach an intersection. Go left on the Slate Creek Trail and contour north for 0.2 mile to a second intersection. Take the right fork and begin a slow, steady climb through mixed forest of redwood, Douglas fir, oak, and madrone trees. At 1.5 miles the trail reaches a narrow saddle (920 feet) and a third intersection. To the right, the Summit Trail offers an alternate descent route. For now, continue on the Slate Creek Trail for another 1.5 miles to the trail camp and intersection (1,020 feet).

From the trail camp, go left and follow the Bear Creek Trail along an old road grade. At 4 miles from the Visitor Center, the road disappears and a narrow trail continues on through open shrub land where you must watch for poison oak and ticks. After 0.5 mile the trail reaches a 1,440-foot high point, then begins a very steep descent to the redwood grove. The state park owns a very narrow strip of land here and the trail builders were forced to forgo some switchbacks.

The grove is reached at 5.2 miles (800 feet). Walk the 0.5-mile loop trail around the grove or just sit by the creek and enjoy the peacefulness of the area. At the base of these hardy trees is a verdant carpet of ferns, redwood sorrel, miner's lettuce, and, in early spring, trilliums.

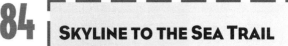

# 84 | SKYLINE TO THE SEA TRAIL

**One-way hike: 32.5 miles**
**Hiking time:** 2–4 days
**High point:** 3,214 feet
**Elevation gain:** 673 feet; loss: 3,887 feet
**Difficulty:** Potentially moderate
**Hikable:** All year

**Driving directions:** Drive to Saratoga Gap, at the intersection of Highway 9 and Skyline Drive (Highway 35). Head south on Skyline Drive for 2.6 miles, then turn right to the trailhead parking at Castle Rock State Park (3,060 feet).
**Maps:** Skyline to the Sea Trail Maps 1 and 2; USGS Castle Rock Ridge, Big Basin, Franklin Point, Ano Nuevo
**Permits:** Big Basin Redwoods State Park Headquarters (Case 9)

From the crest of the Santa Cruz Range to the shores of the Pacific Ocean, the Skyline to the Sea Trail is the reigning monarch of the elaborate Santa

Cruz Mountains trail system. The first segment of this trail, from Saratoga Gap to Big Basin Redwoods State Park, was constructed in 1969 by 2,500 enthusiastic volunteers in a single weekend. Since that time, the idea has grown and the trail has been extended to the ocean.

Since the original rush to get the trail in place, the official starting point has been moved to Castle Rock State Park. From the state park it is 32.5 miles to the trail's official end at Waddell Beach, on the Pacific Ocean. Six trail camps are located at uneven intervals along the route. Two other trail camps, Sunset and Lane, are located on scenic variants off the main route. All camps require advance reservations except Castle Rock Trail Camp, which is on a first-come basis. Fees are charged at all the camps. Drinking water is currently available at the first three camps (Castle Rock, Waterman Gap, and Jay Camp). At the other camps, water must be carried in. No campfires are allowed, so a backpacking stove is required for cooking.

As this is a one-way hike, transportation must be arranged ahead of time. No overnight parking is allowed at Saratoga Gap. Cars are left at Castle Rock State Park. Hikers with trail camp reservations may leave a car at Rancho del Oso Ranger Station, located 0.2 mile east of Highway 1. If you are to be met at the end of the hike, you must walk out to Highway 1 and find your ride at Waddell Beach. Bus service is available from Waddell Beach to Santa Cruz. For information,

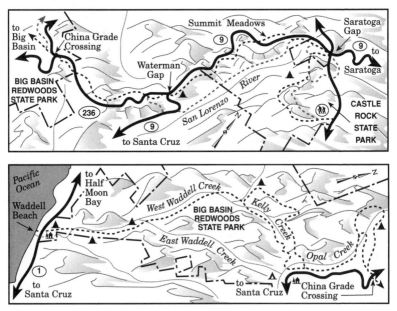

*Trail's end at Waddell Beach*

call Santa Cruz Metropolitan Transit District at (408) 425-8600.

**THE HIKE.** The Skyline to the Sea Trail route begins by following the Saratoga Gap Trail past a waterfall and then along the side of an open ridge with excellent views west over forested hills to the Pacific Ocean. At 2.8 miles reach Castle Rock Camp. From the camp, follow the Loghry Woods and Skyline Trails along the ridge crest for 3.4 miles to Saratoga Gap.

At Saratoga Gap, pick up the official Skyline to the Sea Trail for the 6.3-mile descent to Waterman Gap. Unfortunately, the public right-of-way is very limited in this area and the trail closely parallels Highway 9, crossing it several times. If you prefer a more wilderness feel to your walk, follow the Saratoga Toll Road stock trail for at least part of your descent.

From Waterman Gap, the trail wanders through dense forest while paralleling Highway 236 for the 4.5 miles to China Grade (a road crossing). You then descend through Big Basin Redwoods State Park, past the head-quarters, to reach Jay Camp at 22 miles.

From Jay Camp to the ocean, hikers must choose between three scenic routes: 1) the Howard King Trail, which has views; 2) the Sunset and Berry Creek Falls Trails, which pass three unique and beautiful waterfalls; and 3) the Skyline to the Sea Trail, which winds through majestic redwood groves. The three routes rejoin for the final 6-mile descent along Waddell Creek to the ocean.

**219**

# 85 | BERRY CREEK FALLS LOOP

**Loop trip: 11 miles**
**Hiking time:** 6 hours
**High point:** 1,340 feet
**Elevation gain:** 1,300 feet
**Difficulty:** Potentially moderate
**Hikable:** All year

**Driving directions:** From Saratoga Gap, at the intersection of Highway 35 (Skyline Boulevard) and Highway 9, drive west on Highway 9. After descending 5.8 miles, reach Waterman Gap. Turn right on Highway 236 and follow it to Big Basin Redwoods State Park Headquarters (1,001 feet).
**Maps:** Big Basin Redwoods State Park; USGS Big Basin
**Permits:** Big Basin Redwoods State Park Headquarters (Case 9)

Three waterfalls highlight this very popular hike through stately groves of redwood giants. The first, Berry Creek Falls, appears as a lace curtain in a fern- and moss-covered grotto. The second, Silver Falls, plunges down a sheer cliff right beside the trail, and the third, Golden Falls Cascade, is exotically colorful.

The entire loop can be hiked in one day or divided into two leisurely days with an overnight stop at Sunset Trail Camp. Backpackers must carry their own stove (no open fires are permitted) and either carry their own water or be ready to boil, filter, and then purify the water from nearby Berry Creek.

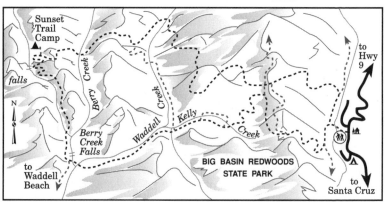

**THE HIKE.** The hike begins opposite the Visitor Center, next to the amphitheater. The trail starts by cutting its way between two impressive redwood groves. Several trails branch off to the right and left, heading into the groves; however, for the loop you need to go straight and cross the Opal Creek bridge, then head left on the Skyline to the Sea Trail.

For the next 3.7 miles, stay on the Skyline to the Sea Trail as it climbs over a ridge and then descends through redwood groves, first along Kelly Creek and then along Waddell Creek. At one point the trail divides, and the right fork crosses the creek to wander through a grove on the opposite side for 0.3 mile before rejoining the main trail.

At the Berry Creek Trail junction (360 feet), go right and begin the climb past Berry Creek Falls, Silver Falls, and Golden Falls Cascades. The final ascent is in a narrow valley, where you climb steps cut into the sandstone at the edge of Berry Creek.

At 5.5 miles (800 feet) a trail branches left to Sunset Camp. Unless you are overnighting, continue straight ahead on Sunset Trail, which climbs and then descends several times before reaching the trip's 1,340-foot high point, on Middle Ridge. Walk across an old fire road and then descend to the Skyline to the Sea Trail at 10.7 miles. Go right and walk along Opal Creek for the final 0.2 mile to the bridge and the Visitor Center.

*Berry Creek Falls*

# 86 | NORTH RIM TRAIL

**Loop trip: 13.5 miles**
**Hiking time:** 7 hours
**High point:** 2,282 feet
**Elevation gain:** 1,282 feet
**Difficulty:** Potentially moderate
**Hikable:** All year

**Driving directions:** From Saratoga Gap, at the intersection of Highway 35 (Skyline Boulevard) and Highway 9, drive west on Highway 9. After descending 5.8 miles, reach Waterman Gap. Turn right on Highway 236 and follow it to Big Basin Redwoods State Park Headquarters (1,001 feet).
**Maps:** Big Basin Redwoods State Park; USGS Big Basin
**Permits:** Big Basin Redwoods State Park Headquarters (Case 9)

From redwood groves to grand vistas, this semiloop along the north rim of Big Basin Redwoods State Park offers excellent scenery and delightful walking. Between the redwood groves and the vistas, the hike passes oddly weathered sandstone formations and a single log house while rambling through a wide variety of

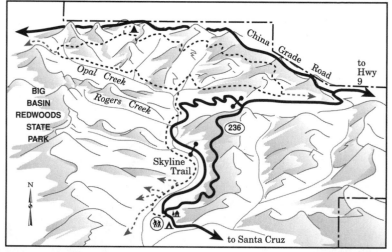

*Opal Creek*

ecosystems. In late winter and early spring, add bubbling creeks and a scattering of wildflowers to the list of attractions.

The North Rim Trail may be hiked in one day or spread out over a 2-day weekend with an overnight stop at Lane Trail Camp. Backpackers must carry a camp stove (no wood fires are allowed) as well as all water needed for the night.

**THE HIKE.** From the trailhead, located opposite the amphitheater, follow the well-defined path across the Opal Creek bridge, then go right on the Skyline to the Sea Trail. The route parallels Opal Creek and North Escape Road, which is gated beyond the picnic area. Head through redwood groves and past the site of the Maddock's Cabin, where the Maddock family built a home from a single giant redwood tree.

The trail brushes along the edge of North Escape Road at several points, then they share a bridge over Rogers Creek. At 2.2 miles pass a fancy information board and picnic table, then use the road a second time to cross Opal Creek. Once across the bridge, go left and follow the trail into a grove of redwoods.

At 2.7 miles (1,320 feet) the trail divides. Leave the Skyline to the Sea Trail and go left on Hollow Tree Trail. After climbing toward the ridge top for 1.4 miles, the trail divides again, at 1,830 feet. Stay on the Hollow Tree Trail and begin a traverse along the northern boundary of the park. Much of this trail parallels China Grade Road, a rarely used access into the backcountry of the Santa Cruz Mountains.

The trail traverses oak- and madrone-covered hillsides, passing a lumber mill site with plenty of old relics to gawk at. Reach the 2,282-foot Lane Trail Camp at the 6-mile mark. The camp is located on the crest of the ridge, ideally placed to take advantage of the afternoon breezes.

From the camp, follow the Basin Trail past several Pacific Ocean vistas and across a couple of weathered sandstone formations. One of these sandstone areas is so steep that steps had to be cut into the rock. The Basin Trail ends at 9.2 miles (1,920 feet). Go right on the Skyline to the Sea Trail for the final 4.3 miles back to the Visitor Center.

# 87 | PINE VALLEY

**Round trip: 12 miles**
**Hiking time:** 8 hours
**High point:** 4,632 feet
**Elevation gain:** 300 feet in; 1,500 feet out
**Difficulty:** Potentially moderate
**Hikable:** April through October

**Driving directions:** Drive Highway 1 to Carmel, then head east on Highway G16 to the town of Carmel Valley. From the center of town, go south, still on G16, for 11.6 miles, then turn right on Tassajara Road. After 3 miles the pavement ends at the Tassajara Zen Mountain Center Monastery. Beyond, the dirt road that continues is best characterized as atrocious and is subject to wet weather closures. At 3.5 miles beyond the end of the pavement, pass a horse packer's station and enter the national forest. Six miles from the pavement the road crosses a saddle. Ignore the unsigned road to the right and head down steeply for the final 1.6 miles to China Camp. The trailhead is located a few yards beyond the China Campground entrance (4,400 feet).
**Maps:** USFS Ventana Wilderness; USGS Chews Ridge
**Permits:** Monterey Ranger District (Case 10)

An oasis of velvet meadows, whispering pines, and cool, clear water lies tucked away in a fold of the hills, hidden among the dramatic terrain of the Ventana Wilderness. This hike can easily be completed in a day; however, the valley is pleasant and peaceful and well worth an overnight visit.

**THE HIKE.** Start the trip by heading up the Pine Ridge Trail, briefly gaining elevation. The views start at the trailhead. The first point of note is Mira Observatory, located to the north, on Chews Ridge.

Before long the trail begins a rolling descent through alternating stretches of old burn and meadow-covered hillsides. Depending on what side of the ridge you are on, the views are either of the Miller Fork of the

*Private inholding in Pine Valley*

Carmel River valley to the north, the Church Creek Valley to the south, or the Pacific Ocean to the west. Early morning hikers will be treated to a calliope of bird songs, while afternoon hikers will need to concentrate on their feet to avoid stepping on lizards.

At 4 miles the trail reaches Church Creek Divide and a major intersection (3,700 feet). A lone campsite is found here, with a seasonal water source just over the divide on the left. More campsites with a better water source are located 0.5 mile farther on the Pine Ridge Trail.

From the intersection, the Church Creek Trail goes left, heading south toward The Mesa. Straight ahead, the Pine Ridge Trail heads west, to Sykes Hot Spring and the Big Sur. Your route is on the Pine Valley Trail, to the right.

For the next 2 miles the Pine Valley Trail descends from the ridge top through the shade of madrone, oak, and pine forest to reach the meadows at the valley floor at 6 miles (3,141 feet). The camping area is located

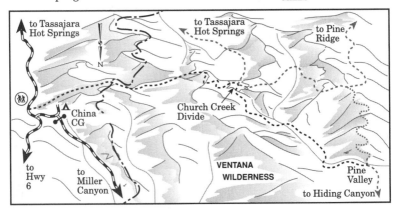

across a small creek from a private inholding with a house. The camp is a great place to just lie back and listen to the wind whisper secrets to the pine trees.

In 2003, it was still possible to make a loop trip out of Pine Valley on the Bear Basin Trail (poorly marked and poorly maintained). This trail will take you back up to the Pine Ridge Trail, which can be followed back to the start, adding an extra 3 miles to your return.

# 88 | MOUNT CARMEL

**Round trip: 9 miles**
**Hiking time:** 5 hours
**High point:** 4,430 feet
**Elevation gain:** 2,580 feet
**Difficulty:** Potentially moderate
**Hikable:** March through October

**Driving directions:** Drive south from Monterey on Highway 1. Check your odometer as you pass the Highway 68 West exit, then continue down the coast for 14 miles. Turn left on Palo Colorado Road and go 7.8 miles to its end, at Bottchers Gap. Park at the small walk-in campground (2,050 feet).
**Maps:** USFS Ventana Wilderness; USGS Big Sur and Mt. Carmel
**Permits:** Monterey Ranger District (Case 10)

Views, views, views, and more views. There is a 360-degree panorama of views from the summit of Mount Carmel, but you had better hurry. Since the fire lookout burned down in the 1950s, the brush has slowly been reclaiming the best viewpoint in the northern Los Padres National Forest. Nowadays, in order to gaze north over the Monterey Peninsula, east across the Carmel Valley to the Sierra de Salinas Range, south over the Santa Lucia Range, or west across the seemingly endless expanse of the Pacific Ocean, you must scramble up a boulder pile or scale a rickety old telephone pole. In another ten years this outstanding view may be gone.

**THE HIKE.** The trail begins at the upper left corner of the parking lot and climbs above the walk-in campsites. The grade varies from moderate (on the chaparral-covered hillside) to steep (in the oak- and madrone-filled Mill Creek Valley). There are two creek crossings before the trail reaches the 3,450-foot crest of Skinner Ridge at 2.5 miles.

On the ridge crest, swing north, entering the Ventana Wilderness, then wander through an arcade of giant oak and madrone trees. After 0.2 mile, leave the ridge and descend to reach Turner Creek Junction (3,200 feet) at 3 miles. To the left a trail descends 300 feet in 0.3 mile to forested Apple Tree

Camp. Continue straight ahead and switchback up the steep hillside.

At 4 miles, cross the 4,158-foot summit of Devils Peak. Views are only moderate here, so head left along the ridge. Where the trail traverses around the second summit of Devils Peak, go left on a well-worn path heading up the meadow-covered hill. Follow this path for 30 feet, then go left on a faint path covered with California blue oak leaves. After a few feet the trail improves. Descend to a small saddle, then head up through manzanita for 0.5 mile to the 4,430-foot lookout site on the summit of Mount Carmel. The final portion of the trail is often very brushy, so have your long pants handy.

Backpackers should return to Devils Peak and continue on for another 1.2 miles to scenic Comings Cabin Camp. Water is usually available at the camp for the entire summer.

*Seeking an unobstructed view from summit of Mount Carmel*

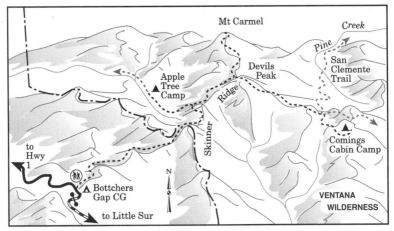

# 89 | MANUEL PEAK

**Round trip: 9 miles**
**Hiking time:** 5 hours
**High point:** 3,379 feet
**Elevation gain:** 3,039 feet
**Difficulty:** Potentially difficult
**Hikable:** All year

**Driving directions:** From Carmel, drive Highway 1 south 25 miles to Pfeiffer Big Sur State Park. At this point you have two options: You may pay the day use fee and park at Picnic Area 3, where the trail begins (340 feet), or you may find a parking place in one of the turnouts just outside the park and walk the extra mile into the park for free.
**Maps:** USFS Ventana Wilderness; USGS Pfeiffer Point and Big Sur
**Permits:** Big Sur Station (Case 10)

Outstanding views keynote this hike, which begins in the redwood groves of Pfeiffer Big Sur State Park and ends overlooking the immense expanse of the Pacific Ocean. Much of this hike is spent on the open and dry slopes of the chaparral-covered hillsides, so during the warm summer months plan to start your hike early and carry plenty of water.

**THE HIKE.** From the entrance to Picnic Area 3, the hike begins by rounding a gate and heading up a paved road through an oak grove. After 500 feet go left on a wide trail, passing a pioneer cabin and then climbing through a beautiful oak arbor.

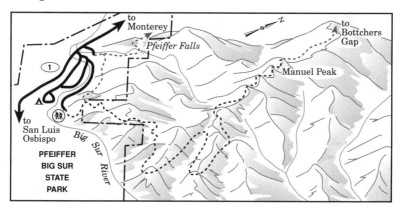

*View of Pacific Ocean from Manuel Peak Trail*

At 0.5 mile from the picnic area is the intersection with the trail from Pfeiffer Falls. Go straight ahead on a wide, well-graded trail, leaving the state park and entering the Los Padres National Forest.

The views begin immediately as the trail switchbacks up the hillside. At first you are overlooking only the park. Soon the steep-walled canyon of the Big Sur River becomes visible and views expand over Island Mountain, deep into the Santa Lucia Range. Not long after, the Pacific Ocean comes into view.

At 2.4 miles the trail rounds a rocky rib and then heads into a deep cut in the hillside. At the shadiest point is a redwood grove and a small, unreliable spring. When you reach the summit ridge at 3 miles, the Mount Manuel Trail turns north for the final push to the crest of Manuel Peak.

Manuel Peak has many summits. The trail passes to the west of the first summit, descends, then climbs to a forested saddle. Go left on a narrow trail, passing a military-looking apparatus to the open and rocky crest of the 3,379-foot second summit. This is a great place to eat lunch and enjoy the view.

The trail continues on. In the next mile it crosses over two more major summits and one lesser summit before dropping down to the Little Big Sur River. However, there is no substantial improvement in the view beyond the second summit.

# 90 SYKES CAMP—THE HOT SPRINGS HIKE

**Round trip: 19.5 miles**
**Hiking time:** 2–4 days
**High point:** 1,640 feet
**Elevation gain:** 2,100 feet
**Difficulty:** Potentially moderate
**Hikable:** April through October

**Driving directions:** Drive Highway 1 south 25.5 miles from Carmel. At 0.5 mile south of the entrance to Pfeiffer Big Sur State Park, turn left to the Big Sur Forest Service Station. Follow signs to the trailhead and overnight parking area (320 feet). A fee is charged for parking.
**Maps:** USFS Ventana Wilderness; USGS Pfeiffer Point, Partington Ridge, and Ventana Cones
**Permits:** Big Sur Station (Case 10)

The Pine Ridge Trail from Big Sur to Sykes Camp is the most popular hike in the Ventana Wilderness. Its popularity has nothing to do with the excellent trail, views of the forest and ocean, the Big Sur River with its deep pools of clear water, or the towering groves of redwoods—although these things help. The reason so many people make the long trek to Sykes Camp is to soak in the famous natural hot springs.

With endless streams of people trekking in to bathe in the pools, this is not the place to go if you are looking for

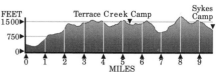

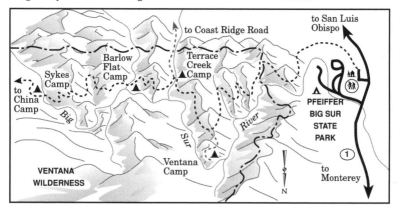

*Big Sur River Valley*

solitude. However, if you are looking for a good introduction to the spectacular variety of flora and fauna of the Ventana Wilderness, this place is hard to beat.

**THE HIKE.** From the parking area, follow the Pine Ridge Trail through the redwood forest around the edge of the state park campground. The trail descends, crosses Post Creek, and then heads steeply up through the chaparral. At the end of the first mile you will enter the Big Sur River Valley. A rock outcropping (880 feet) provides an open vantage point to Island Mountain and the Santa Lucia Range.

The trail contours the hillside, winding in and out of small redwood groves and entering the Ventana Wilderness at 2.5 miles. The next point of interest is an intersection at 4.2 miles. To the left a spur trail drops 700 feet in 1 mile to Ventana Camp, a scenic backcountry camping area on the edge of the Big Sur River.

The Pine Ridge Trail continues up-valley and at 5.4 miles passes Terrace Creek Camp, in a redwood grove. A trail branches off on the right here, ascending to the Coast Ridge Trail. From Terrace Creek Camp, the Pine Ridge Trail climbs a bit, then descends to 900 feet and crosses Logwood Creek. At 7 miles you will pass above a large camp area at Barlow Flat. The trail climbs back to 1,400 feet to cross a rocky rib, then descends to ford the Big Sur River at 9.7 miles (1,100 feet). Sykes Camp is located on the east side of the river. However, if the water level is not too high, you do not need to make the crossing to find the hot springs and campsites. When the water level is low, skip the ford and go left, down the river along the west bank. Campsites are located along the trail. The hot springs are 0.2 mile down-river. The trail is rough, with a challenging scramble over a rock wall to reach the hot springs on the far side. If secluded campsites are preferred, be prepared to wade the river.

# 91 | SANTA LUCIA TRAIL

**Round trip: 12 miles**
**Hiking time:** 7 hours
**High point:** 5,700 feet
**Elevation gain:** 3,540 feet
**Difficulty:** Potentially difficult
**Hikable:** April through October

**Driving directions:** Drive Highway 101 to King City and take the Jolon Exit, located 0.7 mile north of the town center. Head west on County Road G14 for 18.2 miles, then go right on Mission Road, entering the Hunter-Leggett Military Reservation. After checking in at the guard station, head straight north on Mission Road for 5 miles. Just opposite a large hacienda, turn left on Del Ventura Road. Head north for 17.7 more miles to the trailhead, located on the right just before Santa Lucia Memorial Park (2,150 feet).

*Note:* The Del Ventura Road fords two rivers and is closed after heavy rainstorms.

**Maps:** USFS Ventana Wilderness; USGS Cone Peak and Junipero Serra Peak

**Permits:** Monterey Ranger District (Case 10)

The grand view from the site of an old lookout is the objective of this scenic hike along the southeastern edge of the Ventana Wilderness. The only question is what peak the lookouts are standing on. Most maps call it Junipero

*View from old lookout on Junipero Serra Peak*

Serra Peak. Signs along the trail point alternately to Serra Peak and Santa Lucia Peak. However, no matter what name you choose, the hike is excellent.

Carry plenty of water for the long trek to the summit, and plan an early start to avoid the heat of the day.

**THE HIKE.** From the trail-head parking area, where the signs indicate that you are heading to Serra Peak, begin your hike by passing through

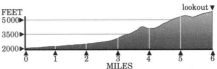

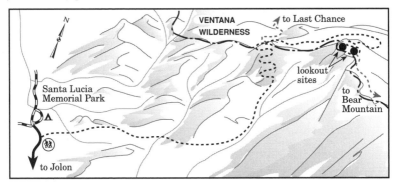

*Cone of giant foothill pine (Pinus sabiana)*

a small gate and heading out into a large meadow with weathered sandstone outcroppings. The trail crosses a small creek and then heads up through an area once used by the Salinan Indians. There are several trails here; take the one that heads up past a couple of large oaks. The trail crosses the rolling foothills, heading steadily east toward the mountains ahead.

The initial shade gives way to sun as the trail leaves the oaks and climbs up to manzanita-covered hillsides. The trail climbs relentlessly to reach the crest of a low ridge and a junction at 4 miles (4,100 feet). The trail to the left heads northwest, to Last Chance Camp. Stay right and continue the steep ascent up the ridge. Near the 5-mile point, the trail reaches the summit ridge and shade of a pine forest (5,400 feet).

The trail now ambles along the north side of the ridge for a mile before popping out of the forest at the base of the remains of the old lookout on Santa Lucia, Serra, or Junipero Serra Peak. A second lookout site is located 100 yards to the east.

# 92 | ARROYO SECO

**Round trip to ridge: 10 miles**
**Hiking time:** 5 hours
**High point:** 4,420 feet
**Elevation gain:** 2,320 feet
**Difficulty:** Potentially moderate
**Hikable:** Mid-March through October

**Round trip to Cook Camp: 12 miles**
**Hiking time:** 6 hours
**High point:** 4,700
**Elevation gain:** 2,600 feet
**Difficulty:** Potentially difficult
**Hikable:** Mid-March through June

**Driving directions:** Drive Highway 101 to King City and take the Jolon exit, located 0.7 mile north of the city center. Head west on County Road G14 for 18.2 miles, then go right on Mission Road, entering the Hunter-Leggett Military Reservation. You will have to stop and check in at the guard station. Head straight down Mission Road for 5 miles. Just opposite a large hacienda, turn left on Del Ventura Road. Go north for 17.9 more miles. After Santa Lucia Mamorial Park, the road divides. Stay left and look for a parking place along the side of the road (1,980 feet).

*Note:* The Del Ventura Road fords two rivers and is closed after heavy rainstorms.
**Maps:** USFS Ventana Wilderness; USGS Cone Peak and Lopez Point
**Permits:** Monterey Ranger District (Case 10)

It is the view from the crest of the Santa Lucia Range that inspires hikers to make the long climb from the valley floor to the top of the ridge. Although you cannot see all the way to China, on a clear day you can see freighters heading in that direction.

The Arroyo Seco Trail climbs along the Arroyo Seco River to the crest of the range, where it meets the North Coast Ridge Trail. Except for an absence of bridges, this is an excellent trail. However, since this area was swept by fire in 1985, storms bring down a new batch of dead and dying trees every winter. Brush grows rapidly in the burned area, particularly the chamise, manzanita, and prickly leaved ceanothus. The Forest Service clears out the trail as often as possible, but expect some rough going in the spring.

**THE HIKE.** The trail starts by following the gated road on the left. Walk around the gate, then head up-valley a short distance to a cabin. The official trailhead is located opposite the second building.

*Forest floor along the Arroyo Seco Trail*

Watch out for poison oak as you walk along the shaded valley floor to reach the first unbridged crossing of Arroyo Seco River, at 0.2 mile. The ford is deep and the water fast, so look for logs to help with the crossing. At 1.8 miles the trail arrives at Forks Camp, an open area along the river with a year-round water supply and fire ring. Just 500 feet beyond the camp, the trail divides. To the right, Rodeo Flat Trail follows an old fire break steeply uphill to meet the North Coast Ridge Trail. Your trail heads left and recrosses the Arroyo Seco River (2,580 feet). Once across, head uphill and soon cross the Arroyo Seco River for the third and last time.

At 3 miles, pass Madrone

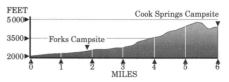

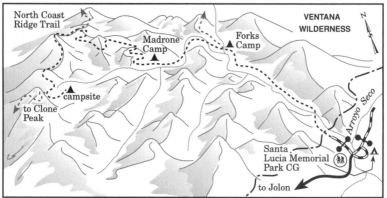

Camp, which has a year-round water source and a fire box. At this point, the trail begins to climb through the old burn, leaving the river and poison oak and entering an area of dense scrub brush. Views begin here and extend across the valley to Junipero Serra Peak, the highest summit in the wilderness.

Following a line of burned telephone poles, the trail reaches the 4,420-foot ridge crest at 5 miles. Go left on the North Coast Ridge Trail for 100 feet for the first views west over the ocean and a great picnic site. Backpackers should continue west along the ridge for another mile to the Cook Springs intersection (4,700 feet). Go left here and descend to the camp. The water supply at Cook Springs is not reliable after midsummer.

# 93 | LOST VALLEY

**Round trip: 11 miles**
**Hiking time:** 6 hours
**High point:** 2,852 feet
**Elevation gain:** 1,372 feet in; 760 feet out
**Difficulty:** Potentially moderate
**Hikable:** April through October

**Driving directions:** Drive Highway 101 to King City and take the Jolon exit, located 0.7 mile north of the Broadway exit, then head west on County Road G14 for 18.2 miles before turning right on Mission Road. You must stop and check in at the Hunter-Leggett Military Reservation before heading straight north for 5 miles. Turn left on Del Ventura Road, just opposite the hacienda. After another 17.7 miles, reach the pavement's end at Santa Lucia Memorial Park Campground. During the rainy season, the hike begins here. When the road is open, continue up-valley another 3 miles to Escondido Campground. The trailhead is located at the lower end of the campground (2,175 feet).

*Note:* The road through Hunter-Leggett has no bridges, fords two rivers, and is flooded after major rainstorms.
**Maps:** USFS Ventana Wilderness; USGS Junipero Serra Peak and Tassajara Hot Springs
**Permits:** Monterey Ranger District (Case 10)

Extensive meadows and a reliable water source make Lost Valley a popular destination for day hikers and backpackers throughout the hiking season. However, regular visitors all agree that springtime is the best, when wildflowers carpet the valley and hillsides, turning the meadows into a brilliant afghan of yellows, blues, and reds. If you wish to time your visit to enjoy the wildflowers, check ahead with the ranger office.

*Fording Arroyo Seco River*

Once the rains begin in the fall (usually in October or November), the access road is gated and the final 3 miles to the trailhead must be walked. The road is usually reopened by the first of May. However, peak wildflower season varies from mid-March to early May, and when the flowers bloom early, the rivers along the trail may still be swollen from the winter rains and be hard to cross.

**THE HIKE.** Find the sign that says "Trail" and begin a 1-mile descent to the Arroyo Seco River (1,680 feet). Once across the ford, spend the next 1.5 miles climbing. Watch for poison oak

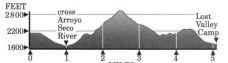

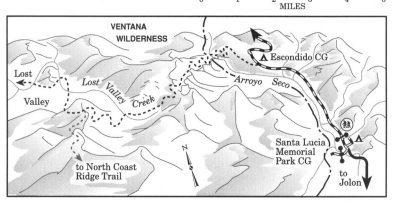

along the creek and for ticks on the dry hillside above. At 2,852 feet, the trail crosses an open divide with excellent views, then descends toward Lost Valley Creek. Just before the final descent to the valley floor, pass a waterfall with a deep bathing pool tantalizingly close to the trail. At 4 miles, cross a small creek to reach Fish Camp (2,030 feet).

The trail climbs again for 0.7 mile to an intersection on a dry divide with the Lost Valley Connector, a steep fire trail. The final leg of the hike is an easy descent to Lost Valley.

Upper Lost Valley Camp is located 0.5 mile below the divide, across a small creek from the trail. The main camp is located 0.2 mile farther down. From your base camp, a day can be spent exploring the meadows and hiking to Higgins Camp and Indian Valley.

# 94 | NORTH CHALONE PEAK

**Round trip: 8 miles**
**Hiking time:** 4 hours
**High point:** 3,304 feet
**Elevation gain:** 2,004 feet
**Difficulty:** Potentially moderate
**Hikable:** November through May

**Driving directions:** Drive Highway 101 for 2 miles south of Gilroy and take the Highway 25 exit. Head south through Hollister on Highway 25 for 42.6 miles. Turn right at the Highway 146 intersection and go 5.2 miles to the Pinnacles National Monument Visitor Center. Park here or continue on another 0.3 mile, to the end of the road (1,260 feet). If spending the weekend during the busy spring season, it is best to stop at the private campground just outside the monument, reserve a site, then take the shuttle bus to the trailhead. When the park is busy, everyone is expected to ride the shuttle bus. (From the south, drive Highway 101 to King City, then go east on Highway 613 to Highway 25. Head north to the Highway 146 intersection.)
**Maps:** USGS Pinnacles National Monument and North Chalone Peak
**Permits:** Case 11

On a normal day at North Chalone Peak lookout, there is a panoramic view of Pinnacles National Monument to the north, the Diablo Range to the east, and across the Salinas Valley to the Santa Lucia Range to the west. If the day is exceptionally clear, it is possible to see all the way to the Pacific Ocean. (*Note:* Although this trail is open for hiking the entire year, temperatures soar to uncomfortable levels during the summer. If hiking during the warmer months, plan to begin your hike at daybreak and carry a minimum of two quarts of water per person.)

**THE HIKE.** The trail begins near the entrance to the upper parking lot. Head up the valley, following signs to Bear Gulch Reservoir. After 0.2 mile the trail divides, offering you two different routes to the reservoir. To the left is the Moses Spring Trail, which is very scenic, with several overlooks of Bear Gulch. This trail has one short section where body and pack must be wriggled through a narrow crevice. To the right, the High Peaks Trail can be followed for another 0.3 mile before veering onto the Rim Trail and following it to Bear Gulch Reservoir. (The Bear Gulch Caves Trail, which parallels the creek up through deep caves, was closed due to bats in 2002. No reopening date had been scheduled.)

From the reservoir a broad, well-graded trail climbs the chamise- and buckbrush-covered hillside to ever-expanding views

*Narrow section of Moses Spring Trail*

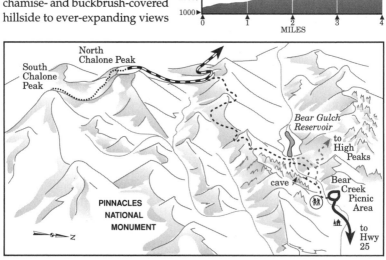

of the monument. At 3.5 miles the trail passes through a gate and heads left up a fire road. After 200 feet the fire road joins the lookout road (gated at the bottom and open to lookout vehicles only). The lookout is now straight ahead and is reached after another 0.5 mile of following the road along the open ridge crest.

The 3,304-foot summit of North Chalone Peak provides a great place to relax and eat lunch. Rest rooms are located just below the summit on the south side. To the south, South Chalone Peak dominates the skyline. The peak can be reached by an easy-to-follow, unmaintained, 1.6-mile trail. To reach the south peak, head back down the road past the switchback to find an unmarked trail on the left. The trail descends along the fence line to a 2,620-foot saddle, then climbs back to the 3,269-foot summit of South Chalone Peak. The view from the south summit is not much better than from the north peak, but it does offer a whole lot more solitude.

# 95 | HIGH PEAKS LOOP

**Loop trip: 9.3 miles**
**Hiking time:** 5 hours
**High point:** 2,580 feet
**Elevation gain:** 1,580 feet
**Difficulty:** Potentially moderate
**Hikable:** All year

**Driving directions:** Drive 2 miles south of Gilroy on Highway 101 and go south on Highway 25 for 42.6 miles. At the Highway 146 intersection, go west for 4 miles, to the east side of the monument. Pass the private campground—the only one near the monument—and enter the park. Where the road divides, go right for 0.3 mile and park at the Chalone Creek Picnic Area (1,030 feet). (When the park is busy, the main road is closed and visitors are required to leave their cars near the campground and ride the shuttle into the monument.)
**Maps:** USGS Pinnacles National Monument or North Chalone Peak and Bickmore Canyon
**Permits:** Case 11

From shaded creeks and underground adventures to cliff-hanging trails skirting under gnome-shaped knobs, this loop samples the most scenic and unique features of Pinnacles National Monument. Although the trails can be hiked year-round, spring is especially appealing. The temperatures are still cool enough to be invigorating, the wildflowers put on a colorful display, and the birds are everywhere, nesting on cliffs and pinnacles, in the trees, and throughout the chaparral-covered hillsides. Summer hikers

*Pinnacles on High Peaks Trail*

should plan to start early to avoid the midafternoon heat. Hikers should always carry plenty water and a flashlight for the caves.

**THE HIKE.** From the picnic area, cross Chalone Creek on a pair of sturdy bridges. After a few feet the trail divides; go left on Bear Gulch Trail and head down-valley through heavy vegetation. Watch for poison oak

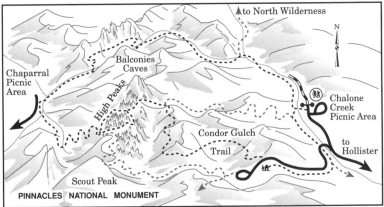

and rattlesnakes. At 0.6 mile, after crossing the park road, the trail divides. Go right and head up Bear Gulch, passing pools and waterfalls (in season) and walking under several impressive sycamore trees.

At 1.2 miles from the picnic area, reach the Visitor Center. Walk to your right, crossing the road, and head up the Condor Gulch Trail. You will immediately start climbing up a series of long and well-graded switchbacks that whisk you up to the chaparral-covered hillsides. Before long you will see pinnacles and rock spires rising out of the hillsides all around. The pinnacles and views increase in number and complexity as you climb. At 2.9 miles, reach the ridge crest, where the Condor Gulch Trail ends at a T intersection. Go left on High Peaks Trail.

At 3.5 miles is another intersection and a choice. The High Peaks Trail heads off to the left, making a very scenic and somewhat exposed traverse along the ridge top. There is a section of trail with a railing, and small steps have been cut into the rock. The alternative is the shorter and very comfortable Tunnel Trail, which descends in smooth switchbacks and includes a tunnel.

If you followed the High Peaks Trail, clamber across the crest of the world for the next 0.7 mile to yet another intersection. Go right and descend 0.6 mile to meet the Tunnel Trail, 4.8 miles from the start. The combined trail continues to descend at a steady pace into Juniper Canyon and reaches the Chaparral parking area at 6 miles.

Go right on the Balconies Caves Trail and follow it down a deep canyon. The valley continues to narrow until the trail heads underground, through the Balconies Caves. If you forgot your flashlight or if you just don't care for dark, damp caves, take the Balconies Caves Trail, which bypasses this area.

Beyond the caves, the trail continues down the valley, crisscrossing the shallow West Fork Chalone Creek. Near the lower end of the valley, leave the trail and follow the old road back to the picnic area at 9.3 miles.

# 96 | NORTH WILDERNESS LOOP

**Loop trip: 9.9 miles**
**Hiking time:** 7 hours
**High point:** 2,083 feet
**Elevation gain:** 983 feet
**Difficulty:** Potentially moderate
**Hikable:** All year

**Driving directions:** Drive Highway 101 to Soledad, then head east on Highway 146 for 12 miles to the road's end, at the Chaparral Picnic Area (1,407 feet). From the east side of the monument you may start the loop from Chalone Creek Picnic Area, adding 2 miles to the total.

**Maps:** USGS Pinnacles National Monument, North Chalone Peak, and Bickmore Canyon
**Permits:** Case 11

The trail along the north boundary of Pinnacles National Monument offers a chance to get away from the crowds and explore the chaparral ecosystem. This is a wilderness trek that wanders along creek bottoms richly covered with grasses, gray foothill pines, junipers, and oaks, then climbs to an impenetrable mixture of chamise, buckbrush, and an occasional manzanita on the ridge crest. In the early spring, wildflowers cover the valley floor and ridges with colorful carpets of yellow, white, and blue.

The North Wilderness Trail has been designated as unmaintained, which means trailheads are not signed, sections of the trail are steep, and maintenance is limited. Hikers must be prepared to crawl over fallen trees and wade shallow creeks. However, when equipped with a map, compass, plenty of water, and a flashlight for the caves, you can hike this trail with little difficulty. (*Note:* In the summer, carry a minimum of two quarts of water per person and start early to avoid the heat.)

**THE HIKE.** From the end of the Chaparral parking area, walk by the rest room and then follow the wide trail to the northwest corner of the picnic area, where an opening in the fence marks the start of the trail. Head up-valley on a faint but discernible path through the deep grass. Points of confusion are marked with white-topped metal fence posts.

After the first mile, the trail heads to the ridge tops and views of the entire park. Once up, the ridge crest is followed to a 2,083-foot high point. Watch for diggings

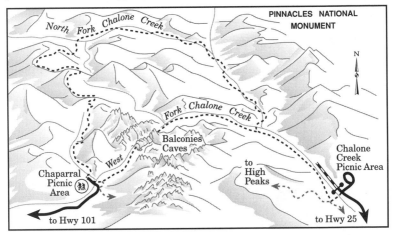

*Shooting stars cover hillsides and forest floors in spring.*

made by wild pigs in this area. The park is working to fence these nonnative animals out, but it is a big job.

From the high point, descend steeply to North Fork Chalone Creek. The trail then heads down-valley, an easy walk except for the fifteen creek crossings. Watch for poison oak.

At 7.6 miles, cross the West Fork Chalone Creek for the last time, then intersect the Old Pinnacles Trail (1,100 feet). Go right, and head up-valley on a broad, well-used path for 1.3 miles, crossing several more creeks. At 8.9 miles the trail divides. The Balconies Caves Trail goes straight, remaining in the cool shade of the valley floor. A flashlight is required to help you negotiate your way around and under the giant boulders that created the caves. The Balconies Cliffs Trail goes right, making a longer but much easier traverse across the dry slopes above the valley. Once the two trails rejoin, it is a quick 0.6 mile to the end of the loop at the Chaparral parking area.

# 97 | WILLSON PEAK

**Loop trip: 7.4 miles**
**Hiking time:** 5 hours
**High point:** 2,651 feet
**Elevation gain:** 1,830 feet
**Difficulty:** Potentially moderate
**Hikable:** All year

**Driving directions:** Drive Highway 101 to Gilroy and take the Leavesley Road exit. Head east for 1.8 miles, then turn left on New Avenue. In 0.6 mile, go right on Roop Road and go 2 miles. Where the road divides at the Coyote County Park entrance, go right on the Gilroy Hot Springs Road and stay with it for the next 3.4 miles, to the Hunting Hollow Entrance parking lot (856 feet). A small day use fee is charged for parking. On spring and summer weekends a park staff member may be available to assist you with backcountry registration and trail directions.

**Map:** Henry W. Coe State Park Trail and Camping Map

**Permits:** Henry W. Coe State Park Hunting Hollow Entrance (Case 12)

Neck-twisting views are the main hazard on this hike into the southwestern corner of Henry W. Coe State Park. Views of the rolling hills, views of the forested valleys, and views of open ridge crests can be addictive.

This popular area is literally laced with old roads and trails. Hike the suggested loop, then come back and try some of the alternative trails the next time. If you have an entire weekend to devote to exploring, there are two excellent backcountry camp areas to choose from a short distance off the main route.

**THE HIKE.** Starting from the upper end of the parking lot, walk around the gate and immediately cross a creek. The road divides here. For now, stay to the right; you will return to this spot on the road to your left. Walk up the Hunting Hollow Road. After crisscrossing back and forth several times across the creek, you will reach a junction at 0.7 mile.

Where the road divides, go left on the Lyman Willson Ridge Trail. (You may want to take a quick detour to inspect the windmill pump, about 200 yards up the Hunting Hollow Road.) Go through a gate, then follow the Lyman Willson Ridge Trail on a brisk climb through an oak forest. In 0.1 mile, Middle Steer Ridge Trail branches off to the left. Continue straight, climbing out of the forest to open hillsides with a view of what seems to be a large portion of California.

At 2.8 miles from the parking lot, the Bowl Trail crosses the Lyman Willson Ridge Trail. Backpackers should head right

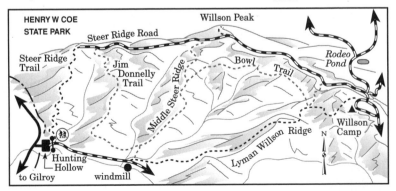

for a mile-long traverse east to Willson Camp. The campsite is an interesting area with an old farmhouse, a horse barn, a couple of abandoned trailers, an outhouse, and running water (purify before drinking). From the camp, backpackers can head east, following the road 0.2 mile to a junction and then heading left on Steer Ridge Road 1.6 miles to the summit.

Day hikers will go straight through the Bowl Trail junction and continue the steady ascent for another 0.5 mile to reach the Steer Ridge Road at 3.3 miles (2,525 feet). Go left and hike the ridge crest for the next 0.8 mile. Pass the Serpentine Trail on the right, then cross a saddle to find an unmarked trail on the right at 4.3 miles. (If you reach the Middle Steer Ridge Trail junction, you have gone 0.2 mile too far.) Follow the unmarked trail for 0.1 mile to the low, rolling summit of Willson Peak at its 2,651-foot high point.

When you are ready to head back, return to the Steer Ridge Road and head west along the rolling ridge crest. The Middle Steer Ridge Trail is passed in 0.2 mile, and the Spike Jones Trail heads off to the right at the 1.1-mile point. Just 0.4 mile beyond pass the Jim Donnelly Trail, which takes off to the left. At this point, the Steer Ridge Road becomes the Steer Ridge Trail and celebrates its new status by heading straight down the steep hillside for 1.4 miles. At 7.4 miles, a right turn takes you back to the Hunting Hollow Road and the parking lot.

*California poppies and an oak tree along Lyman Willson Ridge Trail*

# 98 | KELLY AND COIT LAKES

**Round trip to Kelly Lake: 9.4 miles**
**Hiking time:** 6 hours
**High point:** 2,450 feet
**Elevation gain:** 1,550 feet in; 550 feet out
**Difficulty:** Potentially moderate
**Hikable:** All year

**Round trip to Coit Lake: 11.6 miles**
**Hiking time:** 7 hours
**High point:** 2,450 feet
**Elevation gain:** 2,036 feet in; 650 out
**Difficulty:** Potentially moderate
**Hikable:** All year

**Driving directions:** Drive Highway 101 to Gilroy and take the Highway 152 West exit. Go east on Leavesley Road for 1.8 miles, then turn left on New Avenue and go north for 0.6 mile. At Roop Road, take a left turn and go east for the next 3.3 miles. At the entrance to Coyote Lake County Park, the road divides. Stay to the right, on Gilroy Hot Springs Road, for 3.4 miles to the Hunting Hollow Gate parking area. Go straight and drive the final 2 miles up-valley to the bridge and gate that mark the end of the road. Park along the shoulder (900 feet).

*Note:* Trailhead vandalism is a problem here. Most break-ins occur at night, so backpackers may prefer to park at Hunting Hollow.
**Map:** Henry W. Coe State Park Trail and Camping Map
**Permits:** Henry W. Coe State Park Hunting Hollow Entrance (Case 12)

Kelly Lake is the small and shallow one. It has three arms, which extend up narrow valleys. The lake is surrounded by reeds and scum, making it a good location for fishing and bird watching—but not so inviting for swimmers. If water play is your goal, head to the larger Coit Lake, which has better water access as well as two hikers' camp areas and a horse campground.

Spring is the best time to visit, when the hillsides are colored with mats of yellow gold fields, brilliant clusters of California poppies, and deep blue lupines, to name a very few. This is also an area with seemingly endless possibilities for creating loops and devising hikes to suit your mood and wanderlust. Go with a plan. If you head out without a specific destination, you might be tempted to keep wandering on and on through this exceptionally hikable area.

Temperatures can soar through the 90s during the summer, making the

*Kelly Lake*

spring and fall the most pleasant seasons for long hikes. Few water sources are available after midsummer, and hikers should carry enough water to get them to the lakes. Never use water from the lakes without purifying it first.

**THE HIKE.** From the Coyote Creek Entrance, go right and walk the Coit Road for 0.1 mile to an intersection. Take the right fork and head uphill on Timm Spring Road for 30 feet to a parking lot with a pit a toilet.

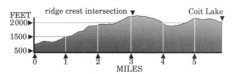

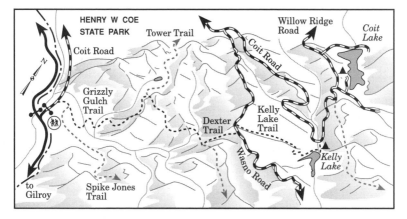

Again go right, on the well-used Spike Jones Trail, and walk uphill through oak forest for 0.2 mile to yet another intersection. Stay left, on Grizzly Gulch Trail.

Initially the Grizzly Gulch Trail makes an easy traverse along the hillside in the cool shade. However, before long the trail dips down and crosses Grizzly Creek. It then begins a steep ascent of the grassy hillside. The ascent gets steeper as you climb. Pass Collen Trail at 0.8 mile from the start and continue up for another 0.5 mile to a small bench and intersection at 1,790 feet. Go right, still following the Grizzly Gulch Trail, and begin a pleasant stroll along the open hillside.

At 2.3 miles from the start, elevation 1,980 feet, leave the Grizzly Gulch Trail and head steeply up the open hillside on Dexter Trail. At 2.9 miles, cross the trip's 2,450-foot high point and descend a few feet to the Wasno Road. Go left for a quick 0.2 mile and then head off to the right for a 1-mile plunge to Kelly Lake (1,900 feet). The camp area and outhouse are located at the outlet below a pretty waterfall.

To continue to Coit Lake, walk through the Kelly Lake camp area and follow the road 0.1 mile, out to Coit Road. Go right for a 0.8-mile ascent, to a 2,386-foot saddle on the ridge crest. Continue over the ridge and down 0.3 mile, then go left for the final 0.2 mile to the campsite. A second campsite is located at the upper end of the lake.

# 99 | POVERTY FLAT LOOP

**Loop trip: 10 miles**
**Hiking time:** 6 hours
**High point:** 3,040 feet
**Elevation gain:** 2,300 feet
**Difficulty:** Potentially moderate
**Hikable:** All year

**Driving directions:** Drive Highway 101 to Morgan Hill. Take the East Dunne Avenue exit and go east through a residential area, then up a steep hill. At the top, the road divides. Stay right, on Dunne Way, a narrow winding road that ends 12.5 miles from the freeway at the Visitor Center and campground (2,640 feet). Pay your day use fee at the Visitor Center.
**Maps:** Henry W. Coe State Park Trail and Camping Map; USGS Mt. Sizer and Mississippi Creek
**Permits:** Henry W. Coe State Park Headquarters (Case 12)

Between the coastal range and the Central Valley lies a group of rolling mountains known as the Diablo Range. This is a beautiful area with steep-sided hills and narrow valleys. Hilltops and valley bottoms are covered

*Wild turkey in Henry W. Coe State Park*

with Pacific madrones, feathery foothill pines, and majestic oaks. Springtime has the added enchantment of green hillsides spotted with colorful flowers.

**THE HIKE.** Begin the loop by walking back up the road for 200 feet from the Visitor Center. Go right and skirt around a gate, then head up the Manzanita Point Road for 400 feet, to the Monument Trail. Go left. At 0.6 mile from the parking lot, the trail divides. Go right for a visit to the Henry

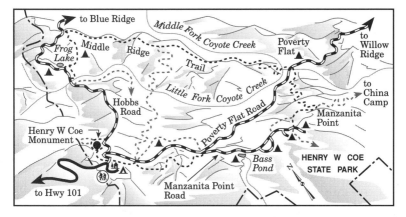

W. Coe Monument and viewpoint, then follow the road over the crest of the hill (3,040 feet). Descend, then climb to reach Frog Lake (2,440 feet) and two backcountry campsites at 1.6 miles. Here you may choose between the trail or the steeper road for the climb to 2,899-foot Middle Ridge.

At the summit of Middle Ridge, turn right on the Middle Ridge Trail and follow it southeast along the ridge crest and then down to the Little Coyote Creek canyon (1,200 feet). Ford the creek at its confluence with Little Fork, then continue down the canyon 0.2 mile and ford the creek again. Watch for poison oak when looking for a dry place to cross.

At 5.5 miles from the Visitor Center, the Middle Ridge Trail ends. If spending the night on the trail, go left, crossing the creek one more time, to reach grassy meadows and five campsites at Poverty Flat. The loop route goes straight on the Cougar Trail. Before long, the trail divides. Stay right for a steep 0.9-mile climb to the crest of a manzanita- and madrone-covered ridge and an intersection with the China Hole Trail (1,840 feet). Go right and keep climbing to reach the Manzanita Point Road and the Manzanita Point group camps. Hike the road along the ridge crest for a mile, then go left on the Springs Trail, which contours pleasantly along the hillside. At 9.4 miles, Springs Trail becomes Corral Trail and climbs a forested gorge to end the 10-mile loop at the Visitor Center.

# 100 | CHINA HOLE

**Loop trip: 9.8 miles**
**Hiking time:** 5 hours
**High point:** 2,640
**Elevation gain:** 1,480 feet
**Difficulty:** Potentially moderate
**Hikable:** March through October

**Driving directions:** Drive Highway 101 to Morgan Hill. Exit the freeway at East Dunne Avenue and head east through a residential area. At the crest of a steep hill, the road divides. Stay right, on Dunne Way, a narrow, winding road that ends 12.5 miles from the freeway at the Visitor Center and campground (2,640 feet). Arrive early to avoid the midmorning parking congestion. Late arrivals will need to retreat 0.5 mile to park in the overflow area. Backpackers need to register at the Visitor Center.
**Map:** Henry W. Coe State Park Trail and Camping Map
**Permits:** Henry W. Coe State Park Headquarters (Case 12)

It would be mighty hard to get bored on this hike. Constantly changing views, fascinating wildlife, and a progression of habitats provide continual

*The Narrows on East Fork Coyote Creek*

visual and mental stimulation as you hike to a narrow gorge on the East Fork Coyote Creek. The destination is an idyllic swimming hole with deep pools and clear, refreshing water. Hikers who have the time to linger for a night or two will find comfortable campsites in the grassy meadows near the creek.

Because of the excellence of this hike, backpackers often outnumber the single available campsite at China Hole. However, the nearby campsites up

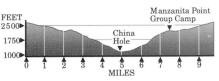

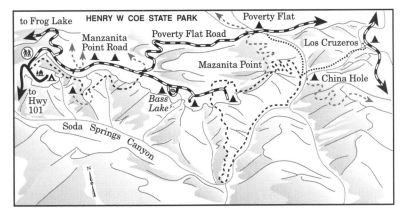

The Narrows, at Los Cruzeros Camp, or at Poverty Flat Camp, on the Creekside Trail are also pleasant.

**THE HIKE.** From the Visitor Center head south on the Corral Trail, which traverses the ridge, descending gradually. The initial section is shady, but before long the trail leaves the trees and heads across grass-covered hillsides spotted with venerable giant valley oaks. The ground shows signs of frequent rooting by wild pigs.

At 0.6 mile Corral Trail ends. Ahead, you have a choice of three trails. The best option for scenery is the Springs Trail. If you are late, the quickest route is the road. You will return on the trail to the left. Just 0.3 mile from the junction, pass a turnoff to Lion Spring Camp, continue straight for another mile.

At 1.9 miles from the Visitor Center, Springs Trail ends. Go right on the Manzanita Point Road, which descends and climbs, passing the Blue Oak Horse Camp, Manzanita Point Group Camp, and little Bass Pond. At 2.7 miles, just past the group camp outhouse, go right on Madrone Springs–Soda Spring Trail for a steep descent into Soda Springs Canyon. The trail drops 750 feet in 1 mile before arriving at the camp area. The soda springs is located across the creek.

The trail heads down the canyon, crisscrossing the creek several times before arriving at China Hole at 4.9 miles (1,150 feet). The campsites are located on the opposite side of the creek, a wet crossing.

For further adventures, or maybe to reach your campsite, the unmarked Narrows Trail makes a delightful afternoon jaunt. China Hole is located at the confluence of the Middle Fork and the East Fork of Coyote Creek. The Narrows Trail heads up the East Fork, which is the one on the right. This is a sandal trail, and you should plan on wandering through the creek at several locations. Some of the creek rocks are slippery, so use caution. Los Cruzeros Camp is located 1 mile above China Hole. Poverty Flat Camp is located up the Middle Fork. There is a rough trail that parallels the creek for 0.6 mile to the campsite.

To finish the loop, from China Hole head up the well-graded China Hole Trail. After 1.5 miles of steady climbing you will pass an intersection with the Cougar Trail from Poverty Flat. Continue up at a leisurely pace to reach the Manzanita Point Group Camp 2.6 miles from China Hole.

Watching for wild turkeys, go right and follow the road for the next 0.8 mile to a multiple road and trail junction. Stay to the right to find the Forest Trail, a self-guiding nature loop that is shaded in the afternoon. Forest Trail is 1.2 miles long and ends 4.6 miles from China Camp. Pass two trails on the right, then walk across the road and head right on Corral Trail for the final 0.6 mile back to the Visitor Center.

# APPENDIX

## WILDERNESS PERMITS, REGULATIONS, AND QUOTAS

In national parks, in state parks, and for many of the national forest wilderness area trailheads, quotas have been set on the number of backpackers who can start hiking from a given trailhead on a given day. A permit must be obtained before you reach the trailhead for all trails with trailhead quotas. Only back-packers are required to have permits. Day hikers do not need permits except on the Mount Whitney Trail.

Once you have your permit, you are free to hike as long and as far as you wish during the time specified. At the end of your trip, you must obtain a new permit if you wish start another trip from a different trailhead. If your hike passes through more than one forest or through a forest and a national park, you need only obtain one permit, issued from the forest or park where your trip begins.

In some high-use areas, such as the Carson Pass area, Paradise Valley in Kings Canyon National Park, and Glen Aulin in Yosemite National Park, backcountry camping is limited to numbered sites. These areas may also have one- or two-night camping limits. When the numbered sites are full, you are required to move on to find a legal and vacant site somewhere else. On busy weekends, searching for an open campsite may require a lot of extra miles or cross-country travel.

Each park and national forest has a different set of rules and regulations governing the acquisition of wilderness permits. The following information will help you understand what steps you can take to ensure you acquire the permits you need. However, regulations are frequently changed. Check the appropriate website for the most up-to-date information.

**CASE 1:** In the Mokelumne, Carson–Iceberg, and Emigrant Wildernesses, permits are required year-round for all overnight trips. As of 2003, no quota system had been established, so you may pick up your permit on the day of your hike from the most convenient ranger station along your route to the trailhead. If you prefer, you may write ahead; in some areas the permits will be mailed to you. For trips in the Emigrant Wilderness, you must pick up the permit from the nearest ranger station on your way to the trailhead. If you are not passing a ranger station during business hours, your permit will be placed on the permit board outside the ranger station. Emigrant and Carson–Iceberg Wildernesses have a maximum group size limit of fifteen people, although in some sensitive areas you may be requested to voluntarily reduce the party size. The Mokelumne Wilderness has a maximum limit of eight per party on overnight trips and twelve for day hikes. Self-registration boxes are available at Ebbetts Pass and Wet Meadows Trailheads. (Call ahead or check the Internet for up-to-date information; this system may see some changes in the next few years.) The one exception is the Carson Pass Management Area, where camping is allowed in specific areas only and permits are issued from the Carson Pass Information Station on a first-come basis.

Permits for Mokelumne Wilderness can be obtained from the Amador Ranger Station in Pioneer; Carson Ranger Station in Carson, Nevada; Carson Pass Information Station at the summit of the pass; and the Eldorado Information Center in Camino. For the Carson–Iceberg Wilderness, permits are issued from Summit Ranger Station in Pinecrest; Calaveras Ranger Station in Hathaway Pines; and Carson Ranger Station in Carson City, Nevada.

For the most up-to-date wilderness regulation information, please log on to *www.r5.fs.fed.us/stanislaus/visitor/wildernessregs.htm.*

**Hikes 1–2:** Call Amador Ranger Station for information about after-hours permits at (209) 295-4251.

**Hike 3:** The only permit required for an overnight hike is a California Campfire permit, which may be picked up at any Forest Service office or, during July and August, at the Information Center at the crest of Carson Pass between the hours of 8:00 A.M. and 4:30 P.M. For more information, contact the USDA Forest Service, Lake Tahoe Basin Management Unit, 35 College Drive, South Lake Tahoe, CA 96150; phone (916) 573-2600.

**Hike 4:** In the Mokelumne Wilderness Carson Pass Management Area, camping is allowed only in designated sites. These sites are located at Winnemucca, Round Top, and Fourth of July Lakes. Overnight permits are issued at the Carson Pass Information Station from July through September, 8:00 A.M. to 4:30 P.M., and from the Amador Ranger District Office the rest of the year. Fires are prohibited in the Carson Pass Management Area, and dogs must be restrained with a leash.

**Hike 5:** Call the Amador Ranger Station for information about after-hours permits at (209) 295-4251.

**Hikes 6–7:** Permits are issued from the Calaveras Ranger Station, Highway 4, P. O. Box 500, Hathaway Pines, CA 95223; phone (209) 795-1381.

**Hikes 8–9:** Permits are obtained by self-registration at the Ebbetts Pass Trailhead.

**Hike 10–11:** Obtain permits from the Summit Ranger Station at the Pinecrest Lake turnoff.

**Hikes 12–14:** Permits are obtained from the Summit Ranger District, 1 Pinecrest Lake Road, Pinecrest, CA 95364; phone (209) 965-3434; or Groveland Ranger District, Groveland; phone (209) 965-3434.

**CASE 2:** Overnight trips in the Hoover Wilderness and its proposed addition areas require a wilderness permit, which can be obtained by mail from the Bridgeport Ranger Station. During the summer many of the trailheads have quotas, and advance applications are advised. Permit requests are accepted up to three weeks before the first day of your trip, starting January 1. No phone reservations are accepted. All other permits are issued on the day of the hike. Permits are also required at nonquota trailheads, such as Sonora Pass, and can also be obtained in Bridgeport. A $3.00 per-person reservation fee is charged for advance reservations and a check for the amount must be submitted with the reservation request. Reservations are mailed to the address specified on the request. Half the daily quota for each trail is available on a first-come basis on the day of departure. Arrive at the Bridgeport Ranger Station very early in the morning to ensure a permit. For the most up-to-date information, log on to *www.fs.fed.us/htnf/hoover.htm.*

**Hike 15:** For information and permits, contact the Bridgeport Ranger Station or Summit Ranger Station.

**Hike 16:** Tamarack Lake lies outside the wilderness boundary, and no backcountry permit is required at this time. Carry a fire permit, and check with the Bridgeport Ranger Station for any changes in regulations.

**Hike 17–18:** These are very popular hikes. Advance reservations from the Bridgeport Ranger Station are recommended.

**CASE 3:** John Muir and Ansel Adams Wilderness. Much of the area administered by the Inyo National Forest is extremely popular with hikers and stock users, and quotas are in effect from May 1 to November 1. To ensure that you will get the hike of your choice, reserve your wilderness permit ahead of time. Sixty percent of the daily quota of spaces are available by advance reservation, except on the Mount Whitney Trail, where all spaces are filled by a complicated advance reservation/lottery system. Forty percent of the quota space is given out on a first-come basis the day of the hike at the locations listed later in this section. Popular hikes often have a line of people waiting all night for a permit.

As of 2003, reservations may be made up to six months before the first day of your trip. The quota system is in effect from May 1 through November 1. The fee for an advance reservation is $5.00 per person. No fee is charged for day-of-hike permits. The phone number for reservations in the Inyo National Forest is (760) 873-2483 from 10:00 A.M. to 4:00 P.M. (Do not call this number if you have questions; this number is only for reservations.) The fax number is (760) 873-2484. If you have questions, call (760) 873-2485 before making your reservation. Electronic filing will be available in the next couple of years. You may want to check the website for the most up-to-date information before calling: *www.r5.fs.fed.us/inyo/vvc/wild_permits/permits.htm.*

**Hikes 19–20:** Day-of-hike permits may be picked up at either the Mono Basin Scenic Area Visitor Center or the Mammoth Lakes Visitor Center. Advance reservations are recommended for this popular area.

**Hikes 21–24:** Reserved and day-of-hike wilderness permits for the Mammoth Lakes area (which includes hikes in the John Muir and Ansel Adams Wildernesses) are issued from the Mammoth Ranger Station Visitor Center. Arrive early for day-of-hike permits. For hikes beginning from the Devils Postpile area (Hikes 21 and 22), there is a mandatory shuttle bus ride from the Mammoth Mountain Ski Area. The bus runs from 7:00 A.M. to 7:00 P.M., leaving from the Mammoth Mountain Main Lodge Gondola Building every 30 minutes. The bus ride is free after you have paid a per-person user fee to enter the area. Hikers are expected to plan their schedules to coincide with the shuttle bus schedule. The only exceptions to driving are given to people who are planning to camp at one of the very busy valley campgrounds. Backpackers will be expected to carry bear-resistant containers, which may be rented at Mammoth Lakes Visitor Center.

**Hikes 25–31:** If you have an advance reservation, your permit will be mailed to you before you leave home. Day-of-hike permits can be issued from White Mountain Ranger Station in Bishop and Mammoth Lakes Visitor Center.

**Hike 32–36:** Plan to arrive at the White Mountain Ranger Station in Bishop very early and guard your place in line if you are hoping to secure a day-of-hike permit for these hikes. Hikers entering Kings Canyon National Park will be required to keep food in a bear-resistant container. These can be rented at the ranger station.

**Hikes 37–41:** Day-of-hike permits can be picked up at the White Mountain Ranger Station in Bishop or at the Mount Whitney Ranger Station in Lone Pine. Arrive early for all permits. Bear-resistant canisters are required for all overnight hikes on the Kearsarge Lakes Trail (Hike 40) and for all hikes entering Kings Canyon National Park.

**Hike 42:** Permits are required for all day and overnight hikes on Mount Whitney. Currently, permit applications are accepted by mail or fax only. At the time of this writing, the application period starts February 1 and ends February 28 for all hiking dates in the quota season. Once all the applications have been received and sorted, a lottery is held. Reservations are $15 per person. A small number—some days none—of day-of-hike permits are issued each morning at the Mount Whitney Ranger Station. (Bring your sleeping bag.) Before applying for a Mount Whitney permit, check the website, *www.fs.fed.us/r5/inyo*, for the most up-to-date information, forms, and changes in application dates. The phone number for the Mount Whitney Ranger Station is (760) 876-6200. All backpackers on the Mount Whitney Trail are required to use bear-resistant canisters, which may be rented at the Mount Whitney Ranger Station in Lone Pine.

**Hikes 43–44:** The quota period for the Cottonwood Pass Trail (Hike 44) extends from the last Friday in June through September 15. Bear-resistant canisters are strongly recommended if you hike the entire New Army Pass Loop. When making advance reservations for Hike 43, request the Cottonwood Lakes Basin Trail on your reservation request form. For Hike 44, you must request the Cottonwood Pass Trail on the advance reservation request form.

**CASE 4:** In Sequoia and Kings Canyon National Parks, 75 percent of the daily trail quotas may be reserved in advance. Reservation applications are accepted starting March 1 for the time period between May 21 through September 21. You must make your advance reservation no later than three weeks before the start of the trip to allow time for processing. All requests must be mailed or faxed; at the time of this writing, the park was not set up to accept electronic reservations. Information needed is as follows: dates to begin and end your trip; trailheads used; method of travel; number of people; your best guess as to where you will camp and the number of nights in each location; and your name, address, and phone number. You must also include a check or credit card number to cover the reservation fee. Mail requests to: Wilderness Permit Reservations, HCR 89 Box 60, Three Rivers, CA 93271. Reserved permits are picked up at the closest issuing station to the start of your hike, up to 24 hours in advance. Reserved reservations may be picked up after 1:00 P.M. the day before the hike and must be picked up no later than 9:00 A.M. the day of your hike. For more information, call (559) 565-3766. To check for the most up-to-date rules and regulations before sending in your reservation request, log on to *www.nps.gov/seki/resform.htm*. Day-of-hike permits must be picked up at the ranger station closest to the trailhead. Some areas require hikers to carry a bear-resistant container for their food and toiletries. These canisters may be rented at the visitor center where you pick up your permit.

**Hikes 45–48:** The Mineral King Ranger Station issues reserved and day-of-hike permits between 7:00 A.M. and 3:00 P.M.

**Hike 49:** Day-of-hike and reserved permits are issued at Grants Grove Visitor Center.

**Hikes 50–52:** Day-of-hike and prereserved permits may be picked up at the Permit Office at the Lodgepole Visitor Center from early June to the end of September. Office hours are 7:00 A.M. to 4:00 P.M. Off-season permits are self-issued outside of the Permit Office.

**Hike 53:** No permits are required for backpacking in the Jennie Lakes Wilderness. Fire permits are required if you intend to operate a camp stove or burn wood in a fire ring. These permits can be obtained from Hume Lake Ranger Station at 36273 E. Kings Canyon Road, Dunlap, CA 93257; phone (209) 784-1500; or at the Grants Grove Visitor Center.

**Hike 54:** Pick up day-of-hike permits at the Grants Grove Visitor Center starting at 1:00 P.M. the day prior to the hike.

**Hikes 55–57:** Permits are to be picked up at the Road's End Issuing Station in Cedar Grove.

**CASE 5:** In the Sierra National Forest, trailhead quotas for the John Muir, Ansel Adams, Kaiser and Dinkey Lakes Wildernesses are in effect year-round. Advance reservations are given for 60 percent of the daily trailhead quota, while the remaining 40 percent of the available spaces are doled out on a first-come basis from the High Sierra Ranger Station in Prather. Requests for advance reservations may be submitted up to a year in advance of the starting date of your trip and no latter than three weeks ahead of time. For trips starting south of the San Joaquin River, send your application and fee payment to High Sierra Ranger District, Attn: Wilderness Permits, P. O. Box 559, Prather, CA 93651. For trips starting north of the San Joaquin River, permits are issued from Bass Lake Ranger District, Attn: Wilderness Permits, 57003 Road 225, North Fork, CA 93643. In 2003, the fee was $5.00 per person. Once your reservation has been placed, you will be sent confirmation of your reservation by mail. This confirmation will instruct you where and when you can pick up your wilderness permit. There is a $10.00 fee for any changes to a confirmed reservation. Phone, fax, and electronic reservations were not available as of 2003. For more information, check *info@sierrawilderness.com* or *www.r5.fs.fed.us/inyo/vvc/wild_permits/permits.htm*.

**Hike 58:** Day-of-hike permits are picked up at the High Sierra Ranger District office in Prather. Ask for the Woodchuck Trailhead on the permit application.

**Hike 59:** Day-of-hike permits are picked up at High Sierra Ranger District office in Prather. Ask for the Maxson Trailhead on the permit application.

**Hike 60:** Day-of-hike and reserved permits are issued from the High Sierra Ranger District office at Prather. On the permit application, specify the Dinkey Lakes Trailhead as your start and end point.

**Hike 61:** Day-of-hike and reserved permits are issued from the High Sierra Ranger District office at Prather. Ask for the Deer Creek or Billy Creek Trailheads.

**Hike 62:** Day-of-hike and reserved permits are issued from the High Sierra Ranger District office at Prather. Ask for the Potter Pass Trailhead.

**Hike 63:** Day-of-hike permits and reserved permit coupons may be redeemed at the High Sierra Ranger District office in Prather. Specify the Florence Lake Trailhead on the permit application form.

**Hikes 64–65:** Day-of-hike permits and reserved permit coupons may be redeemed at the High Sierra Ranger District Office in Prather. Specify the Mono Creek Trailhead on the permit application.

**Hike 66:** Day-of-hike permits are available at the Bass Lake Ranger District Office in North Fork. From May 1 through November 1, day-of-hike permits are issued at Clover Meadow from 8:00 A.M. to 12:00 P.M., and 1:00 P.M. to 5:00 P.M.

**Hike 67:** Food storage in bear-resistant canisters is a requirement for camping at Chain Lakes. Pick up day-of-hike permits at the Bass Lake Ranger District Office in North Fork. From May 1 through November 1, day-of-hike permits are issued at Clover Meadow from 8:00 A.M. to 12:00 P.M., and 1:00 P.M. to 5:00 P.M.

**CASE 6:** In Yosemite National Park, wilderness permits are required year-round for all overnight trips. Sixty percent of the available spaces are filled by advance reservation; the remainder are open to the spur-of-the-moment–type hiker on a first-come basis the day of—or one day before—the start of the hike. The permits are issued at the Wilderness Centers, located at the Hetch Hetchy Entrance Station, Big Oak Flat, Hills Studio in Wawona, Tuolumne Meadows, and Yosemite Valley. Advance reservations are accepted from 24 weeks to 2 days before the start of the trip. In 2003, the per-person reservation fee was $5.00. To make a permit reservation, call (209) 372-0740. For general information about the Yosemite backcountry, call (209) 372-0200 or visit their website at *www.nps.gov/yose/wilderness.* For trailhead transportation within the park, check the YARTS website at *www.yarts.com* or call toll-free (877) 989-2787.

**Hikes 68–69:** Pick up day-of-hike permits at the backcountry office in Wawona or Yosemite Valley.

**Hikes 70–72:** Pick up day-of-hike permits at the wilderness office in Yosemite Valley.

**Hike 73:** Pick up day-of-hike permits at the Hetch Hetchy Entrance Station. If you pick up a permit a day ahead of the hike, you may stay at the walk-in campground at the end of the road.

**Hikes 74–81:** Permits are issued at the Wilderness Center in Tuolumne Meadows.

**CASE 7: (Hike 82)** Wilderness permits are required for all overnight stays in 20 Lakes Basin. In 2002, permits were issued at the kiosk in the backpackers parking area at Saddlebag Lake and from the Mono Lake Ranger Station. At that time there were no quotas or fees. No open fires are allowed in the basin. (As this area is suffering from long-term overuse, rules can be expected to change in the not-so-distant future. Call ahead for current regulations or check the Inyo National Forest website for current rules and regulations.)

**CASE 8:** (Hike 83) Above and beyond the standard fee for parking in California's state parks, backpackers are required to pay for a permit for overnight stays at the Slate Creek Trail Camp. For reservations, write or call Portola Redwoods State Park, 9000 Portola State Park Road #F, La Honda, CA 94020; phone (650) 948-9098.

**CASE 9:** (Hikes 84–86) All hikers are required to pay the standard fee for each vehicle parking in the state park. In addition to the parking fee, a permit is required and fee charged for use of all campsites in Big Basin Redwoods State Park and for all trail camps on the Skyline to the Sea Trail except in Castle Rock Trail Camp, which is on a first-come system. For reservations, call Big Basin Redwoods State Park at (408) 338-6132. For Skyline to the Sea Trail camps, call (831) 338-8861. No fires are allowed at any of the trail camps.

**CASE 10:** (Hikes 87–93) At the time of this writing, wilderness permits were not required for overnight hikes in the Ventana Wilderness except for Sykes Camp (Hike 90). The Sykes Hot Spring hike is very popular and permits help to disperse backpackers throughout the Big Sur valley rather than allowing them to all congregate in the small area near the hot springs. All hikers in the Ventana Wilderness are expected to carry fire permits and have Adventure Pass tags or Golden Eagle Passes for their vehicles. Fires are allowed only in designated trail camps. If camping at a nondesignated camp, you must use a camp stove. Stop at the Big Sur Station for permit information for Hike 90. For more information, contact the Monterey Ranger District Office, 406 Mildred Street, King City, CA 93930; phone (408) 385-5434. For Hike 90, the most current trail information can be obtained at the Big Sur Guard Station; phone (408) 667-5726.

**CASE 11:** (Hikes 94–96) No backcountry camping is allowed in Pinnacles National Monument.

**CASE 12:** (Hikes 97–100) A permit is required and a fee is charged for all overnight stays in the backcountry of Henry W. Coe State Park. The permits are issued on a first-come basis. On spring weekends it is best to arrive early to ensure you will get the permit you want. A self-registration booth is located at the Hunting Hollow Entrance for Hikes 97 and 98. A park staff member may be there on spring and summer weekends to assist with trail information and registration. For more information, write Henry W. Coe State Park, P. O. Box 846, Morgan Hill, CA 95038; call (408) 779-2728; or log on to their website at *www.coepark.com.*

# ADDRESSES

Adventure Pass Headquarters
USDA Forest Service
1824 South Commercenter Circle
San Bernardino, CA 92408-3430

Alpine Ranger Station (1 mile above
    Bear Valley on Highway 4)
Open seasonally, June 1 through
    October 1, 8:00 A.M. to 5:00 P.M. daily
(209) 753-2811

Amador Ranger District
Eldorado National Forest
26820 Silver Drive
Pioneer, CA 95666
(209) 295-4251

Bass Lake Ranger District
Sierra National Forest
57003 Road 225
North Fork, CA 93643
(559) 877-2218 extension 0

Big Basin Redwoods State Park
21600 Big Basin Way
Boulder Creek, CA 95006
(813) 338-8860
*www.cal-parks.ca.gov*

Big Sur Station #1
Multi-Agency Facility
Highway 1
Big Sur, CA 93920
(831) 667-2315

Bridgeport Ranger District
Toiyabe National Forest
P. O. Box 595
Bridgeport, CA 93517
(760) 932-7070
*www.fs.fed.us/htnf/hoover.htm*

Calaveras Ranger Station
Stanislaus National Forest
P. O. Box 500
5519 Highway 4
Hathaway Pines, CA 95233
(209) 795-1381

Carson Ranger District
Toiyabe National Forest
1536 South Carson Street
Carson City, NV 89701
(730) 932-7070

Castle Rock State Park
15000 Skyline Boulevard
Los Gatos, CA 95033-8291
(408) 867-2952
*www.cal-parks.ca.gov*

Devils Postpile National Monument
PO Box 3999
Mammoth Lakes, CA 93546
(760) 934-2289
*www.nps.gov/depo*

Eldorado National Forest Information
    Center (5 miles east of Placerville on
    Highway 50)
3070 Camino Heights Drive
Camino, CA 95709
(530) 644-6048

Henry W. Coe State Park
P. O. Box 846
Morgan Hill, CA 95038
(408) 779-2728
*www.cal-parks.ca.gov*

High Sierra Ranger District
P. O. Box 559
29688 Auberry Road
Prather, CA 93651

Hume Lake Ranger Station
Sequoia National Forest
35860 E. Kings Canyon Road
Dunlap, CA 93621
(559) 338-2251

Groveland Ranger District
Stanislaus National Forest
24545 Highway 120
Groveland, CA 95321
(209) 965-3434

Inyo National Forest Wilderness
   Permit Office
873 North Main Street
Bishop, CA 93514
(760) 873-2485 (information only)
*www.r5.fe.fed.us/inyo/vvc/wild_permits/*
   *permits.htm*

Lake Tahoe Basin Management Unit
35 College Drive
South Lake Tahoe, CA 96150
(530) 573-2674

Los Padres National Forest
6755 Hollister Avenue, Suite 150
Goleta, CA 93117

Markleeville Guard Station
Toiyabe National Forest
Markleeville, CA 96120
(530) 694-2911 (summer only)

Mammoth Lakes Visitor Center
Inyo National Forest
P. O. Box 148
Mammoth Lakes, CA 93546
(760) 924-5500

Mono Basin National Forest Scenic
   Area Visitor Center
P. O. Box 429
Highway 395 North
Lee Vining, CA 93541
(760) 647-3044

Monterey Ranger District
Los Padres National Forest
406 South Mildred Street
King City, CA 93930
(831) 385-5434
*www.r5.fs.fed.us/lospadres*

Mount Whitney Ranger Station
Inyo National Forest
P. O. Box 8
Lone Pine, CA 93545
(760) 876-6200
*www.r5.fs.fed.us/inyo*

Pfeiffer Big Sur State Park
Big Sur Lodge
47225 Highway 1
Big Sur, CA 93920
*www.cal-parks.ca.gov*

Pineridge Ranger District
Sierra National Forest
P. O. Box 559
Prather, CA 93651
(559) 855-5360

Pinnacles National Monument
Visitor Information
5000 Highway 146
Paicines, CA 95043
(831) 389-4485
*www.nps.gov/pinn/index/htm*

Placerville Ranger District
Eldorado National Forest
4260 Eight Mile Road
Placerville, CA 95667
(530) 644-2324

Portola Redwoods State Park
9000 Portola State Park Road #F
La Honda, CA 94020-9717
(650) 948-9098
*www.cal-parks.ca.gov*

San Mateo County Government Center
590 Hamilton Street
Redwood City, CA 94063
(415) 363-4021

Sequoia and Kings Canyon
   National Parks
Park Information
47050 Generals Highway
Three Rivers, CA 93271
(559) 565-3341
*www.nps.gov/seki*

Sequoia and Kings Canyon
   National Parks
Wilderness Permit Reservations
HCR 89 Box 60
Three Rivers, CA 93271
(559) 565-3708
*www.nps.gov/seki/resform.htm*

Stanislaus National Forest
   Supervisors Office
19777 Greenly Road
Sonora, CA 95370
(209) 532-3671
*www.r5.pswfs.gov/stanislaus*

Summit Ranger District
Stanislaus National Forest
#1 Pinecrest Lake Road
Pinecrest, CA 95364
(209) 965-3434

USDA Forest Service
Pacific Southwest Region
Office of Information
1323 Club Drive
Vallejo, CA 94592
(707) 562-8737
*www.r5.fs.fed.us/*

White Mountain Ranger District
Inyo National Forest
798 North Main Street
Bishop, CA 93514
(619) 873-4207

Yosemite National Park
Wilderness Permits
P. O. Box 577
Yosemite National Park, CA 95389
(209) 372-0740
*www.nps.gov/yose/wilderness*

# INDEX

## ABOUT THE AUTHORS

Vicky Spring and Tom Kirkendall are both enthusiastic professional land-scape photographers. The couple travels the hills in summer with medium- and large-format cameras on their backs looking for exotic and exquisite mountain scenery. When the snow falls they step into cross-country skis and keep adding to their expansive collection of photos. Both Tom and Vicky studied at the Brooks Institute of Photography in Santa Barbara, California. Along the way they decided to share their extensive knowledge of scenic mountain trails with others to entice more people to help to protect these sacred places from exploitation. They currently live in Western Washington where their two favorite hiking buddies, eleven-year-old Logan and ten-year-old Ruth, attend school.

*Tom and Vicky with son Logan and daughter Ruth on summit of Mount Carmel*

THE MOUNTAINEERS, founded in 1906, is a nonprofit outdoor activity and conservation club, whose mission is "to explore, study, preserve, and enjoy the natural beauty of the outdoors . . . ." Based in Seattle, Washington, the club is now the third-largest such organization in the United States, with seven branches throughout Washington State.

The Mountaineers sponsors both classes and year-round outdoor activities in the Pacific Northwest, which include hiking, mountain climbing, ski-touring, snowshoeing, bicycling, camping, kayaking, nature study, sailing, and adventure travel. The club's conservation division supports environmental causes through educational activities, sponsoring legislation, and presenting informational programs.

All club activities are led by skilled, experienced instructors, who are dedicated to promoting safe and responsible enjoyment and preservation of the outdoors.

If you would like to participate in these organized outdoor activities or the club's programs, consider a membership in The Mountaineers. For information and an application, write or call The Mountaineers, Club Headquarters, 300 Third Avenue West, Seattle, WA 98119; (206) 284-6310. You can also visit the club's website at www.mountaineers.org or contact The Mountaineers via email at clubmail@mountaineers.org.

THE MOUNTAINEERS BOOKS, an active, nonprofit publishing program of the club, produces guidebooks, instructional texts, historical works, natural history guides, and works on environmental conservation. All books produced by The Mountaineers Books fulfill the club's mission.

*Send or call for our catalog of more than 500 outdoor titles:*

The Mountaineers Books
1001 SW Klickitat Way, Suite 201
Seattle, WA 98134
(800) 553-4453
mbooks@mountaineersbooks.org
www.mountaineersbooks.org

The Mountaineers Books is proud to be a corporate sponsor of The Leave No Trace Center for Outdoor Ethics, whose mission is to promote and inspire responsible outdoor recreation through education, research, and partnerships. The Leave No Trace program is focused specifically on human-powered (nonmotorized) recreation.

Leave No Trace strives to educate visitors about the nature of their recreational impacts, as well as offer techniques to prevent and minimize such impacts. Leave No Trace is best understood as an educational and ethical program, not as a set of rules and regulations.

For more information, visit *www.LNT.org*, or call (800) 332-4100.

# OTHER TITLES YOU MIGHT ENJOY FROM
# THE MOUNTAINEERS BOOKS

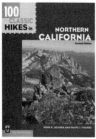

**100 Classic Hikes in Northern California,**
*John & Marc Soares*
Full-color guide to the best trails from the Bay Area
and the Pacific Coast to the Klamaths, Cascades and
the Sierra Nevada

**Best Short Hikes in California's
North Sierra,**
*Shane Shepherd & Owen Wozniak*
Find great, short day-hikes with the
option of extending the adventure sleeping
under the stars in nearby campgrounds

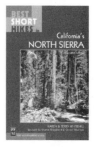

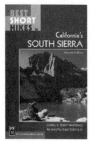

**Best Short Hikes in California's
South Sierra,** *Paul Richins Jr.*
Trips for all ages and abilities in
California's Sierra Nevada

**100 Hikes in Yosemite National Park,**
*Marc J. Soares*
Full-color guidebook to the 100 best
hikes in and around Yosemite
National Park

## ALSO FROM THE AUTHORS

**Bicycling the Pacific Coast: A Complete Route
Guide, Canada to Mexico**

**Glacier-Waterton International Peace Park**

**100 Best Cross-Country Ski Trails in
Washington**

Available at fine bookstores and outdoor stores, by phone at
800-553-4453 or on the web at *www.mountaineersbooks.org*

THE MOUNTAINEERS BOOKS